AFTER APPOMATTOX

AFTER APPOMATTOX

HOW THE SOUTH
WON THE WAR

✠

STETSON KENNEDY

✠

UNIVERSITY PRESS OF FLORIDA

Gainesville Tallahassee Tampa Boca Raton
Pensacola Orlando Miami Jacksonville

00 99 98 97 96 95 6 5 4 3 2 1
Library of Congress Cataloging-in-Publication Data
Kennedy, Stetson.
    After Appomattox: how the South won the war/by Stetson Kennedy.
    p.   cm.
    Includes bibliographical references and index.
    ISBN 0-8130-1341-0 (alk. paper)
    1. Afro-Americans—History—1863–1877. 2. Reconstruction.
3. Southern States—History—1865–1877. 4. United States—History—
Civil War, 1861–1865—Influence. I. Title.
E185.2.K33   1995
975'.04—dc20   94-42910

The University Press of Florida is the scholarly publishing agency for the
State University System of Florida, comprised of Florida A & M University,
 Florida Atlantic University, Florida International University, Florida State
University, University of Central Florida, University of Florida, University of
North Florida, University of South Florida, and University of West Florida.

University Press of Florida
15 Northwest 15th Street
Gainesville, FL 32611

✠

CONTENTS

✠

✠

ACKNOWLEDGMENTS

✠

Work on this book began with the discovery of a complete set of the thirteen volumes of testimony given by former slaves and other victims of the Reconstruction Klan terror before a Joint Congressional Committee in 1872.

These survivals of a historical coverup far more successful and momentous than the attempt at Watergate were found in the Schomburg Center for Research in Black Culture in the New York Public Library. My colleague in the long, hard job of mining, copying, and editing those testimonials included here was Patricia Hemberow.

The entire manuscript might have remained forever among my "unfinished works" had it not been for the prompting and indispensable assistance of my wife, Joyce Ann, who took it upon herself to prepare the chapter notes, bibliography, and index.

My thanks too to Dr. Ann Henderson of the Florida Humanities Council, Dr. Nick Wynn of the Florida Historical Society, and Dr. Raymond Mohl of Florida Atlantic University for their respective support in getting my earlier works back into circulation. Professor René Cherel of Nantes also has my heartfelt appreciation for his prodigious promotional efforts on my behalf in France. Likewise strengthening my arm has been the generous praise of musicologist Alan Lomax of the Association for Cultural Equity.

To the all-seeing eyes of Jack Price I am indebted for decades of clippings keeping me posted on the bitter "shoots of the roots" of racism; and latterly to Gabrielle Ayala who volunteered to join in that effort.

Much appreciated moral support in completing this work came from my lifelong partisan-in-arms, David Lord, who believed that the material it brings to light is important to America's present and future. On his death bed at the age of 90 in 1994, I told him that the book had been scheduled for publication, and asked if it was all right to refer to him therein as a "partisan."

"That's what I've been all my life," he replied, and added in what may have been his last words, "Still am!"

Moral support was also forthcoming from Gerald Hart, no partisan yet best of lifetime friends, who thought it made good reading, but passed away in 1993 without seeing it come to print.

And finally, my thanks to my best-of-profilers, Erick Dittus, whose accolades I have tried to deserve; to my stepdaughter Kathy Jones-Garmil, documentation manager of the Peabody Museum of Archaeology for her valuable assistance in annotation; and stepdaughter Karen Roumillat for clerical services rendered.

It would not be too much to say that what we have here is a stacked oral history sandwich on wry bread with hot mustard. Enjoy!

✠

✠

This book—unlike many another more or less qualified—makes no claim to being *the* history of Reconstruction.

The very idea of a complete history of any decade, particularly that one, is beyond the realm of human capability. The most that can be said is that some histories contain more information and less disinformation than others.

Here the modest intent has been to bring to light the hidden truth that the essence of Reconstruction was a struggle between all those who wanted to see the Emancipation Proclamation and verdict of Appomattox bring closer to realization the American pledge of liberty and justice for all, and all those who through cupidity or bigotry sought to perpetuate the oppression of blacks by whites.

Thus these pages are focused upon what seemed to be the most crucial happenings each year as the drama unfolded to its final curtain. The reader interested in further detail would do well to look not so much to "authoritative works" as to primary sources, and even there to beware of the biases that have always sought to distort the facts.

Those historians, politicians, educators, and critics who have some ax to grind other than that of democracy and equity will doubtless take exception to the evidence and conclusions presented here. Let them. To each his own, as the saying goes. These are mine, and I stand by them.

One reviewer of this work in manuscript observed that it has much to say about the *reactive* role of blacks during Reconstruction but not a great deal to say about the historic scope of their *active* role in politics and the enduring contributions made in introducing universal public education to this country, better care for the aging, penal reform, and much else besides. To the extent that this critique has merit, let it be said that this seeming neglect has been owing to considerations of space, not inclination; and besides, the subject is one that has been very adequately presented by such historians as W. E. B. Du Bois (*Black Reconstruction in America*), Eric Foner (*Reconstruction*), Lerone Bennett, Jr. (*Black Power USA: The Human Side of Reconstruction*), William P. Vaughn (*Schools for All*), Edward Magdol (*A Right to the Land*), and numerous others dealing with individual states.

So far as the present author is concerned, there was action aplenty in the steadfast refusal of so many blacks brutally flogged by the Klan to promise that they would thenceforth vote for white supremacist candidates or not at all. As one of these said to a congressional interrogator who marveled at his fortitude, "I can be strong in a good cause."

✠

CHAPTER I

✠

Anyone who has crossed the Mason-Dixon line dividing the former Confederate States from the United States of America must have been struck by the sudden switch from statues of Confederate general Robert E. Lee to those of U.S. generals Ulysses S. Grant and William T. Sherman—or vice versa, depending upon the direction in which one was traveling.

It is of course only natural that in any conflict one side's heroes are the other side's villains. In international warfare this is usually taken for granted, though methods of dealing with the phenomenon have varied widely, from Genghis Khan's "play it safe" policy of putting conquered populations to the sword to the Allied requirement following World War II that the defeated Axis powers assume a posture of remorse. Hence, no statues of Hitler, Mussolini, or Hirohito have (as yet) arisen.

What happened in the wake of the American Civil War, after the Confederacy ostensibly surrendered to the Union at Appomattox Courthouse in Virginia, was quite different. On both sides there were those who made an effort to refer politely to the war itself as "The Late Unpleasantness." Far from being treated in the traditional manner as armed rebels guilty of treason and insurrection, precious few Confederates were so much as imprisoned, and then only for brief periods. For the most part the North seemed willing to concede that Southern whites had fought valiantly for a cause in which they believed.

It is one thing, however, for a victor to magnanimously write off a war as a sort of misunderstanding between friends (which in this case enabled the white South to erect statues to its generals and pay pensions to its soldiers and their widows), and quite another to permit the loser to dictate the terms of peace—to have its own way not only internally, but to have that way adopted throughout the land of the conqueror.

And that is precisely what the white South succeeded in doing during the decade after Appomattox. It was much the same as though, after World War II, Nazism had not only been allowed to continue to hold sway in Germany but had also been adopted as the official and unofficial creed of the Allied nations. Far from conceding that it had been in the wrong, the white South persisted in telling itself and the world that "Might had triumphed over right."[1]

Within the decade, both sides had reached an agreement to the effect that slavery and secession had been wrong—but that thenceforth racial segregation and white supremacy would be good for the entire nation.

How the white South was able to wrest this ideological and political victory out of military defeat is the subject of this book.

Briefly put, the South did it by changing its uniform from Confederate gray to Ku Klux white and by reverting from open warfare to mass terrorism. Since those at the helm of the nation did not see fit to order the Union army to seek and destroy this Confederate underground, the terrorists did not have to contend with professional soldiers and armament, but were left free to devote all their energies to terrorizing the unarmed black civilian population and those few white Southerners and newcomers from the North who joined with them in an effort to introduce democracy to the region.

Although the Ku Klux Klan did engage in a few pitched battles with U.S. troops, and its imperial wizard within one year of its founding at Pulaski, Tennessee, in 1886, boasted that he was in command of 550,000 klansmen throughout the South and would field 40,000 armed klansmen in Tennessee if that state's militia were called out to protect black voters, the Klan and its various front groups were essentially terrorist organizations.[2] They were not interested in waging guerrilla warfare against government troops but in restoring white supremacist regimes on the state and local levels by driving all opposition, black and white, out of the political process. Their modus operandi was to slay from ambush, to launch sneak attacks in force by night upon families as they slept, using the bullwhip, torch, mutilation knife, and lynch rope to persuade them either to support white supremacy or abandon politics altogether.

With some few exceptions, the black and white targets of Klan terror chose not to arm themselves or band together for protection, counterattack or counterterrorism. They simply stood as individuals against their tormenters, and, for refusing to renounce their rights they were often made to pay the ultimate price. Although the bloodletting did not quite reach holocaust proportions, the fate of Southern blacks in the aftermath of the Civil War was indeed analogous to that of European Jews during World War II. As the Nazis boasted, "We may have lost the war against the Allies, but we won the war against the Jews," so too could unreconstruction Southerners claim that they were perpetuating the subordinate status of blacks in spite of military defeat by the Union.

In their nonviolent resistance to the forces of white supremacy, Southern blacks were pioneering techniques later adopted by followers of Mohandas Gandhi in India and Martin Luther King, Jr., in America. Such a course was dictated by pragmatic as well as idealistic considerations. White supremacists stated publicly that they were fully prepared to resort to the "ultimate solution" of genocide if need be. That this was no idle threat was being demonstrated at that same historical moment by the efforts of the U.S. armed forces to exterminate the American Indian.

Necessary Fictions?

Someone has said, "Every society has its necessary fictions."[3]

The generations of Americans born after Appomattox have all been taught that the Civil War ended then and there, with an unconditional Confederate surrender. As a result of that Union victory, we have been assured, the United States was restored and slavery abolished. We have been further informed that out of that victory came three amendments to the U.S. Constitution: the Thirteenth abolishing slavery, the Fourteenth asserting the equal rights of all citizens, and the Fifteenth specifically forbidding any state to deny the vote on grounds of race.

All this is true enough; but what we are not told is the transcendent truth that, while the Confederacy did lose the four-year military phase of the war, a Confederate underground fought on for twelve more years— using every weapon at its disposal, including the ultimate one of mass terrorism—until the nation finally acceded to most of the Confederacy's modified war aims. It was the "Deal of '76," not Appomattox, that marked the real end of the American Civil War. Under its terms, blacks were sold back down the river into virtual reenslavement, and all three

of the new constitutional amendments—so far as blacks were concerned—
were rendered dead letters for a century to come.

We Americans urgently need to ask ourselves whether this particular
fiction, about what happened during Reconstruction, is at all necessary.

Nations no less than individuals are often obliged to pay a terrible price
for self-deception. Consider Nazi Germany, for example, where the
"good burghers" pretended to think that the smoke rising from the concentration camp crematoria was of garbage being burned. Have not racial
segregation and discrimination as practiced in our country likewise been
acts of mass murder, even genocide? We, too, have paid a price, and accounts are far from being settled.

Once upon a time we castigated the Nazis for their use of the propaganda technique of the Big Lie, which, 'twas said, if big enough and repeated often enough, would eventually be believed by many. Is it too
much to say that the official and unofficial version of what happened after Appomattox, as embedded in American history books and the American public mind, is our Big Lie?

Of course it may well be argued that we have others that are still bigger.
Voltaire said that all of history consists of whatever pack of lies historians
are agreed upon. Indeed, anyone, contemplating writing a *true* history of
the United States—or of almost any other country, for that matter—would
do well first to absent themselves from the land in question.

The well-nigh universal popularity of the Big Lie as a component of
tribal and national histories attests its efficacy in overcoming guilt com-
plexes and inspiring peoples to sally forth and smite their neighbors or
total strangers far afield. So ingrained does this tendency seem to be that
even attempts by the United Nations to rewrite world history in an objective fashion have thus far reeked of big-power, big-religion chauvin-
ism—for all the world as if the histories of little powers and little religions
do not count.

Our Big Lie, though it has to do with what is primarily an internal
matter, has been the root of much evil, and is capable of prolonging those
evils so long as we cling to it. We cannot say that we need it to do battle with an enemy, for the enemy is us. Let us proceed, then, with its in-
terment, in the conviction that a higher form of patriotism requires that
we substitute truth for falsehood, insofar as we are able to discern it.

Our Big Lie about what happened during the decade of Reconstruction was not concocted after the event, nor even entirely during the
course of it, but had its roots in the antebellum racist rationale whereby
the "peculiar institution" of slavery had been justified as a means of bring-

ing "civilization" to "savages." Needless to say, the concept of white supremacy was concocted entirely by whites, and its insistence that black,
brown, and yellow peoples were innately inferior had long served the
slave-trading nations of Europe well. Their reluctant abandonment of
slavery did not carry with it any renunciation of racism, which continued to serve as justification for the European conquest and colonization
of continents peopled by other races. Many whites throughout the world
were thoroughly convinced that "wherever the white man plants his feet,
there he rules or finds his grave."[4]

Such was the white worldview that spawned slavery and racism in the
United States and paved the way for the Big Lie, making plausible the
new order of slavocracy established after Appomattox.

The breaking away of the American colonies from the British home-
land in 1776 had not entailed any abandonment of the Master Race Theory—the extralegal pontification of the Declaration of Independence
that "all men are created equal" notwithstanding, the intent there being
merely to assert the parity of white British colonists with white British
citizens. As American whites, these people energetically set about the
business of exterminating the indigenous Indian peoples, buttressing
black slavery with law, and pursuing their "manifest destiny" to rule
"from sea to shining sea." In its zeal to become a "great power," the ma-
cho young nation joined with the European consortium in seeking to
carve up China, sponsored the infiltration by Anglos of that portion of
Mexico it intended to seize, and turned a covetous eye upon Spain's
crumbling empire.

There was of course no such thing as a uniform national sentiment re-
garding the "peculiar institution" of slavery, and this moral dichotomy
found expression in such things as the Missouri Compromise and Lin-
coln-Douglas debates. The controversy was both inter-sectional and in-
tra-sectional in its scope. When the "irrepressible conflict" came, dis-
senters North and South were abundantly apparent.

In the North, so-called "Copperheads" who strenuously opposed the
Union war effort were so numerous that Lincoln, without waiting for
Congress to act, on April 27, 1861, suspended habeas corpus in certain
areas and ordered the military to arrest persons overtly opposing recruit-
ment or the draft. On July 31 Congress adopted a Conspiracies Act, and
buttressed the same with a "second confiscation act" on July 27 of the
following year. On September 24 Lincoln issued a proclamation formally
subjecting draft opponents to martial law. An estimated 38,000 arrests
were made.

In the South, draft-dodging was endemic, and in the course of the war 100,000 deserted the Confederate Army. What's more, a tabulation of whites who volunteered to serve in the Union forces came to 54,137, not including Virginia, South Carolina or Georgia, and non-Confederate Kentucky added 75,760 volunteers to the armies of Lincoln. (Not included in these figures were 179,000 blacks who, experiencing no ambivalence as to slavery, donned Union uniforms and fought for its abolition.)

Given this prefab American national mindset, Ole Massa, home from the Civil War, knew just what he had to do. Post-Appomattox Confederate strategy called for, on the one hand, imposition of a reign of terror to deter blacks from asserting any rights and, on the other, psychological warfare to deter the nation from interfering. As the Ku Klux Klan served as the primary instrumentality for creating the terror, our Big Lie became the primary vessel for brainwashing the nation. Neither could have succeeded without the other.

The drama evolved in the course of being acted out on stage. As Appomattox rang down the curtain on chattel slavery as such, it rang up the curtain on a contest to determine whether the South and nation were to evolve as a truly democratic society, or be cast in the racist mold of white supremacy. When the curtain rose, Ole Massa—in his role as Author, Producer, Press Agent, and Master of Ceremonies—put the plot rather differently. What it was about to see, he assured the onlooking nation, was but the latest chapter in the age-old struggle of civilization versus barbarism. It being understood that white folks represented civilization, and black folks barbarism, the rest was easy. The Good Guys and the Bad Guys fell into their respective places as naturally as the proverbial sheep and goats.

When the final curtain descended after the tableaux known as the Deal of '76, the script was at last complete, and ready for copying by historians. In its classic form, in the language of Ole Massa himself, the play consisted of four Acts, somewhat as follows.

The Dark Decade
A National Tragedy with a Happy Ending
Act I. Lincoln Points the Way

In which Ole Abe, for all his demonism, points the way to "bind up the Nation's wounds . . . with malice toward none, with charity toward all." While revealing his malice by appointing pro-Union Southern Scalawags to public office (at least they were white, and men of some substance), he offers to pay slaveowners for their slaves, makes no mention of treason trials, confiscation, land reform, or rights for blacks—thus proving there is some good in even the worst of men.

Act II. Johnson Sees the Light

In which Ole Andy, Southern born and bred, overcomes his po-white antipathy for the landed gentry (following a few visitations to the White House by Southern Ladies seeking pardons for their husbands). Proudly flying his new colors as a True Southerner, Ole Andy pardons the Rebels, pulls out the Yankee troops, proposes to send blacks back to Africa, and puts the reins of government back into the hands of the Better Elements of Southern Society without regard to their previous condition of servitude to the Confederate Cause. When Congress convenes in December 1865, he presents 'em with a Southern contingent of staunch Confederates, and announces that he has completed the job of Reconstruction.

Act III. The Radicals' Revenge

In which Congress responds it will be damned if that is so. Slamming the door on the Southern delegation, it ushers in a decade of strife, bloodshed, depravity, graft, and corruption. Incited by those Radical fiends-out-of-hell Thaddeus Stevens in the House and Charles Sumner in the Senate, Congress carves the South into five military districts, each under the command of a Yankee General. The Army of Occupation presides over voter registration, barring many Loyal Confederates and registering more than 100 percent of the blacks in some localities. Northern Carpetbaggers, Southern Scalawags, and their gullible black followers conspire to get themselves elected to public office at all levels. Congress tries to impeach the President for pardoning Rebels and pulling nigger-loving Generals out of the South; Ole Andy hangs in there by a margin of one vote. Southern whites up in arms, swear to drive Radicals out of office, or kill them to the last man.

Act IV. The Klan to the Rescue!

In which High-minded Southern Men band together in the Invisible Empire of the Knights of the Ku Klux Klan. Riding by night in robes and masks, they drive out the vulturous Carpetbaggers, convert the rascally Scalawags, and push the unruly blacks away from the polls, out of public office, off the land, and back into the place ordained for them by Almighty God. Thus the Dark Decade is brought to an end, law and order, home rule, and white supremacy restored, and the sanctity of Southern Womanhood assured for all time.

(Curtain)

Depiction of a typical visitation of the "night assassins" (Library of Congress).

A Card in the Deal

Such was the play that Ole Massa put on, improvising as he went, to brainwash the nation into letting him resume business pretty much as usual. And although Southern blacks and their allies across the country resisted mightily, the acceptance of this Big Lie as official doctrine was an integral part of the Deal of '76 that finally brought an end to the war; and it has continued to serve as one of our "necessary fictions" ever since. Though it came cloaked in fraudulent trappings, and was agreed to under the duress of intimidation, terrorism, and political blackmail, it has not yet been repudiated.

Scarcely less shameful than the spectacle of Southern chefs preparing and serving this racist concoction was that of the North devouring it en toto with mucho gusto. Not only Northern racists and the uncaring gobbled up this recipe for "national reconciliation"; at table with them were many former "friends of the Negro" and even some abolitionists.

Since the Deal was entered into under the aegis of the Northern financial and industrial establishment, it was hardly surprising that a succession of Northern scriveners came forth to write the lie into American history. After all, the theory of a white master race and system of apartheid fit in very nicely with the international company Uncle Sam was keeping, and the things they were up to.

Western imperialism had already taken as its bible the *Essay on the Inequality of Human Races,* penned by Count Arthur de Gobineau, a fiction writer, sometime between 1853 and 1857.[5]

One of the first to implant our Big Lie in the textbooks of the nation was James Ford Rhodes, whose jingoistic multivolume "history" of the United States, published during the 1890s, endorsed the Confederate contention that Congressional Reconstruction had been "repressive and uncivilized" and had "pandered to the ignorant negroes, the knavish white natives and the vulturous adventurers who flocked from the North."[6]

During that same decade, Professor John W. Burgess of Columbia University jumped on the bandwagon with a description of Reconstruction as "the most soul-sickening spectacle that Americans have ever been called upon to behold."[7] This was also the decade in which Uncle Sam drove the Spaniards out of Cuba and picked up Puerto Rico and the Philippines as prizes of war. As if to cap it all, an Englishman, Houston Chamberlain, published his apologia for imperialism, *Foundations of the Nineteenth Century,* in 1899. (Not surprisingly, he turned up working for the German Kaiser during World War I.)[8]

Soon after the turn of the century, another Columbia professor, William A. Dunning, did such a superb job of piecing together all the components of the Confederate version of Reconstruction that all subsequent propagators of the legend have been said to belong to the "Dunning School."[9]

It remained for a motion picture, however, to embed the Legend of Reconstruction in the American public mind as deeply as that of Washington and the cherry tree. This was *Birth of a Nation,* filmed by D. W. Griffith in 1915 and based upon a novel, *The Clansman,* written by a North Carolina preacher named Thomas Dixon, Jr.[10] At first, premier showings in New York and Boston evoked storms of protest, but these were cleverly allayed by Dixon, who arranged for private viewings in the White House by President Woodrow Wilson and his cabinet, and subsequently for the chief justice of the Supreme Court. With the blessings of such dignitaries as these, the film went on to gross $18 million.[11]

Taking advantage of all the free publicity generated by *Birth of a Nation,* a preacher/salesman named William Joseph Simmons bused some fifteen colleagues to Stone Mountain, Georgia, on Thanksgiving Eve of 1915 and, by the light of a fiery cross, proclaimed the "reincarnation" of the Ku Klux Klan.[12] Although the Klan had never ceased to exist, carrying on under a wide variety of pseudonymns, the terrorist functions of the Reconstruction-era Klansmen had indeed been taken over by lawmen in police uniforms. Under the aegis of Imperial Wizard Simmons, however, the "modern" Klan swept the nation. Making use of much of the original Klan's nonmenclature, symbolism, and ritual, Simmons wrote and copyrighted *The Kloran* which continues in use to this day.[13] Along with all the Klan's super-secret rituals and the "Way of the Klavern," *The Kloran* contains the Klan's own version of the role it played during Reconstruction. Designated "Lecture No. 1, K-Uno," this inflammatory briefing has been fed to millions of Klansmen, living and dead. Its roots go far deeper than Washington's cherry tree, and it read in part as follows.

The Klan's Own Version

The noble achievements of the Ku Klux Klan shine with undiminished effulgence through the gathering mist of accumulating years, an eloquent tribute to the chivalry and patriotism of the past, and the holy heroism of our fathers in preserving to us the sacred heritage of a superior race—political supremacy, racial integrity, social peace and security, and to humanity the boon of cultured civilization. . . .

When the shuddering peals of the thunder of the impending storm of the American Reconstruction were heard above the fading echoes of the battles of the great Civil War, the chosen victims stood aghast and pale, wondering at the meaning and purpose of the gathering gloom . . . They had been promised protection in the possession of property, in the pursuit of peaceful employment and in every political and civil right formerly possessed by them as citizens of the National Commonwealth, but the National Government, by the shameful deviltry of its unscrupulous manipulators, repudiated that solemn promise and inaugurated the most disgraceful epoch in the annals of the nations against that unarmed, defeated, defenceless and submissive people . . .

Constitutional law was stripped by profane hands of its virtuous vestments of civilized sovereignty of four thousand years in the making, and was mocked by polluted political pirates in legislative assemblies . . . Carpetbaggers, the vultures of gluttinous greed, swooped down from their aerie on the lofty peaks of the mountains of national authority o'er the dismal plain of human helplessness . . . and the Scalawags—the conscienceless, cadaverous wolves of treason—gnawed the bones remaining in a baleful state of ghastly bleaching.

North Carolina Klansmen with captive. Conical hoods tipped with tassels, and the cross emblem, remain in vogue with the modern Klan, while such decorations as cow horns have been abandoned (Stanley Horn, *Invisible Empire,* 1939).

The chastity of the mother, wife, sister and daughter was imperiled and their sacred persons were placed in jeopardy to the licentious longings of lust-crazed beasts in human form. Might ruled over Right . . . Ignorance, Lust, and Hate seized the reins of State; and riot, rapine, and universal ruin reigned supreme . . . the very blood of the Caucasian race was seriously threatened with an everlasting contamination.

That anguish-laden cry of that defenceless people of the Southland was heard and answered by the gallant knights of the Invisible Empire, and not one faltered or failed as Duty pointed the way in the cause of humanity and civilization; with a grim smile of sacred duty resting upon their manly countenances, impelled by an instinct of the race, they leaped into the saddle, borne upon the back of their faithful steeds, baptized with a suffusion of tears, they came; they came, they saw, they conquered!

From over the mysterious borderland from the Empire of the Soul, the Ku Klux came. They were knight errantry in the highest, noblest and gravest form personified . . . They dissipated the cruel storm of the American reconstruction and won the plaudits of an intelligent, unprejudiced world. They stemmed the murky tide of despotic usurpation and tyrannical greed, and rescued the entire country from utter disgrace and ruin. They re-established racial rights, and the sovereignty of constitutional law, redressed the wrong, made secure political supremacy, started anew the wheels of industry and made possible the birth of the greatest nation of all time—the Re-United States of America.

With a 'fiery cross,' symbol of the purest and most loyal patriotism, as their beacon, the Ku Klux rode through the darkness of Reconstruction's night . . . and at the rising of the sun of a glorious day, they saw the shades of that awful night receding. Right had been by them established over Might. The voice of music was again heard in the land . . .

The noble ride of the Ku Klux Klan is immortalized by their accomplishments, and is memorialized by the men of today who appreciate the chivalric, holy and patriotic achievements of the original Klan in the permanence of this our great fraternity.

> ". . . ride on and on, thou spirit of that mystic klan,
> In your noble mission for humanity's good,
> Until the clanish tie of klancraft binds man to man
> For our country, our homes and womanhood.
> *Non Silba, Sed Anthar.*
> (All say in unison)—"Not self, but others."

With the Invisible Empire peddling the legend on one side of Main Street, U.S.A., and the Dunning School on the other, the lie has gone marching on. On the world stage, racism was given a boost by World War I, which gave rise to such master race delusions as Lothrop Stoddard's *The Rising Tide of Color*,[14] Madison Grant's *Conquest of a Continent*,[15] and Adolf Hitler's *Mein Kampf*.[16] In America, new matriculates of the Dunning School included Claude Bowers (*The Tragic Era*, 1929)[17] and James G. Randall of the University of Illinois, who gave the legend a modern twist by describing Reconstruction as "a kind of racket."[18]

The Revisionists Revised

And so it came to pass that even black Americans were obliged to recite the Legend of Reconstruction if they wanted to pass their courses in American history. But all along, blacks, and some whites, knew that it wasn't true and that some day the truth would have to be told.

One of the first to tell it was the distinguished black scholar, Dr. W. E. B. Du Bois, who in a paper delivered before the American Historical Society in 1909, served notice on the history-writing establishment that the legend was a forgery. He had hinted as much in his *Souls of Black Folks* (1903),[19] but it remained for his monumental work *Black Reconstruction* (1935) to reveal the heroic role played by blacks and the class nature of the struggle that had been waged to democratize the South's economy and government.[20]

Needled or inspired by Du Bois's legend-pricking, and no doubt also by the impact of the Great Depression, a number of white historians were forthcoming with economic interpretations of Reconstruction. Charles and Mary Beard, Howard K. Beale, William Hesseltine, and Matthew Josephson were prominent among those who provided insights into the economic determinants that had been at work behind the scenes; but these contributions tended to be tacked onto the legend instead of being substituted for it.[21]

In time those who sallied forth to tilt at one or more of the windmills turning to the tune of the Dunning School came to be denominated the Revisionist School. But by and large, these worthies have been content to take issue with some aspect of the legend, leaving its mendacious essence intact. What they have said in effect is "It can't have been all that bad; let me give you an example . . ."

At that rate, we shall be revising a very long time indeed before our Big Lie is nailed as a whole. The need is for renunciation, not revision.

By way of explaining their reluctance to pick the lie to pieces, the revisionists are well-nigh unanimous in asserting the dearth of reliable information about what happened and who did it. Although it is true that the terrorists and their sponsors went to great pains to cover their tracks through systematic destruction of evidence,[22] the revisionists protest overmuch. The record *is* there, as Du Bois pointed out early on. One has only to look to the minutes of the constitutional conventions and legislatures, to courthouse records, to files of the Freedmen's Bureau, War Department, and Congressional Record, and to contemporary press reports in order to cut through the phony fog invoked by the revisionists.

This book proposes to do just that, with special reference to the Congressional Record.

But before any successful attempt can be made to set the record aright, there is a need to propose and define an appropriate terminology. Ever since Appomattox, America's acceptance of the counterfeit terminology coined by the Confederates has obliged us to think of Reconstruction in Confederate terms. Even the revisionists have been so steeped in the legend as to find it difficult not to parrot its familiar formulations. In the very act of trying to depict the "carpetbaggers" and "scalawags" in more kindly light, they can think of no better names for them, and even let slip such qualifying adjectives as "notorious." This is much the same as trying to extol the merits of blacks and Jews while referring to them the while as "niggers" and "kikes." It simply can't be done. One might as well try to negotiate a nonaggression pact between the superpowers while referring to "the running dogs of capitalism, party of the first part" and "the power-mad men of the Kremlin, party of the second part."

If, in our search for objectivity, we begin by repudiating the Confederate contention that Reconstruction represented a struggle between civilization and barbarism, and look upon it instead as an effort to supplant the old racist oligarchy with a peoples' democracy, we shall be off to a good start. Beyond that, the most urgent need is for a sort of "Revised Who's Who in Reconstruction." This is what I propose:

Conservatives. This label has always been more honorific by definition than it has in practice. Those Southern whites who laid claim to it during Reconstruction were intent upon conserving their wealth, property, privileges, and ruling position. To say that they were conservative was to put it politely; they were in fact reactionary to the point of hoping to restore the status quo antebellum, including some form of slavery if at all possible.

This "Conservative Club" was liberal enough, however, to maintain an open-door-policy for augmenting its ranks and adding power to its political arm. No poor white was too poor to bask in the reflected glory of the rich whites and share in the privileges and immunities afforded by the system of white supremacy, provided only that they comport themselves in all respects as true racists. If you weren't a racist, you couldn't be a conservative.

In their pragmatism, the conservatives even made room for reformed members of the opposition. There was no scalawag, high or low, and no matter how intensively villified, who could not gain overnight acceptance as a gold ole boy simply by confessing the error of his ways and pledging to forevermore toe the line of white supremacy. So, too, with the carpetbagger from the North: rich or poor, all he had to do to be accepted into Southern society (including the bonds of matrimony) was to abandon the blacks and pledge allegiance to white supremacy. Even blacks, though they could not change their color and so could not be accepted into "Southern society," were allowed to support the conservative cause, and thereby assure themselves a modicum of patronage as "good darkies."

For these reasons, then, I propose to refer to these people not as "conservatives" but as "white supremacists."

Radicals. This brand, applied by self-styled conservatives to their intended victims, has always been more honorific in practice than it is by definition. During Reconstruction, it was affixed to all those, black and white, North and South, who supported rights for blacks and/or land for the landless. Since no Southern Democrat in those days believed in *that* kind of democracy, the Democratic and conservative labels were interchangeable. Among the nation's Republicans of that time, however, a fluctuating segment did endorse some rights for blacks, and there were even those (especially blacks) who, after Appomattox, continued to espouse land reform. All such were contemptuously referred to by the conservatives as "radicals." On the national level, distinction was made between the radical wing of the Republican Party, and moderate Republicans who were willing to let the white South have its own way. In the narrower Southern context, the Republican ticket came to be regarded as the radical ticket, and anyone who supported congressional Reconstruction and the constitutional amendments extending the rights of citizenship to blacks was a radical in the eyes of the white supremacists.

I propose to refer to these people not as "radicals" but as "Reconstructionists." It would be too much to call them all nonracists, for some of the whites harbored a degree of racism within their bosoms. Needless to say, blacks were regarded as natural-born radicals, unless they publicly disavowed any claim to rights and free land.

Carpetbaggers. Every white Northerner who settled in the South after Appomattox ran the grave risk of being called a carpetbagger, unless he speedily adopted the racist *mores* of the region and supported the perpetuation of white supremacy. Many of these settlers had served in the Union Army and had been favorably impressed with the South's climate and economic potential. Some were men of property, and some were not. Some were imbued with a desire to assist the liberated blacks in assuming the rights and responsibilities of citizenship, whereas others were apolitical. In the polarized political climate of the postwar South, however, most felt obliged to support the Republican Party's efforts at Reconstruction, as a patriotic duty not to betray the Union's war aims. Though there were undoubtedly some who fit the white supremacists' description of a carpetbagger, there were many who voluntarily sacrificed much, including their lives, on behalf of human rights and democratic principles.

I shall refer to them, then, not as "carpetbaggers" but as "Reconstructionists from the North." (The *real* carpetbaggers were those Northern railroad, banking, lumbering, and mining interests who conspired to cart off the South's resources, not in any carpetbag, but by the train- and boat-load.)

Scalawags. This opprobrious label was reserved for white Southerners who in any wise supported black rights, i.e., did not support white supremacy. Southern whites who had opposed secession, and/or the Confederate war effort, were readily forgiven if, after Appomattox, they were in favor of "keeping blacks in their place." But white Southerners who voted Republican, supported Reconstruction, or fraternized with blacks were denounced not only as scalawags, but as "nigger-lovers" and "traitors to their country and their race." That many of them were men of principle who sacrificed much for their beliefs was not to be conceded by their racist brethren.

We shall speak of them not as "scalawags" but as "Southern white Reconstructionists."

In addition to presenting its cast of characters under the misnomers of "conservatives," "radicals," "carpetbaggers," and "scalawags," the legend has relied heavily upon other obfuscatory usages. The Klan, the Dunning School, the Revisionist School, and white America generally is wont to speak of "the South" when in reality it has only the *white* South in mind. That the six million emancipated slaves were Southerners too is seldom taken into account. In the same way, it has been understood that when someone speaks of a Southern "Unionist," the reference is to a white person, when, needless to say, every black man, woman, and child was also a Unionist.

I propose when speaking of the white South to say so.

There is need, moreover, to make it clear that even the white South was never of one mind. The prevailing fashion has been to refer to the ruling class as "the aristocracy," or "the big planters," or "the former slaveholders." But after Appomattox, as well as before it, the class that called the shots down South was considerably more diverse than any of those terms would indicate. Not all were aristocrats or planters; among them were merchants, bankers, timber and mining men, and industrialists of various sorts. With few exceptions, however, they were of one mind where matters of class, race, and politics were concerned.

When speaking of this group as a whole, I shall do so in terms of their least common denominators: they were at once the "proprietary class" and (by virtue thereof) the "ruling class."

Finally, there is that misleading misnomer with which we have been saddled by historians, the "Johnson Reconstruction." Inasmuch as Johnson's efforts were devoted to the restoration of the South's antebellum political structure (white rule) rather than any restructuring of it, I shall refer to that period as the "Johnson Restoration."

✠

CHAPTER 2

✠

"This war was got up drunk, but it will have to be settled sober," President Abraham Lincoln sagely opined when the sanguinary conflict was yet in its infancy.[1]

Some say that U.S. General Ulysses S. Grant was not all that sober when, on April 9, 1865, Confederate General Robert E. Lee tendered at Appomattox Courthouse his sword in token of the South's surrender. In any event, Grant was magnanimous enough to permit Confederate officers to keep their mounts and sidearms.

The "irrepressible conflict" had lasted four long years. Johnny Reb, the Confederate rank-and-filer, had a song that summed up its course rather succinctly, as folk songs will:

Johnnie, Fill Up the Bowl![2]

In 1861
The cruel war had just begun.
In 1862
We all had enough to do.
In 1863
Abe Lincoln swore the niggers was free.

In 1864
We drove em back to Baltimore.
In 1865
Scarcely a Rebel was left alive.
In 1866
Ole Marse Jeff was in a damn bad fix.

Chorus:
So come up boys and we'll all take a drink.
Hussah! Hussah!
We'll give Marse Jeff the one-eyed wink,
And we'll all drink stone-blind:
Johnnie, fill up the bowl!

From the Union point of view the war had been fought, as Lincoln put it in his famed Gettysburg address, "to determine whether this Nation, or any nation, can long endure half slave and half free." Resolution of that question had cost (including death by disease) 622,511 American lives (as compared to 126,000 in World War I and 407,000 in World War II).[3] Physically and economically the ravages of war had left the South in ruins. As for its people, the census of 1860, taken just before the war got under way, indicated there were then 11,000,000 whites and 4,097,000 blacks; 258,000 of the latter were "free persons of color," the rest being slaves. Throughout the rest of the country there were reported to be an additional 230,000 blacks.

Although news of Lee's surrender traveled fast enough, it took quite some time to sink in. Lincoln had less than a week to savor the victory before being felled by an assassin's bullet on April 15.

Two weeks after having laid down his sword, General Lee was still feeling feisty enough to tell the *New York Herald* on April 24 that "should arbitrary or vindictive policies be adopted, the end is not yet. There remains a great deal of vitality and strength in the South." Indeed, even as Lee spoke, the forces under Confederate General Edmund Kirby-Smith were still fighting, and they continued to fight until May 26 when they finally put down their arms at Shreveport, Louisiana, some seven weeks after Appomattox.

Confederate President Jefferson ("Marse Jeff") Davis, on the lam, had the nerve to say: "The Confederate Cause is not lost, it is only sleeping."[4]

Forsooth, it scarcely paused for a cat-nap.

Most of the Confederate state governors—Pendleton Murrah of Texas, Charles Clark of Mississippi, Joseph E. Brown of Georgia, A. G. Magrath of South Carolina, Zebulon Vance of North Carolina, Abraham Allison of Florida, and William Smith of Virginia— had the temerity to continue to conduct business as usual, as though there had been no war and no surrender. Some proceeded to call their legislatures into session. Georgia Governor Joseph E. Brown, in a telegram on May 7 to Lincoln's successor, President Andrew Johnson, stated their case in this fashion: "The complete collapse of the currency and the great destitution of Provisions among the poor makes it absolutely necessary that the legislature meet to supply this deficiency and with a view to the restoration of peace and order."[5]

Four days later, on May 11, leading Confederates met in the Confederate capitol of Montgomery, Alabama, and sent Johnson a letter commending him for espousing the doctrine that the Southern states were states still and were "not to be lost in territories or other divisions."[6]

Johnson was not, however, in any position to go along with any such prolongation of Confederate power. On his order, Secretary of War Edwin M. Stanton dispatched a telegram to all U.S. generals in the South, as follows: "You will prevent by force the assembly of any persons assuming to act as a Legislature, and to exercise any civil or political authority, jurisdiction or right claimed by, through or under the Rebel Confederacy or the Rebel State Government."[7]

Some of the rebuffed Confederates were highly miffed. Mississippi's Governor Clark went so far as to send the following letter to U.S. General Embury Osband on May 22: "I am relieved from the duties of the Chief Executive of the State of Mississippi, and for the grave consequences that may result, the President of the United States has assumed responsibility."[8]

As for the mood of the South's people after Appomattox, the white mood and the black were of course two very different things. While most blacks were ecstatic in their newfound freedom, taking it for granted that the U.S. government would thenceforth assure them the same rights as anyone else, most whites were unwilling to accept blacks as fellow citizens.

It was a time of absolutism.

Rather many whites felt that if the blacks would not leave the country, they would. Some did, in fact, emigrate to Brazil.

"I'm a foreigner," one planter swore. "I scorn to be called a citizen of the United Sates. I shall take no oath of allegiance, so help me God!"

Rather many blacks felt that they too had had enough of America, and were ready to leave.

"There is nothing in this country for a blackman that has common sense but cruelty starvation & bloodshed," a group of freedmen resolved at Halifax, North Carolina, in a bid for financial assistance to relocate in Africa.[9]

But the great mass of both whites and blacks chose to remain where they were, posing the question of how the two races would continue to coexist.

Surrendered but Unsubdued

The smoke of battle had scarcely lifted when a host of journalists and dignitaries descended upon the South for the avowed purpose of assessing its "temper." What they found was fraught with portent for the years to come.

At first the former Confederates, numbed by defeat, confidently expected that their lands would be confiscated and their leaders hung or imprisoned. A friend of President Johnson, Benjamin C. Truman, took a quick trip through the South and reported to the president that the ex-Confederates "lived in a state of the most fearful suspense . . . looking for judgment," and an "hourly apprehension of the beginning . . . of Northern vandalism and butchery."[10]

Describing this same initial period, Whitelaw Reid, on tour for the *Cincinnati Gazette,* reported: "The National Government could have prescribed no condition for the return of the Rebel States which they would not have promptly accepted. They expected nothing; were prepared for the worst; would have been thankful for anything."[11]

The white South was not to remain pacified for long, however. With a stroke of a pen on May 29, scarcely seven weeks after Appomattox, President Johnson put most of their fears to rest by granting amnesty to all but the top military and civil leaders of the Confederacy. Only a few were ever imprisoned, and then only for a few months. Confederate President Davis was eventually captured and jailed, only to be released two years later. The sole Confederate to be executed was Henry Wirtz, commandant of the Andersonville, Georgia, prison camp, where 12,912 Union soldiers lie buried, having perished from disease, malnutrition, and maltreatment.[12]

It no sooner dawned upon the former Confederates that neither confiscation nor prison nor the gallows awaited them than their rebellious spirits soared. If only they could be rid of the Union occupation forces, they reasoned, the road would be clear to doing pretty much what they pleased. With governing power back in white Southern hands, they could deal with the blacks with impunity, secure in the knowledge that white Southern politicos, lawmen, judges, and juries would hold them blameless.

Securing the withdrawal of Union troops thus became the white folk's first order of business. The proprietors put their presses to work, pulling all stops to convince Northern public opinion of the evils of prolonged military occupation.

"It will hardly be possible for a people to remain at peace, or be allowed to do so, with armed and probably insolent garrisons quartered among them," the *Columbia* (S.C.) *Phoenix* solemnly warned. Occupation, it continued, would lead to "a neglect of all regular habits of industry [by blacks], and a sense of surveillance and annoyance [among whites], which in the end must drive them [the whites] into exile."[13]

In such manner, having failed to take their region out of the country, they now threatened to take themselves out. Even some white Southern Unionists joined in the call for prompt troop withdrawal. Prolonged occupation, argued A. G. MacKay of Charleston, would be regarded as "quasi-continuance of the war."[14]

Under such promptings, demobilization proceeded at an astounding pace. At the time of Appomattox, more than a million men were wearing the Union uniform; but by the end of that Year of Surrender, a mere 57,000 remained in army service. During 1866 this number was further reduced to 28,565, and the bulk of these had been pulled out of the South and sent West.[15] Their four-year mission to liberate black folk having been "accomplished," they were reassigned to exterminate red folk.

There is more than passing significance in the rapid disposition that was made of the 179,000 blacks who had donned the uniform of the Union army to fight for their people's freedom. These "Black & Blues"— as white supremacists derisively referred to them— were mustered out so fast that by the end of 1866 there was not a single black man in blue uniform left in the South. Those still in service had been transferred elsewhere, as General Grant explained it, "for obvious reasons."[16]

What few occupation forces remained were spread so thin that in vast expanses of the South whites were able to boast that they had never, during the war or after, cast eyes upon a blue uniform. There was, moreover, some tendency among these remaining occupying forces, particularly the officers, to identify with the defeated whites rather than the liberated blacks. (The situation was not unlike that which came to pass nearly a century later, when white American soldiers sent to occupy defeated Germany exclaimed in astonishment, "These are our kind of people!")

In those post–Civil War days, distance meant far more than it does now, the latter-day axiom that "political power comes out of the mouth of a gun" was if anything even more true then than now. With federal guns virtually gone from the South, and the monopoly on firepower by Southern white supremacists restored, it was well-nigh inevitable that they would soon monopolize political power as well.

The Northern journalists who toured the South after Appomattox were unanimous in attesting that, once retribution and compulsion were ruled out as national policy, the rebels waxed as rebellious as ever. When, not long after the surrender, U.S. Supreme Court Chief Justice Salmon P. Chase announced that he would like to inspect the South, a correspondent for the *New York Tribune* who had already done so said he feared for the Justice's life. Signing himself "E. S." (rather many journalists resorted to initials, presumably for their own protection), this correspondent reported on May 8: "The temper of the masses . . . is as yet unchanged, and as to their aristocratic and Rebel class par excellence, they are as haughty, exacting, unsubdued, and, if possible, more devilish than ever." The prevailing view, "E. S." further reported, was that "might has crushed right," and that "the right of the white man to make the negro work for him has not changed."

There was a concensus among these journalists that while the *power* of the rebellion had been crushed by the war, its *spirit* was undiminished. "With the exception of the younger class of hot-headed rebels, the external conduct of all is proper, and shows an outward respect for authority," reported "H. V. N. B." in the *Cincinnati Gazette* on June 17. "But underneath this calm, society is seething and boiling, as if a volcano were struggling beneath it. All here is chaos, and designing politicians are very busy with schemes to save all that can be saved of the old order or things. Everything looks as if the South had only laid down the sword and rifle as weapons, and changed the fighting ground to the political arena."

So rapid was the transformation of the white Southern mood that Charles Sumner was moved to report to the Senate on July 12: "Two months ago the whole South was ready to accept the rule of Justice, prescribed by the Declaration of Independence. Now it is perverse, recalcitrant, and rebellious."[17]

The resumed bellicosity of the white supremacists, fed as it was by the federal abstention from retribution and compulsion, was rendered positively exuberant when it became evident that, far from being dictated to, the white South was to be accorded the privilege of either consenting to or dissenting from any peace terms. That is to say, the U.S. government let it be known that tolerance of civil disobedience was official policy.

No rebel could ask for more, and they made the most of the limitless opportunities thus afforded them. One early strategy came to be known as "masterly inactivity."[18] It called for refusal to take any oath of allegiance to the U.S. government, boycotting of any elections held under that government's auspices, and above all a refusal to be "Reconstructed" by Yankees of any description. They even had a song that summed up such sentiments very nicely:

Good Ole Rebel

Oh, I'm a good ole Rebel, that's what I am,
And for this Yankee Nation, I do not give a damn!
I hates the Constitution,
This "Great Republic" too;
I hates the Freedmen's Bureau,
In uniforms of blue.

I hates the nasty Eagle,
With all his brag and fuss;
And them lyin' thievin' Yankees—
I hates em wuss and wuss!

I followed ole Marse Robert,
For four years nearbout;
Got wounded in three places,
And starved at Point Lookout.

I cotched the rheumatism,
A-campin in the snow,
But I killed a chance of Yankees—
And I'd like to kill some mo'.

Three hundred thousand Yankees
Lie stiff in Southern dust;
We got three hundred thousand
Afore they conquered us!

They died of Southern fever,
And Southern steel and shot;
And I wisht it was three million,
Instead of what we got!

I can't take up my musket,
And fight em now no mo'—
But I ain't a-goin to love em,
And that is sartin sho!

Chorus:
For I'm a good ole Rebel,
That's what I am:
And for this Yankee Nation,
I do not give a damn!
I don't axe no pardon,
For what I was or am;
I won't be Reconstructed,
And I don't give a damn![19]

So much for the preponderant mood engendered by Appomattox in the white South. Let us turn now to the very different effect it had upon the black South.

Uncertain Freedom

To the slaves of the South, Appomattox meant being "born again" as human beings instead of beasts of burden. As for the slavers of the South, they were as discomfitted as a flock of fleas whose dog has just died.

Slaveowners, like the military and civil leaders of the Confederacy, were extremely reluctant to accept the implications of the surrender. Ole Massa kept the news to himself as long as he could and kept on working his slaves as if nothing had happened. As had been true after Lincoln signed the Emancipation Proclamation in 1863, freedom was obliged to wait until the sound of Union gunfire could be heard on the plantation.

"The big gun fired on Saturday, and meant that the Yankees had come and the slaves was free," the onetime slave Margaret Nickerson recalled years later. "Black folks came out of the woods from all directions. The next day Mr. Carr got us all together, and read a paper to us that didn't none of us understand, except that it meant we was free. Then he said that them that would stay and harvest the cotton and corn would be given the net proceeds. Them what did found out that the net proceeds wasn't nothin but the stalks."[20]

In up-country South Carolina when slaves finally heard a rumor that they were free, some slipped off the plantations and went to Columbia or Charleston to find out if there was any truth in it. One such, Toney, declared that when he got back to the plantation at Pendleton he intended to strike a "bargain" with Ole Massa.

Patience Johnson, who served as a house slave, was asked by her mistress to remain and work for wages. "No, Miss," she replied. "I must go. If I stay here I'll never know I am free."[21]

Phoebe, house servant to the Reverend Cornish of the Aikin (S.C.) Baptist Church, had her feelings hurt when the Reverend first sought to force freed slaves to sit in the balcony of his church, and then closed the church when they refused. "Whose servant are you?" Phoebe was asked. "My own," she replied. Asked to apologize or leave, she left.[22]

At the Holmes plantation in Camden there were twelve adult slaves. Their mistress, while informing them of the Confederate surrender, would not release them "because it was not at all certain that they would be freed." Some left anyway, causing one of the daughters of the household to complain that "Ann, poor deluded fool, informed mother she could not wash any longer, nor would she remain to finish the ironing, and off she went."

"In every direction we hear of families being left without a single servant, or those who stay doing almost nothing," bemoaned another member of the Holmes family. "All have turned fool together."[23]

In some localities the liberated blacks celebrated their newfound freedom with "jubilees." One of the most elaborate was staged in Charleston on March 29. The freedom parade was led by two black marshals on horseback. Then came the U.S. 21st Colored Troops (Third South Carolina Volunteers), followed by a "Liberty" float bearing the thirteen black girls representing the thirteen original states. A cart carrying a mock slave-auction block had a number of black men tied to it with ropes, several black women with their children, and an auctioneer who hawked their merits while a boy rang a bell beneath a sign reading "A Number of Negroes for Sale." Behind this came a coffin marked "Slavery Is Dead!" and "Who Owns Him?—No One!" Then came eight companies of black firemen, fifty sailors, eighteen hundred schoolchildren, and a number of black craftsmen—tailors, coopers, blacksmiths, painters, carpenters, wheelwrights, barbers—all carrying the tools of their trade.

"Good order and appreciation for freedom was evident," a white spectator reported. However, when the paraders announced their intention to stage a similar celebration come Independence Day, they were reminded that the slave codes forbade any assemblage by blacks on national holidays.[24]

During the first month after Appomattox everyone looked to Washington for some definitive statement about slavery. When none was forthcoming by mid-May, General Q. A. Gillmore, in command of the Department of the South, took it upon himself to publicly declare: "It is deemed sufficient, meanwhile, to announce that the people of the black race are free citizens of the United States, that it is the fixed intention of a wise and beneficent Government to protect them in the enjoyment of their freedom and the fruits of their industry."[25]

This did not in the least deter many slaveholders from keeping their blacks in bondage, and in darkness about such an order having been issued. Three months later, in mid-August, General Gillmore felt obliged to issue another order, commanding all slaveholders to inform their slaves of his initial order without further delay.

Even so, both the U.S. military and the Freedmen's Bureau (then attached to the War Department) backed a demand by former slaveowners that blacks be kept on the plantations until the year's crops had been harvested. To this end, all (except blacks) were agreed that "labor contracts" were the way to go. Most former slaves, familiar as they were with the ways of Ole Massa, were exceedingly loath to sign, instinctively fearing that to do so might result in their reenslavement.

"They signed with great reluctance," reported E. J. Parker, who had operated a turpentine camp with slave labor. "Isaac Reed would not do it and had to be taken to Kingstree. He cut up all sorts of Shines. Said he would suffer to be shot down before he would sign it. That he did not intend to do anything for any man he had been under all his life."[26]

Many were forced to sign under duress—and thus obliged to look forward to New Year's Day 1866, when the contracts would run out, as their real Emancipation Day. "The poor negro," wrote Augustine Smythe of Lang Syne Plantation in South Carolina. "Besotted with ignorance, & so full of freedom, looking forward to January as to some day of Jubilee approaching."[27]

Idleness, though always regarded as a virtue as practiced by the planters themselves, was considered to be utterly intolerable when indulged in by former slaves. No doubt, many slaves felt they were entitled to a bit of vacation. One woman reported that she practiced freedom by sitting down whenever she felt like it.[28]

A white observer of the Southern scene reported "negroes generally very idle, wandering about the country enjoying their freedom, tho to my mind wonderfully civil, under the circumstances."[29]

Further attesting the demeanor of the blacks, a former slaveowner declared: "I have been very agreeably disappointed in the behavior of the negroes. They are as civil and humble as ever. All I met greeted me enthusiastically as 'Mass Gus.' "[30]

That these were not isolated instances was made manifest by many "gatherings" of blacks that took place all over the South, where what might now be called "position papers" were adopted. One such resolution, from Petersburg, Virginia, was typical of the lot: "That we have no feelings of resentment toward our former owners, but are willing to let the past be buried with the past, and in the future treat all persons with kindness and respect who shall treat us likewise."[31]

In social relationships with blacks, however, white supremacists were willing to be civil upon occasion but drew the line there. Taboos against all sorts of interracial relationships (excepting of course sexual liaisons between white males and black females), which had been stringent enough under slavery, were now tightened as a means of compensating for the abolition of slavery. The purpose of the codes and mores enforced to this end was to keep blacks "in their place."

"We must make the negro our friend," wrote James Lusk Alcorn of Mississippi. "We can do this if we will. Should we make him our enemy under the prompting of the Yankees, whose aim is to force us to recognize him on a basis of equality, then our path lies through a way red with blood and damp with tears."[32]

It was with good reason that black enthusiasm over their liberation was tempered by anxiety lest they be reenslaved.

The antislavery aspect of the Union war effort had never been very pronounced, and vacillated from beginning to end. Early in the war, when U.S. generals John C. Fremont in Missouri and David Hunter in South Carolina had taken it upon themselves to declare slaves in U.S.-occupied territory to be free, President Lincoln as commander in chief had countermanded their order.[33] In the Western theater, U.S. General Henry W. Halleck delivered back to their owners all slaves who fled to his ranks in search of freedom.[34] Still other U.S. generals, like Benjamin F. Butler of Virginia, had declared refugee slaves to be "contraband of war" and put them to work for the Union army.[35] Even the Emancipation Proclamation, when it finally came in the midst of the war, was frankly adopted as a war measure with the primary aim of weakening the Confederacy. Time and again Lincoln had offered to pay for all slaves, if the Confederacy would but lay down its arms.

Little research has been done on the extent to which the rank-and-file Union soldier was intent upon liberating blacks. In all probability they were no more nor less dedicated to this war aim than the Yanks were to "making the world safe for democracy" in World War I, or establishing the Four Freedoms during World War II, or "Defending the Free World" in Korea, Vietnam, Grenada, or Lebanon.

After Appomattox Ole Massa made no bones about his hopes for salvaging slavery. "I fear there are many of them . . . who say that . . . if the people of the South will watch and wait, take no oaths and remain as they are, slavery will yet be saved," George W. Williams, a South Carolina planter, wrote his state's provisional governor at the time.[36]

Such hopes were founded upon far more than a policy of watchful waiting and civil disobedience. In many quarters, North as well as South, there were those who fancied that the U.S. Supreme Court might yet declare the Emancipation Proclamation to be unconstitutional. This particular anticipation was based not only upon the technical shortcomings attending the Proclamation but also upon the Supreme Court's position as stated in the Dred Scott decision of 1857.

Each of the nine justices had issued separate decisions. That written by Chief Justice Roger B. Taney declared that a Negro "whose ancestors were . . . sold as slaves" could not become a citizen of the body politic created by the U.S. Constitution by virtue of the fact that their ancestors were not regarded as "people" by the framers of that Constitution. The Chief Justice went on to declare: "It is difficult at this day to realize the state of public opinion in relation to that unfortunate race, which prevailed in the civilized and enlightened portions of the world at the time of the Declaration of Independence, and when the Constitution was framed and adopted. But the public history of every European nation displays it in a manner too plain to be mistaken.

"They had for more than a century before been regarded as beings of an inferior order, and altogether unfit to associate with the white race, either in social or political relations; and so far inferior, that they had no rights which the white man was bound to respect; and that the negro might justly and lawfully be reduced to slavery for his benefit . . . This opinion was at that time . . . universal in the civilized portion of the white race . . . The legislation of the different colonies furnishes positive and indisputable proof of this fact."[37]

At the time when the Dred Scott decision was handed down, and subsequently, it was generally agreed that Taney's reference to slave ancestry was but a literary flourish and that the decision in intent and effect barred any and all persons of African descent from American citizenship.

Two of the justices dissented: Benjamin R. Curtis and John McLean, the latter pointing out that there were rather many free persons of color who held citizenship in various states prior to the Constitution and adding that he could find nothing whatever in that document that could be interpreted as barring persons of African descent from American citizenship.

Although the Thirteenth Amendment abolishing slavery was pushed through during the Year of the Surrender, Mississippi and Texas never did ratify it, insisting that the Constitution already reserved such powers to the several states, in perpetuity. Hard-core slavers continued to harbor a hope that the Supreme Court might some day agree with them, or at least rule out the enforcement clauses of the amendment. The fact that the U.S. Congress had given slavery its stamp of approval in the Fugitive Slave Act of 1850, and again in the Missouri Compromise, was recalled by some die-hard slavocrats in support of their contention that congress might be prevailed upon to do so again.

As for the Southern states themselves, blacks knew them to be expert in the art of returning "free persons of color" to slavery, and a number of states still had statutes on their books to facilitate the process. There was many a reason, then, for blacks to feel both jubilant and uneasy about their newfound freedom.

With this assessment of the diametrically opposed mindsets that Appomattox precipitated among the white and black *people* of the South, let us, before embarking with them into the tumultuous decade of conflict that lay ahead, take additional time-out to familiarize ourselves with some of the instruments of *power* that were destined to be the focal points of that struggle.

✠

NEW CHAINS FOR OLD

✠

CHAPTER 3

✠

The havoc the war had wrought with the South physically was nothing compared to what it threatened to do to the South's institutions. The question confronting the postwar South was whether the old order, which had endured for centuries, was gone forever, or whether its essence could yet be salvaged by changing it somewhat.

Although the war had arrived at a military solution for the questions of secession and chattel slavery, the erstwhile Confederates were determined to preserve both white supremacy and black bondage throughout the region, albeit within the framework of the Union. Needless to say, they could not have the one without the other. Given the manifest resolve of the former slaves to take hold of, exercise, and defend their new-found freedom, it was obvious that strenuous measures would be required to deprive them of it. But the white supremacists were old hands at this, and they set about the task with evident zeal. Given also a perception by most Northerners that it was not for such a Southland that they had fought and won, continued conflict on an intensive scale was inevitable.

While reconstructionists had to start from scratch, white supremacists already had in place all the makings for an integrally racist society. The entire infrastructure of the Southern states—their statutes, ordinances, institutions, and traditions— had been meticulously calculated to insure white supremacy throughout every facet of human existence. No conceivable eventuality had been overlooked; every individual of both races knew full well what sort of behavior the system demanded in any given situation.

After Appomattox the white supremacists were determined to keep just as much of this racist infrastructure in place as possible. In the legalistic sphere this entailed retention where possible, and modification where necessary, of the elaborate Black Codes that had governed the conduct of slaves and "free persons of color" before Appomattox. As a starter, the all-white legislatures created under the Johnson Restoration hastened to adopt such measures as the following (from Mississippi): "All penal and criminal laws now in force . . . defining offenses and describing the mode of punishment of crimes and misdemeanors committed by slaves, free negroes, or mulattoes, are hereby re-enacted, and decreed to be in full force and effect, against freedmen, free negroes, and mulattoes," except insofar as the mode of punishment may have been "changed and altered by law."[1]

Far from being satisfied with such reaffirmations of the old order, the neo-Confederates busied themselves with the enactment of new provisions under the Codes. It was Mississippi that again led the way in fashioning new links, among them a tax on blacks only "to take care of their poor and infirm," and a prohibition against the lease or sale of farmland to blacks. The Freedmen's Bureau saw fit to negate the latter piece of legislation, and U.S. general Daniel E. Sickles found South Carolina's Black Code so infamous that he rejected it en toto and substituted military authority for it.[2] At times a mustering of troops and show of force by the Bureau was necessary to set aside certain provisions of the Codes.

Rights that the white supremacists were willing to concede to blacks as a result of Appomattox were few and far between. These included the right to move about (unless one was said to be in debt), assemble (under certain circumstances), get married (to members of their own race), own property (if anyone would sell to them), make contracts, attend schools (of their own), and sue and be sued. At the same time, blacks were expressly forbidden to bear arms, attend school with whites, sit on juries, or testify in court when the personal or property interests of any whites were involved. On this last point, Alabama's Governor-elect Benjamin Humphreys put this question to President Johnson: "Members feel that one Concession will only lead to others. What assurance can I give on the subject?" To which the president would only reply: "The admission of negro testimony, they all being free, will be as much for the protection of the white, as the colored."[3]

The question of what effect the abolition of slavery would have upon relations between members of the two races was one that attracted particular attention. Under slavery, which had required a certain intimacy in working relationships between whites and blacks, it had hardly been necessary to spell out, in the form of law, the terms of such relationships. An intricate web of interracial etiquette took care of these matters, and any white who was not entirely satisfied with a black's behavior or demeanor had only to say so. Separation of the races was the rule in all things, except when service to whites required proximity. Even then, a certain amount of prudence on the part of blacks was in order. As one house servant said, "I feeds white folks with a long spoon."[4]

With the absolute dictatorship of whites over blacks that slavery had afforded abolished by Appomattox, white supremacists felt an urgent need to erect legalistic barriers to keep black and white individuals and communities strictly apart. Segregation laws already on the books were strengthened, and an all-pervasive network of new ones were enacted. On state, county, and municipal levels the rush was on to use legal compulsion to assure racial segregation in housing, transportation, education, and all areas of public accommodation. With true Southern decorum, whites were forbidden to intrude upon assemblies of blacks, and vice versa. A double standard reared its head in matters sexual, however, with a fine of one thousand dollars and three months' imprisonment being provided for any white woman who had sex with a black man, but with no penalty for white men who had sex with black women.[5]

In time, facilities set aside for blacks, and the laws compelling their usage, came to be referred to as "Jim Crow" provisions, the name apparently deriving from an early blackface minstrel song and dance:

> Jump—jump—jump Jim Crow,
> Take a little twirl, and away we go!
> Slide—slide—stamp—stamp—stamp,
> Take another partner, and jump Jim Crow!

When the first Jim Crow coach for blacks was hitched onto the rear of a Southern train, the African Methodist Episcopal Church— perhaps seeing a vision of the century that was to come—led its flock out onto the tracks to bar the way, but to no avail.[6]

Lost—Forty Acres and a Mule

Such skills as blacks had acquired after being brought to or born in the U.S.A. were confined in the main to agriculture and stock-raising. It was abundantly clear to everyone, therefore, that if the freedom were not to be relegated to the status of serfdom, they would have to somehow come into possession of arable land. Only the economic security and independence that ownership of farmland afforded could render the freedmen immune to lynching—economic and otherwise—and insure that their political, civil, and human rights would be respected.

Southern blacks and whites were equally aware of this. The latter were therefore resolved that the former not be allowed to acquire good land, either by lease or by purchase. At first, as has been noted, they sought to achieve this by making such leases and sales illegal. When the "forces of occupation" ruled out such measures, they achieved the same end by entering into an informal Southwide conspiracy not to lease or sell to blacks any viable tracts of cultivable land.[7] And as it turned out, ostracism and terrorism were quite as effective in enforcing the conspiracy as any law might have been.

While the war was still in progress, Union spokesmen promulgated many a laudable war aim, as wartime spokesmen will. Prominent among these was the promise of "40 acres and a mule" to every adult freedman. At the very least, it was said, the 180,000 blacks who had fought in the Union army, and perhaps also the 200,000 who had been put to work for the army, were entitled to such a reward. The same entitlement should be offered, it was said, to white Union soldiers who were interested. The most generous of the advocates of land reform were even willing to count Southern poor whites in. If free land was the way to win the West, why not the South as well?

The difference, of course, was that whereas the former holders of the West had been forcibly dispossessed and largely annihilated, the South's big planter class was, though decimated in numbers, still very much alive and on the scene, ready to do battle to cling to their holdings.

One of the most insistent and persistent advocates of breaking up the big plantations in the South and redistributing the land to the landless was Thaddeus Stevens in the House. "I would seize every foot of land and every dollar of property as our armies go along, and put it to the uses of the war and the payment of our debts," he had declared in July of 1862, when the war was yet young. "I would sell Confederate lands to the soldiers of independence: I would send those soldiers with arms in their hands to occupy the heritage of traitors and build up there a land of free men and of freedom."[8] Stevens's vision included the distribution of land to freedmen, who together with and backed by former Union soldiers, would build a free and democratic society in the South.

But throughout the war, that lawyer in the White House, Abraham Lincoln, evinced little enthusiasm for the confiscation of Confederate property. When Congress adopted a Confiscation Act in 1862, it was in part owing to Lincoln's opposition that a proviso was added that any lands confiscated would be returned to the heirs upon the death of the original rebel owners. A somewhat more stringent act, passed later in the war, was modified when Lincoln threatened to veto it; and even after it was passed he refrained from using it.

As for Andrew Johnson, during his wartime antiaristocracy mood he had waxed as militant as any of the champions of land reform. During October of 1864 he had declared that he favored breaking up the large plantations and distributing the land to "free, industrious and honest farmers" and had gone on to assure blacks, "I will indeed be your Moses . . . and lead you to a fairer land of liberty and peace."[9] (Perhaps even then he had Africa in mind.)

Not only Southern blacks were led to believe land distribution was a Union war aim; U.S. General Sherman evidently believed also, for as the war drew toward its close he issued on January 16, 1865, Field Order No. 15, inviting blacks to take possession of a thirty-mile-wide strip along the Atlantic coast, from Charleston, South Carolina to Jacksonville, Florida, to build homes and establish farms thereon, and to govern themselves. White people were ordered to keep out.[10] Some 40,000 blacks proceeded to occupy some 485,000 acres. Similar steps were taken under Union military auspices in the Carolina Sea Islands, and General Grant sponsored another self-governing black community at Davis Bend, Mississippi.[11]

Flushed with the impending victory, Stevens in the House in that spring of 1865 urged the confiscation of no less than 394 million acres of plantation land, and distribution of 40 million of these in parcels of forty acres per adult male. The remainder he proposed to sell at auction, and to use the proceeds toward retiring the Union war debt, increasing the pensions of Union soldiers, and compensating loyal citizens who had suffered property damage as a result of the war. But despite the fact that Stevens's proposal had far more to offer whites than blacks, it got nowhere.[12]

Congress did adopt, in March (Appomattox came on April 9) a bill establishing the Freedmen's Bureau as an adjunct of the War Department, authorizing it to provide food, clothing, and fuel for Southern blacks and whites in distress. A final report issued by the Bureau indicated that it did distribute fifteen million food rations (not only to blacks), established fifty hospitals which had served a million patients, and established elementary schools staffed by ten thousand teachers who had provided instruction for three hundred thousand pupils, not all of whom were children. The measure also contained a watered-down land distribution provision, whereby both blacks and whites could have access to U.S.-held lands under a use/right-to-purchase agreement. This act read: "The Commissioner [of the Freedmen's Bureau], under the direction of the President, shall have authority to set apart, for the use of loyal refugees and freedmen, such tracts of land within the insurrectionary states as shall have been abandoned, or to which the United States shall have acquired title by confiscation or sale, or otherwise, and to every male citizen, whether refugee or freedman . . . there shall be assigned no more than forty acres of such land, and the person to whom it was so assigned shall be protected in the use and enjoyment of the land for the term of three years . . . At the end of said term, the occupants of any parcels so assigned may purchase the land and receive such title thereto as the United States can convey."

Southern planters never ceased to inveigh against confiscation, and their proprietary-class counterparts in the North heard their cry and joined with them in seeing to it that the war was going to have no such result. "Division of rich men's lands among the landless . . . would give a shock to our whole social and political system from which it would hardly recover without the loss of liberty," opined the *Nation* in a typical broadside.[13]

The case for land reform was stated by the black emancipator Frederick Douglass, among others. Pointing out that the Russian serfs had been given land upon being set free in 1861, he called attention to the contrasting fate of American slaves, who he said "were sent empty-handed, without money . . . without a foot of land upon which to stand. Old and young, sick and well, were turned loose to an open sky, naked to their enemies."[14]

And so this question of who was to own the land was accurately perceived by both the haves and the have-nots as being the basic determinant of what sort of society was to evolve in the South.

Cash or Kind?

To keep blacks landless was not enough to serve the multifarious purposes of white supremacy; ways and means had to be found to compel them to work for little or nothing. The latter, from the "employers' " point of view, was the preferable of the two, and no effort was spared in an attempt to achieve this goal.

Immediately after Appomattox, the payment of cash wages to blacks was looked upon by many Southern whites as positively seditious. If blacks had money in their pockets, it was reasoned, they would be free to stop work, go where they pleased, and spend where they pleased. So abhorrent was this prospect that vigilante bands were formed to raid and vandalize railroad construction camps and other employers who began to pay cash wages to blacks.

The vigilante tradition as a means of enforcing black bondage had a long history in the South, and it was not to be inhibited by the loss of the war. Before the war, it had been the "paderollers" (patrollers)—mounted bands of men who caroused about the countryside at night—who made it their business to apprehend runaway or rambling slaves, often "touching them up" with a bullwhip before collecting a reward for returning them to their owners. During the war, white men too young or old to fight had carried on, calling themselves "home guards." And after Appomattox it was the "regulators" who were on the prowl. That these latter were indeed intent upon imposing some sort of involuntary servitude upon blacks was made clear by such dispatches as the following in the *New York Herald* (which at the time had the largest circulation of any newspaper in the country): "The 'regulators' go to the bottom of the matter, and strive to make it uncomfortably warm for any new settler with demoralizing innovations of wages for 'niggers.' "

Resistance to cash wages for blacks was coupled with a determination to keep them from acquiring or practicing skilled trades. Keeping blacks skill-less as well as landless was considered essential for assuring employers the pool of cheap labor they desired.

It so happened—as was noted in the lineup of Charleston's freedom jubilee parade, that a substantial number of blacks had already managed to acquire skills in the trades. In fact, in the mechanical trades they were reported to outnumber whites five to one. This of course meant that they not only had to be henceforth barred but also squeezed out. To accomplish this, laws were enacted requiring black tradesmen to pay prohibitory license fees. In many instances, white tradesmen conspired with white employers to bar blacks from skilled jobs. As Isaac Myers, a ship caulker, protested at the time: "American citizenship for the black man is a complete failure if he is proscribed from the workshops of the country."

Even while barring blacks from the trades, whites devised a system of so-called "apprenticeship" for black youth, whereby those who were orphans or whose parents were said to be unable to provide for them, were "apprenticed" to white masters. The purpose, however, was not to teach blacks trades but to obtain menial labor at relatively little cost. Masters were empowered by law to whip "moderately" apprentices under the age of eighteen; beyond that age, a magistrate's approval had to be had.[15]

Northern employer interests, being fully appreciative of the advantages to themselves of casting blacks into a pool of cheap labor, lent tacit support to all these schemes of Southern white supremacists to make blacks vulnerable by denying them land, credit, skills, and rights.

In such fashion were the "freedmen" set up for resubjugation. The actual process of placing them in bondage required still other measures, however. The procurement of peons was not quite the same as the procurement of slaves had been. To obtain slaves, one had only to capture, buy, or breed them. To secure peons, on the other hand, it was necessary to employ cajolery, fraud, economic pressure, intimidation or coercion, or some combination thereof.

Just as the blacks had not had much choice about being enslaved, they were not given much more when it came to being peonized. In most instances, dire economic necessity was enough to drive them to accept any sort of work that seemed to hold forth a prospect of subsistence for themselves and their families. But just to make sure that none escaped his dragnet, Ole Massa added a few other forms of compulsion.

One of these was a head tax, levied against blacks only. Those who were unable or unwilling to pay could be jailed, and Ole Massa would offer to pay their fine if they would commit themselves to "work it out" on his plantation. Alternatively, he could lease convicts (mostly black, then as now) to work his holdings.

One of the strongest links in the new chains being forged by Ole Massa proved to be vagrancy laws, lifted en toto from the statute books of New England. These catchall enactments were broad enough to ensnare almost anyone (again, then as now). A typical statute, as adopted by Florida, provides as follows:

> Rogues and vagabonds, idle or dissolute persons who go about begging, common gamblers, persons who use juggling, or unlawful games or plays, common pipers and fiddlers, common drunkards, common night-walkers, thieves, pilferers, traders in stolen property, lewd, wanton and lascivious persons, keepers of gambling places, common railers and brawlers, persons who neglect their calling or employment, or are without continuous employment or regular income and who have not sufficient property to sustain them and misspend what they earn without providing for them-

selves or the support of their families, persons wandering or strolling around from place to place without any lawful purpose or object, habitual loafers, idle and disorderly persons, persons neglecting all lawful business and habitually spending their time by frequenting houses of ill-fame, gaming houses, or tippling shops, persons able to work but habitually living upon the earnings of their wives or minor children, and all able-bodied male persons over the age of 18 years who are without means of support and remain in idleness, shall be deemed vagrants and upon conviction shall be subject to penalty.[16]

Such vagrancy laws were made to order for the purposes of Ole Massa, who first saw to it that the freedmen were denied bona fide opportunities for earning a living, and then invoked the vagrancy laws to force them to work on his terms. To justify this arrangement in the eyes of the nation, an intensive propaganda campaign was launched.

"Now that the negro is free he has no idea of working more than is barely necessary to keep in pork and grits," O. M. Crosby averred in a typical broadside in his book *Florida Facts*. "Few colored men will agree to work faithfully by the month. Their sense of honor is low, and they cannot be trusted at the stores."[17]

Only occasionally did the real facts of this matter leak out, as in *A Winter in Florida* by Ledyard Bill: "We suspect the chief reason why the negro is loth to labor is the uncertainty of his wages. Finding they received nothing but promises, the negroes naturally became idle."[18]

With hunger, head taxes, vagrancy laws, and convict parole/lease system all going for him, Ole Massa still hankered after something tantamount to the hold that the bill of sale had given him over his slaves. He satisfied this longing by devising the labor contract, which he carefully couched in language that few black laborers understood. Understood or not, the labor contract gave Ole Massa the legalistic and physical control over his workers that he so fervently desired. In practice, blacks were rigidly bound by the terms of the contracts, while Ole Massa was not. It became a widespread practice among planters to dismiss their "hands" without recompense, so soon as the harvest was in. Little or no excuse was required for this: racist etiquette dictated that blacks not act "uppity" or "sass" white folks, and allegations of such offenses were quite enough to warrant turning them off without a penny. There was far more than symbolism in the fact that the contracts referred to the respective parties not as "employer" and "employee" but in the old familiar terms of "master" and "servant."[19]

Having thus rendered the freedmen vulnerable by denying them rights and resources, and having impaled them neatly upon vagrancy laws and labor contracts, Ole Massa figured that all he needed to complete his new order of slavocracy was some equivalent of the paderollers and fugitive slave laws to keep his peons from making a run for freedom. For the freedman as peon felt the same urge he had as a slave. It was an urge that he had already been memorialized in this bit of dialogue between Ole Massa and Ole Black Joe:

"I've always treated you right, haven't I?"

"God knows you have!"

"You do love Ole Massa, don't you?"

"God knows I do!"

"If I was to turn by back, you wouldn't run, would you?"

"God knows . . ."

The chief instrumentality for making peons stay put was soon seen to be the innovation of the plantation commissary or company store. As a condition of their "employment," workers could be charged rent and required to get the necessities of life from the commissary. With born-again Ole Massa fixing the prices and keeping the books, the hired hands could be kept perpetually in debt. To make doubly sure, some employers paid any earnings due in scrip good only at the commissary rather than in cash.[20] In such manner involuntary servitude could be assured, despite the new state constitutions and the Thirteenth Amendment.

In time the black peon came up with the song "Po Lazarus" to protest his plight:

Didn't Lazus crap on the commissary counter,
And walk away,
Lord, Lord, walk away?

Camp told the High Sheriff,
"Go bring me Lazus, dead or alive!"
Lord, Lord, dead or alive.

They found Po Lazus way up 'tween two mounds,
With his head hung down,
Lord, Lord, head hung down.

Judge give Po Lazus 99 years in Atlanta,
For crappin in town,
Lord, Lord, crappin in town.

Most planters were resolved to rely upon their own talents to keep their peons from "running off without paying their debts," and bringing them back if they did. To facilitate the process, families and possessions (if any) were held hostage. Anyone making a "citizen's arrest" of a runaway was paid a bounty of five dollars, plus ten cents per mile. If need be, lawmen could be called upon to apprehend a fugitive on a charge of fraud, for parole back into the custody of the employer. Sometimes the culprit was given the option of "working it out with the county." Either way, it meant working under a gun.

Only slightly more refined than the labor contract was the sharecropper system that some planters set about establishing on their former slave plantations. Under this system, the owner (of the land), the merchant (who provided tools, seed, fertilizer, and provisions), and the cropper (who did all the work), were each to get one-third of the crop's proceeds. At year's end, however, records would be produced purporting to show that the cropper had little or nothing coming to him.

"We worked for them as though we were slaves, and they treated us like dogs," three black croppers told a congressional investigator. When they refused to surrender the crop for nothing, they were flogged and driven off.

THE JOHNSON RESTORATION

✠

CHAPTER 4

✠

The question of *what* was to be done with the "liberated" South, and *who* was to do it, had of course been passionately debated while the war was still in progress.

Much depended upon point of view. It could be argued, on the one hand, that the states as such had committed suicide by the act of secession, and hence could be regarded as U.S. territories like those in the West, with Congress legislating for them as provided by the Constitution. Or one could take the position with lawyer/president Lincoln that the U.S. government was contending with disloyal *citizens* rather than disloyal *states,* a position that implied that *loyal* citizens in those states were entitled to form new governments and resume the functions of statehood.

The Lincoln Formula

The question was legalistic and theoretical to a degree, but it was also one with vast practical ramifications. Although the concept of a War Powers Act, conveying extraordinary powers to the presidency, was still something for the distant future, Lincoln had proceeded as though he had the benefit of one. Among many other things he did during the war without overmuch regard for the Constitution was to devise a formula whereby liberated Southern states could reconstitute their state and local governments, and be readmitted to the Union, whenever ten percent of the number of white citizens who had been registered to vote in that state in 1860 had taken an oath of never having voluntarily supported the Confederacy. Blacks, though prepared almost to a man to take such an oath, were not invited to do so. Loyal or not, they didn't count—except, pursuant to the Constitution, as three-fifths of a person in determining how many representatives whites could send to Congress.

Early in the war, even before promulgation of the Lincoln Formula, loyal citizens in West Virginia were encouraged to establish civil authority and govern themselves. And when Union troops proceeded to occupy Louisiana, federal supervision was applied to the same end. On July 2, 1862, Congress had adopted an "iron-clad" loyalty oath to standardize the procedure.

During late 1864 and early 1865, Tennessee and Arkansas had joined Louisiana in setting up new governments based upon Lincoln's ten percent formula. Few people took exception when the Louisiana regime proclaimed itself to be "a government of white people, made to be perpetuated for the exclusive benefit of the white race." When all three states dispatched representatives to both houses of Congress, however, they were rejected as being unrepresentative.

Throughout the North, throughout the war, there had been a rather widespread conservative sentiment that the nation's war aims should be limited to "preserving the Union as it was, and the Constitution as it is."[1] Lincoln and his party, some said, were doing things—and contemplating doing things—that were potentially even more subversive of the republic and the Constitution than the rebels and their Confederacy.

On the other side of the scale, men like Charles Sumner in the Senate and Thaddeus Stevens in the House were urging the confiscation of Confederate property; the breakup of the plantations for the distribution of small holdings to blacks, poor whites, and Union soldiers; and federal backing to enable these three elements to coalesce into a new democratic society in the South.

It was in the midst of such conflicting currents that Appomattox came to pass, making urgent the transformation of debate into decisions. Nine days after Appomattox, a so-called "Generals' Agreement" was entered into by U.S. Major-General William T. Sherman and Confederate General Joseph E. Johnston, stipulating that Confederates need only lay down their arms to regain full U.S. citizenship and statehood. But Lincoln, and subsequently Johnson and the Congress, were quick to repudiate the simplistic terms of this cease-fire agreement. It was enough, nonetheless, to enable Confederates in the years that followed to complain that they had been tricked into quitting, and that the U.S. should be bound by the Generals' Agreement.

Po-White in the White House

The accession of Vice President Andrew Johnson to the presidency upon the assassination of Lincoln prompted both reconstructionists and racists to claim him as their own.

"Mr. Johnson," quoth Senator Ben Wade of Ohio, "I thank God that you are here. Lincoln had too much of the milk of human kindness to deal with these damn Rebels. Now they will be dealt with according to their deserts."[2]

Many rebels were inclined to agree that they were in for a hard time. Andy Johnson, a "po-white" raised in Tennessee, had been the only senator from the South to remain loyal to the Union after the Rebels fired upon Fort Sumter. During the war, as chairman of the Joint Congressional Committee on the Conduct of the War, he had championed many a "no-quarter" measure. Serving as military governor of Tennessee in 1864, he ruled with an iron hand, and in a torchlight parade he orated: "I, Andrew Johnson, hereby proclaim freedom, full, broad, and unconditional, to every man in Tennessee! This damnable aristocracy must be pulled down!"[3]

Chosen that same year to be Lincoln's running mate for the vice presidency, Johnson evoked this comment from *Harper's Magazine*. "There is no man in the country, unless it be Mr. Lincoln himself, whom the Rebels more cordially hate. He fought them in the Senate when they counted on his aid, and he has fought them steadily ever since."[4] As if to confirm this view, one Isham G. Harris, a rebel from Tennessee, had this to say: "If Johnson were a snake, he would lie in the grass and bite the heels of the rich men's children."[5] The *Houston Telegraph* direly predicted: "Abolition, confiscation, the gallows, revenge in its most sweeping decrees and direct forms, are all in his heart, and will soon find utterance in his programme."[6]

There were, however, some more astute rebels who refused to write off the South's wayward son in the White House. Citing Johnson's Southern birth and rearing, the *New Orleans Times* ventured hopefully: "He has never peddled a clock or palmed off a wooden nutmeg . . . The wonderful effects of New England culture are not manifested in any growth of horns upon his forehead."[7]

White supremacists all over the country pinned their hopes on the known racist streak in Johnson. Although he had endorsed the Emancipation Proclamation as being "right in itself" and an effective means of destroying the "odious and dangerous aristocracy," he had also at one time expressed the wish that every white family in America could have a black slave "for drudgery and menial service."[8]

With such as this in mind, the antislavery *New York Tribune* somewhat apprehensively reminded its readers that Johnson could hardly be called a "negro-worshipper," since "he had always till now voted and acted as though Blacks had no rights which whites are bound to respect."[9] (This absolutist concept embodied in the Supreme Court's Dred Scott decision of 1857 was to become the cornerstone of the Klan's Kreed and the new order of white supremacy in the South.)

Johnson had no sooner entered the White House when he received a letter from a Tennessee friend, reminding the president that he remembered well "your remark, and that was, 'I am for a white man's government in America.' "[10]

Johnson had evidently neither forgotten nor changed his mind, for he shortly sent an emissary, a personal friend named Harvey Watterson, into the South to tell the U.S. generals stationed there that he, their commander in chief, was "for a white man's government, and in favor of free white citizens controlling this country."[11]

In short, it was evident from the start of his term that he had always been more antiaristocracy than he had been problack. It was the plantation system, rather than the system of slavery, that had been the target of his ire.

With the president of the United States openly espousing their white supremacist doctrine for the exclusion of blacks from politics, the former Confederates felt with good reason that their continuing battle was at least half won.

It soon turned out, moreover, that the po-white president's antipathy to the Southern aristocracy was no more than skin-deep. Coteries of Southern ladies converged upon the White House, seeking pardons for their Confederate husbands and sons, and exemption of their plantations from confiscation. In the process they evidently convinced Johnson that Southern aristocrats were not such a bad lot after all, for on May 29 (less than two months after Appomattox) he issued a General Amnesty Proclamation,[12] offering political rights and immunity from confiscation for former Confederates who would pledge to support the United States in the future and abide by any federal laws against slavery.

While there were thirteen excepted categories—including high civil officials of the Confederacy, army officers above the rank of colonel, and anyone owning more than twenty-thousand dollars' worth of property—provision was made whereby these might also seek presidential pardons. To expedite the pardoning process, Johnson appointed Confederate Colonel M. F. Parsons to supervise the operation. Pardons were soon being handed out at the rate of more than a hundred per day, with lawyers and brokers raking in fees ranging from $150 to $500 per person, depending upon how big a traitor the applicant had been.[13]

So taken with the "Johnson Plan" for reconstructing the South was Confederate General Lee that he came out of seclusion to give it his enthusiastic endorsement.[14] Southern black spokesmen, on the other hand, said they "could not understand the justice of denying the elective franchise to [black] men who have been fighting for their country, while it is freely given to men who have just returned from four years of fighting against it."[15]

The Soft Peace

In keeping with his belief in white supremacy and a right of white Southerners to impose and enforce it, Johnson proceeded to recognize the all-white governments already established in four states under the Lincoln Formula and to appoint provisional governors in the remaining seven states. Instead of limiting his choices to loyal white Southern Unionists, however, as Lincoln had, Johnson's gubernatorial appointees included a former slaveowner (Sharkey of Mississippi) and a former Confederate judge (Perry of South Carolina). By these and countless other official and unofficial acts, Johnson made it clear that he intended for the reins of power to be handed back to the former Confederates, and not to Southern Unionists.

The Johnson agenda for the restoration of Southern white rule included the restoration of political rights for most whites, who would elect delegates to constitutional conventions that would repeal the articles of secession, abolish slavery, and reaffirm allegiance to the United States. That done, elections would be held for state offices and seats in the U.S. House and Senate.

"In our opinion, the less the state conventions do, at the present time, outside of that which is absolutely necessary, the better," was the way the *Augusta* (Ga.) *Chronicle* viewed the situation.[16]

And so they did, the South Carolina convention refusing to so much as fly the American flag over its meeting place. Soft though the proposed peace terms were, all of the neo-Confederate conventions sought to do some horse-trading with Uncle Sam. In Mississippi, Georgia, and Florida, these gentlemen proposed to "repeal" the articles of secession rather than "nullify" them, as the latter word might cast some shadow of doubt upon their right to secede in the first place. Others wanted to know what sort of trade-off they could make in order to be allowed to honor Confederate war debts. As for abolishing slavery, some said they would do it if the U.S. would pay for them. Others, still insisting that the decision of whether to permit slavery was exclusively a right of the states, hinted that they would abolish it only if the federal government would cease insisting upon adoption of the Thirteenth Amendment. There were even those who did not want to go that far, preferring simply to "acknowledge" that slavery had been done away with by force of federal arms. As for any right of blacks to sit on juries, some conventions said they would consider the matter if the U.S. would promise not to press for votes for blacks.

Johnson let it be known that any state that balked could expect to be occupied indefinitely. Eventually the conventions did what they had to do, consoling themselves the while with resolutions to the effect that such things as voting, officeholding, and attending public schools would be limited exclusively to whites. "Neither the white man nor the black is prepared for the radical change" of allowing blacks to take part in politics, was the way one convention put it.[17]

That the enfranchisement of blacks was no less important than their emancipation was clearly foreseen by such staunch abolitionists as Wendell Phillips, who rightly predicted that without the vote blacks would be doomed to a century of peonage.

Johnson and his newfound friends in the South were keenly aware that whatever they were going to do by way of forging new chains for the old had to be done before Congress reconvened in December in that year of 1865. Their big idea was to present the Congress with a fait accompli—and urge it henceforth to mind its own business.

Ole Massa Regains the Whip Hand

In the elections that were feverishly held pursuant to the new constitutions, the men who had ruled the South before and during the war made short shrift of the relative handful of Southern white Unionists who were brave enough to enter the political arena. With no blacks voting, and precious few Unionists around to vote, the white supremacists had a field day. For all practical purposes, it was a mock, no-opposition affair. When the elections were all over, the proprietary class was firmly back in the saddle in every Southern state except Tennessee. So thorough was this power play that historians would do well to refer to it as the Johnson Restoration rather than Presidential Reconstruction.

L. E. Parsons, the provisional governor of Alabama, summed up the Southwide situation when, after mouthing the customary platitudes about "safeguarding the legitimate rights" of blacks, he went on to say, "At the same time it must be understood that politically and socially ours is a white man's government."[18]

The neo-Confederate legislatures busied themselves in making similar pronouncements, and the Mississippi body even refused to ratify the Thirteenth Amendment, which in its final form read: "Neither slavery nor involuntary servitude, except as a punishment for crime, whereof the person shall have been duly convicted, shall exist within the United States or any place subject to their jurisdiction."

On the question of Confederate war debts, South Carolina joined with Mississippi in refusing to repudiate them. Assessing the effect of the Johnson Restoration upon the South generally, the *North Carolina Standard* (Republican) had this to say about what had been going on while Congress fiddled: "We agree with our contemporary (the *Raleigh Progress*) that there is much disloyalty in the South, but we do not agree that there is more now than there was six months ago; it has been here all the time, but, a few months ago it crouched and snivelled at the feet of the victorious national forces, and now, as leniency and mercy has warmed it into life and the troops have been withdrawn, treason becomes bold and defiant."[19]

Further evidence of such defiance was to be found in the campaigning of the men who offered to represent the South in the halls of Congress. One Virginia candidate boldly campaigned on a platform of (1) Federal compensation to owners for all slaves emancipated, (2) Payment of all Confederate war debts, and (3) No use of federal taxes paid by Southerners for satisfying Union war debts.[20] This latter sentiment, widespread in the South, spread panic in the North, where patriotic citizens who had invested in war bonds began to fear they might never get their money back. An unanticipated result of the threat was to convince many such Northerners that the best way to insure their bonds was to see to it that Southern blacks were allowed to vote.

As the Year of the Surrender drew toward its close, and Congress prepared to end its long vacation, the *New Orleans Times* happily predicted that the South's newly elected representatives to Washington would be "proudly welcomed back to their long vacant seats."[21]

The seventy-four-member contingent that the South sent to the nation's capitol read more like a Who's Who of the Confederacy than anything else. Among them was none other than the former vice president of the Confederacy, Alexander H. Stevens, still under parole on a charge of treason. With him were no fewer than six former Confederate cabinet members, fifty-eight former members of the Confederate Congress, plus an assortment of Confederate generals, colonels, and legislators.

President Johnson displayed no sign of embarrassment in commending these gentry to their respective houses of Congress, even though many of them had never been given amnesty or pardoned, or taken the oath of allegiance to the United States. He simply issued a blanket pardon for all those members of the delegation standing in need of one.

The Congress, however, was in no mood to accept the president's handiwork. "I thought I had made my last anti-slavery speech," Charles Sumner said in the Senate, as the Year of the Surrender was about to expire. "I was mistaken . . . neither the rebellion nor slavery is yet ended . . . Slavery has been abolished in name, that is all."[22] To his abolitionist friends in New England he sent word: "Hold the anti-slavery societies together! The crisis is grave."

And a French correspondent stationed in Washington solemnly informed his countrymen that the American Civil War was about to break out all over again.[23]

CONGRESSIONAL RECONSTRUCTION

✠

CHAPTER 5

✠

The threatened resumption of the "Irrepressible Conflict" was not, this time, attributable to any determination on the part of the white South to resort to open war. It had what it wanted: no prosecution or confiscation for having committed treason, no war reparations to pay, restoration of the absolute monopoly on political power traditionally exercised by the white proprietary class, and a free hand in holding Southern blacks in continued subjugation. None other than the president of the United States had served as the chief architect of this new order of slavocracy. Some, looking back to the U.S. Supreme Court's Dred Scott decision of 1857, said that the judicial branch of government was likewise in the corner of white supremacy.

So Johnny Reb had no reason to take up his musket and fire upon Fort Sumter once again. This time it was the Congress of the United States, responding to the insistent demand of Southern blacks and a growing segment of public opinion in the North, that was determined that the Union's war aims be honored, at the point of a gun if need be.

Into this explosive atmosphere, Andy Johnson saw fit to hurl torches. He had, he solemnly assured the joint session that assembled to hear his state of the union message, substantially completed the task of restoring civil government in the South, so the Congress would have no need to consider the matter. Far from having any apologies to make for the lily-white complexion of the new Southern governments, or for the former Confederates who were waiting to be seated as U.S. senators and congressmen, the president seized upon the opportunity to lecture the lawmakers on the manifold evils, as he saw them, of anything but white rule. "[Negroes] have shown less capacity for government than any other race of people," the president declared. "No independent form of government has ever been successful in their hands."

To permit Southern blacks to vote, he went on, would endanger the rights of property, put the white man at the mercy of the black, destroy the South economically, and impose upon the region "such a tyranny as this continent has never yet witnessed."[1]

But if the president was in a bellicose mood, so was the Congress. By nearly unanimous votes, both houses slammed the door on the Southern delegations and sent them back where they came from. The house of cards so hastily yet laboriously erected by the white South with the patronage of the president was put on notice that its powers were to be limited and its days numbered. The Congress made it clear that it was going to turn the clock back to Appomattox and make a fresh start at restructuring the South, and that this time it, not the president, was going to call the shots.

The basic question was could the neo-Confederate regimes be replaced with a republican form of government as guaranteed by the Constitution, and the subjugation of one race by the other brought to an end, by investing Southern blacks with the full powers of citizenship—or would the process require a prolonged military reoccupation of the region?

In the House, Stevens declared that Southern representation in Congress would have to be based upon "voters"—white and black without distinction.

In the Senate, Sumner introduced bills to assure "equality before the law, whether in the courtroom or at the ballot box."

In the White House, Johnson denounced all such moves as an opening wedge that would lead "to a war between the races which would result in great injury to both and the certain extermination of the negro population."[2]

When Congress asked the president for a report on the state of the South, he presented them with a document that had been prepared earlier by General Grant, based upon five days of chitchatting with a few big planters. Not at all satisfied with this, Sumner introduced a detailed report by Secretary of State Carl Shurz, who had spent weeks traveling through the South, talking to people in all walks of life, including hospitalized victims of terrorist violence. Schurz wrote:

> The emancipation of the slaves is submitted to only in so far as chattel slavery in the old form could not be kept up. Wherever I go— the street, the shop, the house, the hotel, or the steamboat—I hear the people talk in such a way as to indicate that they are yet unable to conceive of the Negro as possessing any rights at all . . . The people boast that when they get the Freedmen's affairs in their own hands, to use their expression, "the niggers will catch hell."
>
> In parts where there are no Union soldiers I saw colored women treated in the in most outrageous manner. They have no rights that are respected. They are killed and their bodies are thrown into ponds and mud holes. They are mutilated by having their ears and noses cut off.
>
> All expect the Negro to be killed in one way or another by emancipation . . . If the Northern people are content to be ruled by the Southerners, they will continue in the Union. If not, the first chance they get they will rise again.[3]

To get a line of its own on what was going on down South, Congress created a "Joint Committee of 15 on Reconstruction" to take a close look at the region and make recommendations as to what Congress should do about congressional representation, the future status of blacks, and the future relationship of the federal with state governments in the fields of civil rights, labor, and industry.

Needless to say, President Johnson took a dim view of all such as this. By this time he was openly agreeing with Southern Democrats that the "radical" wing of the Republican Party was revolutionary and as much to blame for starting the Civil War as the secessionists. When, on January 18, Republicans in the House passed (without a Democrat concurring) a bill to enfranchise blacks in the District of Columbia, he said it was "the mere entering wedge to the agitation of the question throughout the states, and was ill-timed, uncalled for, and calculated to do great harm."[4]

In a hopeful effort to dispel some of the racist miasma with which Johnson had infused the White House, Frederick Douglass on February 7 led a deputation of eleven blacks to tell him what they thought was wrong with his scheme of things. Instead of listening to them, Johnson lectured them for forty-five minutes on his reasons for not enfranchising blacks and for encouraging them to emigrate to Africa. Reiterating his contention that permitting blacks to share in the political process would provoke race war, the president went on to aver that blacks were themselves to blame for Southern poor whites hating them because even as slaves they had looked upon the poor whites with disdain.[5]

According to a presidential secretary who attended the meeting, when the "darkey delegation" had departed the president exploded: "Those damned sons-of-bitches thought they had me in a trap! I know that damned Douglass, he's just like any nigger, and he would sooner cut a white man's throat than not!"

Having been given no opportunity to voice their own views, the Douglass delegation sent Johnson a written response, which said in part: "Peace between races is not to be secured by degrading one race and exalting another—by giving power to one race and withholding it from another—but by maintaining a state of equal justice between all classes. First pure, then peaceable."[6]

As for the president's proposal that blacks in America should remove themselves to Africa, the group declared: the worst enemy of the Nation could not cast upon its fair name a greater infamy than to admit that Negroes could be tolerated among them in a state of the most degrading slavery and oppression, and must be cast away, driven into exile, for no other cause than having been freed from their chains."

The First Reconstruction Acts

As a first step toward remedying conditions in the South, the Thirty-ninth Congress addressed itself to extending the life of the Freedmen's Bureau. "We have turned loose four million slaves without a hut to shelter them or a cent in their pockets," Stevens reminded his colleagues. "The infernal laws of slavery have prevented them from acquiring an education, understanding the commonest laws of contract, or of managing the ordinary affairs of business life. This Congress is bound to provide for them until they can take care of themselves. If we do not furnish them with homesteads and hedge them about with protective laws; if we leave them to the legislation of their late masters, we had better have left them in bondage."[7]

A bill to continue the Freedmen's Bureau, sponsored by gradualist Republicans, was adopted in February and sent to the White House. Johnson vetoed it, stating that the intent of emancipation was that the slaves become self-sustaining. "It was never intended that the Freedmen should be fed, clothed, educated and sheltered by the United States," his veto message said.

There was no need for federal legislation to assure that freedmen were compensated for their labor, the president said, because the law of supply and demand would settle the question of their wages. Should they have any problems on this score, they should look to their state courts for relief, he added. Each Southern state had a right to look after its own freedmen, he insisted, and could be expected to deal fairly with them "in order to benefit from their labor."

An attempt to override Johnson's veto of the Freedmen's Bureau Act failed. By way of explanation, House Speaker James G. Blaine had this to say: "The bankers of the great cities . . . believed harmonious cooperation was needed . . . Against obstacles so menacing, against resistance so ominous, it seemed an act of boundless temerity to challenge the President."[8]

So encouraged was Johnson by this turn of events that, speaking to a torchlight crowd gathered on the White House lawn to celebrate Washington's birthday, he declared that the nation's worst enemies were Stevens, Sumner, and the abolitionist Wendell Phillips. "Do they want more blood?" he cried in a frenzy.[9]

Interpreting all this to mean that they had nothing to fear from Congress, the South's white regimes went gleefully back to the business of elaborating ever more stringent Black Codes. This in turn prompted Congress to enact a Civil Rights Act, the first in the nation's history. Based upon the rights of enforcement bestowed upon Congress by the Thirteenth Amendment, the act interpreted the amendment as not only abolishing slavery but also guaranteeing "free institutions." The act explicitly conferred citizenship upon all persons born in the United States, with full and equal rights under the law without regard to race or color, and made it a federal offense for *anyone* to deprive a citizen of federally assured rights. The law specifically asserted the rights of freedmen to vote and sit on juries, and ruled out compulsory racial segregation in places of public accommodation.[10]

Again, Johnson vetoed. The Civil Rights Act was racially discriminatory, "in favor of the colored and against the white race," he declared in his veto message. He was also opposed to it because it would make citizens of U.S.-born Chinese, [American] Indians, and Gypsies as well as blacks, he said. He went on to point out that under such a law, white immigrants would still have to wait five years before applying for citizenship, while native-born blacks would become citizens automatically.

This would be all wrong, he said, because native blacks were just as unfamiliar with American laws and institutions as immigrants. Finally, he denounced the measure as an attempt to force racial equality by federal authority in the face of the fact that "it had often been held to be expedient to discriminate between the two races."[11]

As he had done in vetoing the Freedmen's Bureau bill, Johnson insisted that Congress had no right to enact *any* sort of legislation applying specifically to the South, whose state governments, he said, had been "fully restored" and were thus entitled to all rights of self-government under the Constitution.

But on this occasion his veto was overridden. It was the first time in American history that the Congress had vetoed a president on a major issue. The event also served to bring into sharp focus the fact that Johnson and the Republican Party had parted company.

Flushed by its victory, Congress reenacted its Freedmen's Bureau Act and sent it back to the White House. Johnson again vetoed it, even though his own cabinet voted four to three against veto. This time, however, Congress overrode him.

Meanwhile, the U.S. Supreme Court had elated some and disappointed others by upholding the constitutionality of the Civil Rights Act. In *U.S.* v. *Rhodes,* a case involving the robbery of a black man by whites, it held that a federal circuit court was within its rights in accepting jurisdiction because the laws of Kentucky, where the crime was committed, did not permit blacks to testify against whites.[12]

Bill of Rights for Blacks Too?

There was widespread agreement, even among rights advocates, that an additional Constitutional Amendment was needed to put to rest for all time the contention that American citizenship, and the rights pertaining thereto, were up to each state to decide.

Such a Fourteenth Amendment was strongly recommended by the Joint Committee on Reconstruction, which turned in its report on April 30, following five months of intensive investigation. The report consisted of 776 pages of testimony, records, and other documents. One hundred and fifty thousand copies were printed, and many of the recommendations made were incorporated in the Republican platform adopted that year.

Taking its stand upon the constitutional guarantee of a republican form of government in every state, the committee reported that the do-it-yourself approach sanctioned by President Johnson had signally failed

Opposition to the Freedmen's Bureau was by no means confined
to the South. This flyer was circulated in Pennsylvania in 1866
(Library of Congress).

to produce anything remotely resembling republican government in the
Southern states.

The report was replete with gruesome accounts of widespread exploitation, intimidation, mutilation, and assassination of blacks and any
others who supported black rights and truly representative government.
From General George A. Custer, for example, came a report stating that
the murder of blacks in Texas was a "weekly, if not daily, occurrence."[13]
An estimated 68 percent of the atrocities cited were attributed to private
parties. Life, liberty, and property could not be made secure without still
further congressional action, the committee concluded.

Responding to the committee's recommendations, Congress in heated
debate hammered out the Fourteenth Amendment. In its final form as
adopted and sent to the White House it read: "All persons born or natu-
ralized in the United States, and subject to the jurisdiction thereof, are citizens of the United States and of the State wherein they reside. No State
shall make or enforce any law which shall abridge the privileges or immunities of citizens of the United States, nor shall any State deprive any
person of life, liberty, or property without due process of law, nor deny
to any person within its jurisdiction the equal protection of the laws."

By way of enforcement, the amendment stipulated that any state curtailing voting on grounds of race would have its congressional representation reduced proportionately. Other sections disqualified for federal or state office anyone who had held such an office before the war and then supported the Confederacy. Payment of the national debt was assured, and payment of any Confederate debts or compensation for slaves was prohibited.

The amendment instantly polarized political thinking, North as well as South. The South's white supremacists chose to interpret it to be a virtual declaration of war, and swore to oppose its ratification by all means within their grasp. In exceedingly great haste the South's white legislatures convened, and with the sole exception of Tennessee, voted by well-nigh unanimous votes not to ratify the amendment.

In the Northern states, on the other hand, ratification proceeded apace, despite the fact that many of these states also had restrictions against black voting. This latter fact did not deter them, however, from setting up a hue and cry that the South was seeking to nullify the verdict of the war.

Southern rejection of the amendment took place even though there was a general appreciation among whites that, while forbidding the *states* to curtail the rights of citizens on grounds of race, it had nothing to say about *individuals* and *bands* doing the job. Moreover, racists were pleased to note that the amendment, unlike the Civil Rights Act before it, made no mention of equal access to places of public accommodation. While seeking to establish political and civil equality, the amendment as they saw it stopped short of insisting upon "social equality."

But these considerations were by no means enough to secure Southern white support for the amendment. The central issue in the standoff had asserted itself in stark terms: Democrats said they feared black rule of the South if the freedmen were allowed to vote; Republicans said they feared rebel rule of the nation if blacks were not permitted to vote. To gain their respective ways, the Democrats proposed to bar blacks from the polls by force if necessary, and the Republicans proposed to bar the South from the Union so long as it refused to acknowledge black citizenship.

Massacre

Far from bowing to the national will as expressed in the Civil Rights Act and the proposed Fourteenth Amendment, the South's white supremacists zealously set about the business of entrenching themselves in power and elaborating upon their legalistic mazes for ensnaring blacks in serf-dom.

Hand in hand with this maneuvering went a proliferation of mob vi-olence against blacks. In a number of states, the antiblack terror assumed the proportions of massacres. When mob violence erupted across Missis-sippi, the Johnson-appointed provisional governor William L. Sharkey blamed it all on the Freedmen's Bureau and the presence of black troops in the state. "(Blacks) are destined to extinction, beyond all doubt," he direly predicted, in effect urging the mobs to carry on.[14]

In Memphis in May, following an altercation between white police-men and black militiamen, police-led white mobs went on a three-day rampage through the black community, slaughtering forty-six and wounding eighty more.

In Louisiana, the planter-dominated legislature resolved by two-thirds vote to abandon that state's constitution—adopted in 1864 under the Lincoln Formula—and to return to the prewar constitution of 1861. The presence of Union occupation forces under General Philip Sheridan did not seem to inhibit the legislators in the least in taking this action. Louisiana's provisional governor, James M. Wells, a big planter who had opposed secession, decided that the best way to counter the legislature's move was to reconvene the constitutional convention of 1864, which under wartime federal tutelage had included blacks.

With the governor and legislature thus embarked upon a collision course, tensions rose—and the governor conveniently disappeared. Be-fore dropping out of sight, however, he arranged for a member of the 1864 convention to issue a call for it to convene July 30 in New Orleans.

The mayor of New Orleans, who headed a terrorist band calling itself the Southern Cross, proceeded to issue arms to any white terrorists will-ing to take them up and to mobilize the city's white police force. To-gether the police and mob marched upon the convention hall, where some 150 delegates, a majority of whom were black, were in session. The attackers laid siege to the building.

"I beseech you to stop firing; we are non-combatants!" called out one delegate, a Reverend Horton, waving a white handerchief. "If you want to arrest us, do that."

"We don't want any prisoners!" the police reportedly replied. "You've all got to die!"[15]

When the massacre was over, nearly 50 had died, and 170 had been wounded.

General Sheridan, who had done nothing to prevent or stop the bloodshed, nevertheless reported: "It was no riot. It was an absolute massacre by the police . . . At least nine-tenths of the casualties were perpetrated by the police and citizens by stabbing and smashing the heads of many who had already been killed or wounded by policemen. It was murder which the mayor and police of this city perpetrated without the shadow of necessity."

Outside the South, the nation was horrified. Three members of Johnson's cabinet—Secretary of Interior James Harlan, Attorney General James Speed, and Postmaster General William Dennison—resigned in disgust.

The South's white supremacists, on the other hand, not content with reducing the black constituency through physical annihilation, busied themselves with additional Black Codes to keep those left alive "in their place." In some Northern quarters these codes evoked as much protest as the massacres.

"The men of the North . . . will turn Mississippi into a frog pond before they will allow such laws to disgrace one foot of soil . . . over which the flag of freedom flies!" the *Chicago Tribune* boldly declared.[16] So strong was the tide of Northern reaction to the codes that when some military commanders stationed in the South saw fit to nullify certain of their provisions, Johnson dared not intervene, even though he had but recently assured Southern delegations that only *their* courts had any right to pass judgment on the codes.

The Arm-in-Arm Convention

President Johnson's postwar gravitation away from the Party of Lincoln and into the arms of the white supermacist Democrats called urgently for some sort of political realignment. The combination of codes and massacres was driving more and more of the "let-the-South-do-it" Republicans into the ranks of the equal rights Republicans. In the hope of somehow amalgamating what was left of the antirights Republicans with the racist Democrats in time for the 1866 congressional elections, Johnson issued a call for a "National Union" convention to be held in Philadelphia in June. Preparatory to the convention, he purged his cabinet of everyone who would not pledge support for a "National Union" ticket. All resigned rather than do so, except Lincoln-appointed Secretary of War Edwin M. Stanton, who would neither pledge nor resign.

Leaders of the Democratic Party were reluctant to assemble under Johnson's National Union banner for fear of losing their party's identity. Given assurances that this would not happen, they went to the Philadelphia meeting, which came to be known as the Arm-in-Arm Convention after delegates from South Carolina and Massachusetts symbolically entered the hall arm-in-arm.

No such national unity was to be forged under the banner of white supremacy during the months remaining before the fall elections. As a counterbalance to the National Union convention, a National Loyalist convention was convened in September, also in Philadelphia. Although dedicated to more-or-less-equal rights between the races, this gathering was scarcely less white than that of the white supremacists that had preceded it. Frederick Douglass, en route by train as a delegate from Rochester, New York, was confronted by a deputation of white delegates who passionately urged him not to attend and not to march in the parade. Douglass resolved to attend and march. Later he wrote: "We were marching through a city remarkable for the depth and bitterness of its hatred of the abolition movement. A city whose populace had mobbed anti-slavery meetings, burned temperance halls and churches owned by colored people, and burned down Pennsylvania Hall because it had opened its doors upon terms of equality to people of different colors. But now the children of those who had committed these outrages and follies were applauding the very principles which their fathers had condemned . . . The victory was short, signal, and complete."[17]

Southern white Loyalists in attendance from the ten un-Reconstructed states appealed for congressional action to protect themselves and the freedmen and pledged their support for black suffrage (which rather many of their Northern colleagues were inclined to look upon with some trepidation).

As the elections drew closer, things did not look at all bright for Johnson's National Unionists. For the most part, the slates they presented were straight Democratic. As for the Republicans, events had served to convince ever more of them that their Party's advocacy of the Fourteenth Amendment and a long, strong federal arm was the only hope for establishing a republican form of government in the South.

Johnson, having tested the wind and found it not to his liking, embarked upon a "swing around the circle" speaking tour of key Northern cities. For show, he took with him a discomfited General Grant, who sat silently on stage and puffed furiously on his cigar. In town after town Johnson was met with black crepe, bands that played funeral dirges, and governors who refused to be seen with him. So frenetic—or drunken, some papers said—were Johnson's harangues that they served to turn still more people away from the racist ticket.

"Hang Thad Stevens and Wendell Phillips!" the president of the United States repeatedly cried from the hustings.[18]

On the state level, the elections of 1866 saw Republicans emerge in complete control of every Northern state and three border states—Tennessee, West Virginia, and Missouri (where restrictions on voting by former Confederates were still in effect). Democrats won only in Delaware (which they had carried throughout the war), and in Kentucky and Maryland, where barriers to voting by ex-Confederates had been relaxed.

On the congressional level the Republicans increased their House seats by four, giving them a majority of 129 to 35. Moreover, some "go slow" Republicans were replaced by "rights now" advocates.

Although the congressional majority felt it now had a firm mandate to pursue its Reconstruction policies and oppose those of the president, white supremacists would concede nothing of the sort. Persisting in their refusal to ratify the Fourteenth Amendment, they harped upon the undeniable fact that throughout the so-called "Free States" of the North there were still special restrictions on voting by blacks. It was a significant fact that, by the end of 1866, in referendums held after Appomattox, such solidly Republican states as Wisconsin, Connecticut, Minnesota, and Nebraska had voted to deny suffrage to blacks within their own borders (New Jersey and Ohio were to follow suit in 1867, and Pennsylvania and Michigan in 1868).

While the prospect for ratification of the Fourteenth Amendment continued grim at the end of 1866, the Thirteenth Amendment abolishing slavery was finally ratified in December. That same month, however, the Supreme Court of the United States struck a powerful blow in support of white supremacy by ruling, in *ex parte* Milligan,[19] that the Freedmen's Bureau had no right to bring civilians before military courts in any Southern state where civil courts were operative.

This decision, Thaddeus Stevens declared, was "perhaps not so infamous as the Dred Scott decision" but was "far more dangerous" in that it had "taken away every protection in every one of these rebel states from every loyal man, black or white, who resides there."[20]

✠

CHAPTER 6

✠

Starvation stalked the South as the fateful year of 1867 began. Not only the former slaves were suffering; whites were dying of hunger in the mountains of northern Alabama, and the governor of South Carolina said there were 100,000 people in his state, white and black, who had not tasted meat in a month. The Freedmen's Bureau fed whites and blacks alike. Rather many of the recipients took note of the fact that the people who were handing out free food were also the ones who were saying they were entitled to free elections, free schools, and free land.

Congress was indeed in a mood for drastic action—but nothing quite so drastic as land reform. Nevertheless, Stevens gave it another try in the House. "More than $2 billion of property belonging to the United States, confiscated not as rebel but as enemy property, has been given back to enrich traitors," he roared. But his plea to reactivate the Confiscation Act of 1862 to make good the promise of forty acres fell upon deaf ears.[1]

In this second session of the Thirty-ninth Congress (those elected in 1866 were to serve in the Fortieth Congress), the gradualist Republicans were still more interested in finding a formula for restoring the South to the Union than they were in reconstructing the region. They had taken hope when Tennessee, in July of 1866, had been readmitted after having endorsed the Fourteenth Amendment; but the other Southern states failed to follow suit.

On February 13 the House adopted a bill introduced by Stevens, providing for dissolution of the existing white state regimes and a reoccupation of the region by Union forces. Under this plan, the South would be divided into five military districts, each under the command of a U.S. Army general (to be appointed by General Grant, not President Johnson).

The Senate, still seeking some middle ground between white self-reconstruction and federal rule, came up with a proposal to declare the state governments to be provisional rather than abolishing them outright. Even so, however, the federal power would be given the right to "abolish, modify, control, or supersede" them. The requirement for ratification of the Fourteenth Amendment was reiterated, and in addition the states were called upon to hold new constitutional conventions, this time with black participation as voters and delegates, and adopt constitutional guarantees of universal male suffrage in a form acceptable to Congress.

Not entirely satisfied with this, the House insisted upon disfranchising all those categories of ex-Confederates who would be disfranchised by the Fourteenth Amendment when ratified. In final form as sent to the White House the bill permitted the president to appoint the occupation generals, the Congress consoling itself with the thought that if he abused this privilege it would seek his impeachment. Finally, the bill provided that no more Southern states be readmitted to the Union unless and until the Fourteenth Amendment was ratified.

Johnson tabled the measure until Congress adjourned March 4 and then promptly vetoed it. Not only was it unconstitutional, he declared, but it would force "the right of suffrage out of the hands of the white people, and into the hands of the negroes, who have not asked for the privilege of voting, the vast majority of them having no idea what it means." Should it be enacted over his veto, he warned, it would have the effect of "Africanizing the Southern part of our territory."[2]

Congress promptly called itself back into session, denying Johnson the interregnum he had hoped for, and overrode his veto. Southern blacks also let themselves be heard from, refuting the president's claim that they had no desire to vote. In large "gatherings" held throughout the South, they adopted resolutions reminding the nation of black participation in all of its wars, and concluding on the familiar note that taxation without representation was tyranny.

Whose Army Was It?

In further moves to prevent the president from thwarting its intent, the Congress on March 11 adopted a "Command of the Army Act" and on March 23 a "Tenure of Office Act." The former required that all orders issued by the president as commander in chief of the armed forces be disseminated through Commanding General Grant. Moreover, it forbade the president to dismiss Grant or send him away from Washington without his concurrence (Johnson was plotting to send Grant to Mexico on a "diplomatic" mission). Finally, the act forbade any Southern state to organize a militia of its own without prior congressional approval. The Tenure Act was designed to curtail Johnson's use of his powers of patronage in support of white supremacists. It even went so far as to bar him from dismissing his own cabinet members before they had served full terms (this, to protect Lincoln-appointed Secretary of War Stanton, a supporter of congressional reconstruction).

Although Grant had concurred in the compromise that left the president the privilege of appointing the occupation generals, he was highly apprehensive about the result and urged Congress not to adjourn until the appointments were made. To everyone's surprise, Johnson appointed all five of the nominees submitted by Grant: generals John Schofield, Daniel Sickles, George Thomas, Edward C. Ord, and Philip Sheridan—all considered to be staunch reconstructionists. Some said this signified not any change of heart on Johnson's part, but merely his fear of impeachment.

After thus asserting itself, Congress adjourned, being obliged to entrust *implementation* of its reconstruction program to the army, Freedmen's Bureau, federal courts, and the president.

Grant took the position that each of the occupation generals was free to interpret and administer the Reconstruction Acts as he saw fit. For a brief period, the president did not interfere. But when, pursuant to the law, the generals began to bar former Confederates from voting, and forcibly removed some of them from public office, the president's puppet regimes set up a howl that galvanized him into action. Bypassing both the secretary of war and the commanding general, he sent secret orders to the occupation generals and did all that he could to uphold the white civil authorities over the military.[3]

Soldiers as Registrars

The Thirty-ninth Congress had made special provision for the Fortieth to convene without delay. It did so, with the ranks of its equal rights advocates augmented by the previous fall's elections. Noting that the neo-Confederate regimes down South were dragging their heels about registering blacks to vote, the Congress ordered the military to take over the task—and to get the job done by September 1. In this Second Reconstruction Act the disfranchisement of former Confederates was also vastly extended. Whereas the first act barred all those who had ever taken an oath to support the U.S. Constitution and then betrayed it by supporting the Confederacy, the new act went on to also bar all those who had, before the war, held any executive, legislative, or judicial post and thereafter supported the Confederacy—regardless of whether or not they had ever taken an oath to support the U.S. Constitution. This move was of course designed to prevent the traditional white ruling elements from dominating the political scene before the foundations for government representative of the poorer whites and blacks could be laid.

Like its predecessor, the Fortieth Congress was fearful of presidential sabotage. It resolved, therefore, to meet again on July 3, at which time if quorums were present it would remain in session to deal with whatever exigencies might exist.

With Congress temporarily out of the way, the president saw fit to ask his attorney general Henry Stanberry for an "opinion" as to the relative powers of the white regimes and the U.S. Army commanders in the South. Stanberry obliged by opining that the two were "co-equals." The military could not remove any state or local officials, or alter any state laws, he further declared. The sole legitimate function of the occupation forces was to protect life and property, he went on to say. The right to abolish, modify, or supercede incumbent regimes was given by the law to Congress, not to the military commanders, his opinion held. Finally, he attempted to set aside the law by stating that only those persons who had violated an oath to support the U.S. Constitution could be barred from voting.[4]

This was quite enough to assure quorums when Congress reconvened July 3. There were those in the House who wanted to tighten the requirements for readmission to the Union by giving Congress power to decide whether an applicant state had proven itself loyal "by decisive and trustworthy majorities, and had in good faith endorsed equal suffrage, public education, and land reform."[5] This was too much for most of the lawmakers, however; it was decided not to make any additional demands upon the South, and to concentrate instead upon securing compliance with the demands already made. (This was the last to be heard of the wartime promise of forty acres and a mule.)

In what was to be called the Third Reconstruction Act, passed over Johnson's veto, Congress negated the attorney general's interpretations by explicitly giving the occupation commanders full powers to deal with the provisional white regimes. The act went on to state that in the future the military commanders would not be bound by the opinions of any civil officer of the United States (such as the attorney general). Authority to approve or disapprove removals or appointments of public officials by military commanders was vested in General Grant. The commanders were precluded from appointing anyone who could not take the ironclad oath of never having supported the Confederacy, and the military registration boards were given final authority to determine who could and could not vote under the law.

"Masterly Inactivity"

The adoption of all these Reconstruction Acts posed problems for the reconstituted regimes of white supremacy, to say the least. Some were inclined to blame the outspoken racism of the president for provoking the Congress to such stringent action, when in reality it was the Black Codes and massacres, for which they themselves were to blame, that were largely responsible. At any rate, they were painfully aware that they were involved in a different game, and were being dealt from an entirely new deck of cards.

The strategists of the neo-Confederate high command were of two minds as to how best to react. One die-hard school felt that, despite the acts and military occupation, they should cling to a policy of "masterly inactivity," boycotting the new constitutional conventions and refusing to ratify the Fourteenth Amendment.[6] Others had finally concluded that such opposition and noncooperation were no longer feasible. These latter argued that, during the two years since Appomattox, white supremacy had pressed its case "with honor" but now had no alternative but to go along with the political emancipation of blacks.[7] Propagation of this view was tempered by a spoken and unspoken notion that even as voters the blacks could be manipulated and dominated by methods both old and new.

As early as February of that year of 1867 the governor of Georgia, an ex-Confederate named Charles J. Jenkins, returned from a trip to Washington to urge the South to go along with Congress's 1866 demand for a Fourteenth Amendment, as the only means of avoiding more stringent measures in 1867. For a brief spell, Ole Massa did take to the hustings to try his hand at persuading his erstwhile slaves to vote for him. On March

18, for example, a black political rally in Columbia, South Carolina, was treated to the spectacle of Confederate General Wade Hampton and a black man named Beverly Nash making a joint call for black enfranchisement and an alliance of black and white Southerners in politics.[8] What white advocates of such an alliance were not saying, just yet, was that they envisioned that the blacks would be "just voters" (not officeholders).

Just Voters?

By this time many Northern Democrats, while themselves adopting resolutions against black voting, had nonetheless concluded that their Southern brethren should let blacks vote. Such influential organs as the *New York World, Boston Post,* and *Chicago Times* took the position that, since Northern public sentiment made black suffrage inevitable, the Southern states should themselves initiate "qualified" black suffrage in order to avoid having "unqualified" black suffrage forced upon them. "Qualified" persons were identified as those who could read and write, and who were possessed of at least $250 worth of property—criteria that disqualified the great mass of Southern blacks, along with many a Southern white. By going this route, it was argued, more Democrats could be elected, who would in turn work for repeal of the more objectionable features of Reconstruction.

The Southern Democratic flirtation with black voters was not helped by the fact that, during 1867, Democratic state conventions in Ohio, Iowa, California, Kansas, and Pennsylvania adopted planks in opposition to black voting. Northern Democrats, moreover, were every bit as keen as their Southern counterparts in abhoring the perils of "social equality" and "sexual miscegenation." On the other hand, Republican conventions in the non-Southern states, with the exceptions of Pennsylvania and California, all resolved in favor of suffrage for blacks. This polarization of the issue so alarmed the *New York World* that it direly predicted that race war would ensue if Southern blacks were allowed to gravitate into the Republican Party.

The prospect of somehow persuading blacks to vote Democratic proved to be a forlorn one, however. Too often, before the war and after, blacks had put their faith in Ole Massa and invariably been betrayed. Typical of their reaction across the South was that of a gathering of Florida blacks, who listened respectfully to appeals by white planters for political support, and then resolved: "We cherish no ill-will against our former masters, but the loving people of the North deserve our thanks for our freedom; we resolve, therefore, to identify ourselves with the Republican Party."[9]

Black perception of the issues involved was crystal clear. One, in attendance at a political rally in Selma, Alabama, first held up a blue (Democratic) ticket and shouted "No vote! No land! Slavery again!" and then raised on high a red (Republican) ticket and cried "Votes! Freedom! Forty acres! A mule! Equal of a white man!" Instinct had told them, and experience had already confirmed, that their human, civil, and political rights were dependent upon having a foothold on the land. Although many of their supporters had been obliged to abandon hope for land distribution, they had not.

Occupation Preferred

At the same time that some Ole Massas were making the rounds entreating the blacks to trust them "just one more time," others were sticking to their guns and insisting that rights for blacks would never do. Some were so bold as to assert once again that Reconstruction in its entirety was in violation of the spirit of Appomattox and, still more, of the no-strings accord concluded by generals Sherman and Johnston on the battlefield. The Confederacy had been enticed into laying down its arms and then betrayed, said they. These were the same men who had once denounced Johnson as having no right to unseat their Confederate state and local governments—but had forgiven him after he helped them set them back up again.

In early April Georgia's Governor Charles J. Jenkins abandoned his conciliatory position and, in a widely published open letter, called upon the white South to totally reject congressional Reconstruction and elect to remain under military occupation however long it might take to bring about a reversal of national opinion. In a joint action with Mississippi officials he petitioned the U.S. Supreme Court to declare the Reconstruction Acts unconstitutional.[10] The Court, however, took the position that it "could not interfere with Presidential powers." Whereupon General Pope, in charge of the Georgia occupation district, ordered Governor Jenkins to comply with the laws or be put out of office.

Boycott or Terror?

South Carolina's Governor Benjamin F. Perry took up the cry for open defiance of Reconstruction, and in a series of statements published throughout the South pressed forward the contention that continued military rule was preferable to governments controlled by "ignorant, stupid, demi-savage paupers," who he said would do little but tax the affluent and take away their property.[11] In Georgia, Benjamin H. Hill picked up the standard of open defiance after Governor Perry had been forced to drop it, and in South Carolina Wade Hampton became the standard-bearer, abandoning his vain attempt to persuade blacks to follow him.

As for the Ku Klux Klan, it never entertained any doubt that the only appropriate response to congressional Reconstruction was terror and armed resistance. A "fiery summons" went out to the five thousand Klan dens then said to be in operation, to attend an "Imperial Klonvokation," which was held in Nashville's Maxwell House hotel in April.[12]

Presiding as imperial wizard was the former Confederate cavalry general Nathan Bedford Forrest, a wealthy slavetrader before the war, whose troops had been accused of the massacre of three hundred black men, women, and children at Fort Pillow, Tennessee, on April 12, 1864.[13]

Any doubt that the Ku Klux Klan constituted a veritable Confederate underground was dispelled at this meeting, where ex-Confederate General Albert Pike assumed command as grand dragon of the Arkansas Realm of the Klan's Invisible Empire; General John B. Gordon the Georgia Realm; General W. J. Hardee, Alabama; and General Wade Hampton, South Carolina.[14] These men brought the Southwide terrorist campaign of the Klan under professional, centralized military command and discipline. Its role in the struggle for political power that lay ahead was seen to be crucial.

When the first opportunity for the former slaves to vote rolled around, it was in the month of August in the state of Tennessee, and Ole Massa's worst fears were realized when they cast their ballots solidly Republican. This event, coupled with some Democratic victories in the North, served to renew Ole Massa's conviction that blacks should not be allowed to vote at all. Democratic conventions were called across the South to state that while Southern whites accepted the "legitimate" results of the war and were willing to assure blacks equal protection of person and property, Reconstruction should be brought to an end and "white man's government" proclaimed in perpetuity.[15]

Since the Reconstruction Acts prescribed that the calling of new constitutional conventions be approved by a majority of voters registered, whites proposed to register but not vote. Congress promptly changed the law to read a majority of those casting ballots—and Ole Massa was once again checkmated. With so many blacks enfranchised, and so many whites disfranchised, he concluded that his only remaining hope was to bring economic sanctions, intimidation, and terror to bear to keep blacks from going to the polls. A deviant school of thought contended that if Southern whites would abstain from politics altogether, Congress and the North would repudiate the all-black results. In the end, however, terrorism won out over boycott.

By the time Ole Massa finally made up his mind to get into the political arena and fight, the September 1 deadline set by Congress for voter registration was close at hand. Louisiana whites petitioned President Johnson to extend the deadline, and he obliged. So great was the congressional and public protest that Johnson asked Attorney General Stanberry for another of his opinions. Stanberry promptly ruled that the president was within his rights.[16]

Good Ole Generals

White House support for white supremacy did not stop there. Enactment of the Third Reconstruction Act had compelled the president to abandon his efforts to *control* the occupation commanders and prompted him to exercise his remaining powers to *replace* them. Preparatory to this, he had on August 5 asked Secretary of War Stanton for his resignation. And although Johnson had, four months earlier, declared Grant to be "as radical as anyone," he now named him Secretary of War ad interim, presumably in the hope that he would have more control over him as a member of his cabinet. He then proceeded to remove generals Sheridan and Sickles and on September 7 issued another of his sweeping amnesty decrees, with a view to enabling many of the ruling class whites disfranchised by Congress to get back into politics.

In November and December, when most of the constitutional conventions were meeting, Johnson pulled out of the South two more of the occupation commanders (General Pope in Georgia and General Ord in Mississippi) and also sent the subdistrict commander in Alabama, Wager Swain, on an assignment elsewhere. In making these moves Johnson bypassed Grant, who demanded that the transfers be rescinded, but to no avail. Typical of Johnson's charges against the removed generals were those levelled against Pope and Swain: that they had plotted to reopen the registration books to increase black majorities.

Ole Massa was for the most part delighted with the replacements sent in by the president. General Winfield Scott Hancock, replacing Sheridan, promptly rescinded Sheridan's order opening jury service to blacks, restored to office white politicos who had been booted by his predecessor, came up with a more liberal interpretation of what sorts of whites should be allowed to vote, and asserted the preeminence of (white) civil authority over the military.[17] The president, too, was so pleased that he called upon Congress to commend General Hancock "for his dedication to the Constitution," but that body took a contrary view of the matter.

Another apple in the president's eye was General Alvin C. Gillem, whom he sent to replace Ord in Mississippi. Gillem got along very well indeed with the landed gentry. He even made a deal with one wealthy planter, Edmund Richardson, whereby state convicts, most of whom were black, were put to work on Richardson's plantation. The general further ordered that Richardson be paid thirty thousand dollars per year out of state funds, to reimburse him for transporting and feeding the convicts.[18]

One of the president's appointees, however, General George C. Meade, proved to be a great disappointment to him. Despite a "conservative" reputation, Meade turned out to be a staunch supporter of black rights and congressional Reconstruction. Too often, in Johnson's view, the generals he had sent in as replacements continued to look to Grant for guidance. When some of them persisted in denying the vote to men who had been amnestied by him, who then appealed to him for help, the president told them he dared not countermand his generals, for fear of impeachment.[19]

Voting and Dying

Whites who had anticipated that the former slaves would not miss their first opportunity to vote—no matter how intense the terrorism—were proven to be quite right. When the Southwide voter registration conducted by the U.S. Army was over, the tally showed 627,000 white registrants, and 703,000 blacks.

In every state the calling of new constitutional conventions was approved. White support for the conventions was heaviest in those areas that had not been keen on secession in the first place. The delegates elected were predominantly Republican, but blacks demonstrated their astuteness by not voting along strictly racial lines; many a white candidate who showed some sign of fairness was elected by black votes.

The ratio of black delegates to whites varied widely from state to state. There were but eight blacks in the Arkansas convention, in Texas they were outnumbered 81 to 9, in North Carolina 118 to 13, in Alabama 59 to 18, Virginia 80 to 25, and Georgia 132 to 37. In Florida the proportion of black delegates rose to 40 percent, in Louisiana to 45, and in South Carolina—the only state where black delegates were a majority—to 60 percent.[20]

But of course the political complexion of these conventions was not determined by race alone. Despite the rather rigorous exclusion of former Confederate officials, nearly half of the 53 percent of all delegates who were Southern whites belonged to the camp of white supremacy. The other half, together with the 30 percent of all delegates who were black, and the 17 percent who were white newcomers to the South, added up to something like a majority of 75 percent who were supportive of black rights and the congressional Reconstruction program. On the state level, however, this balance of power was in many cases far more tenuous.

When Congress reconvened in November of 1867 it faced the questions of continuance of Reconstruction and impeachment of the president. Some hoped that the results of that fall's elections would dampen the fervor with which the man in the White House pressed the cause of white supremacy. Not so, however; in his state of the union message Johnson declared the Reconstruction Acts to be unconstitutional and said he had "enforced" them thus far only to prevent a resumption of civil war. The Republicans, he charged, were trying to turn the South over to blacks, despite "the clear evidence of history that they are incapable of self-government."[21]

ELECTION YEAR

✠

CHAPTER 7

✠

The year 1868 was to be a decisive one for the South and the nation. For one thing, there was a president to be elected. It had been eight years since the Southern states had taken part in the election of a president of the United States. During the first four of those years the Confederacy had been locked in military combat with the Union over the issues of secession and slavery; the succeeding four had seen a continuation of that struggle in the form of a terrorist campaign to preserve white supremacy and thwart every effort to establish a republican form of government in the region.

As the year dawned, only Tennessee had been readmitted to the Union and was thus entitled to take part in the election. Before the other Southern states could participate they had to meet the conditions laid down by Congress: adopt new state constitutions, elect new state governments with black participation, and ratify the Fourteenth Amendment. These were bitter pills to many a white Southern palate, and many were resolved never to swallow them—or to regurgitate them at the first opportunity.

Congress, on the other hand, was convinced that it had prescribed just the right medicine to cure the South's ills. And so when the president set a bad example by spitting it up in the face of Congress in his state of the union message, the House responded, in January, by adopting a measure declaring that the legislative, executive, and judicial branches of the federal government did not recognize the legitimacy of the incumbent all-white regimes that had been restored in the South under Johnson's auspices. The Senate, however, proved unwilling to go along with this measure, which would have also given General Grant full control over the occupation commanders. The Supreme Court, for its part, did on February 10 turn down a bid by the Georgia regime asking it to declare the Reconstruction Acts unconstitutional.[1]

Johnson's next move, which came on February 21, was to fire Edwin M. Stanton as secretary of war, thus openly defying the Tenure of Office Act. Stanton refused to budge, and, backed by Grant and armed supporters, remained in his office day and night.

Almost Impeached

On the following day, Stevens, on behalf of the Committee on Reconstruction, moved that Johnson be impeached. The issue, he said, was who was to represent the American people—an elected Congress or a president who had upon twenty-three occasions used his veto to thwart the will of the people as expressed by Congress. Seventy-three years of age and in poor health, Stevens's voice failed him after five minutes. But on February 24 the House adopted, by a vote of 126 to 47, nine Articles of Impeachment. Carrying Stevens in an armchair, the House proceeded in a body to the Senate, where he announced its decision.

Two weeks later, Thaddeus Stevens was dead. He was laid to rest in a black cemetery, with this inscription over his grave: "I repose in this quiet and secluded spot, not from any natural preference for solitude, but finding other cemeteries limited as to race by charter rules, I have chosen this that I might illustrate in my death the principles which I advocated through a long life: the Equality of Man before his Creator."[2]

The impeachment trial conducted by the Senate focused upon the central question of whether a president has any right not to implement or any right to subvert a law once it has been passed over his veto. The vote finally came on May 16, with thirty-five senators holding that Johnson was guilty, and nineteen saying he was not. Impeachment had failed by one vote, that vote being cast by Senator William P. Fessenden of Maine. Had he voted otherwise, the nation might have been spared at least some of the ugly events that were to mark the remainder of Johnson's last year in office.

One of the first effects of the failure to impeach was Stanton's surrender of the office of secretary of war, and Johnson's interim appointment of General John M. Schofield to replace him. And so, while Union troops were back in the South as decreed by Congress, there was now grave doubt as to whether they would serve the democratizing role prescribed by Congress. Before, General Grant had been able to rely upon the backing of the secretary of war in carrying out the congressional intent; now it was the president who had the backing of the secretary in his efforts to thwart congressional Reconstruction.

The Constitutional Conventions

The initial battleground for the struggles of 1868 was on the floor of the constitutional conventions. These assemblies—the fruit of the first free elections, not counting ex-Confederate bigwigs, the South had ever known—set about their appointed tasks with all the zeal that characterizes democracy aborning. The first to convene was that of Alabama, which met in November of 1867, while most of the remainder began their deliberations in January of 1868.

The voice of the U.S. military had been heard in behalf of moderation, with General Pope (prior to his transfer by Johnson) urging both restraint and speed[3] and General Ord (likewise before removal) predicting that if extreme measures were adopted by the conventions the proposed new constitutions would go down to defeat when submitted to referendum.[4] The question of course was "how much was enough?" Black delegates displayed a willingness to compromise on some issues, such as segregated schools, in order to get public schools started; but they stood firm against efforts to rob them of more basic rights.

"It is a patent fact that, as colored men, we have been cheated out of our rights for two centuries," Francis L. Cardozo reminded the South Carolina convention. "Now that we have the opportunity, I want to fix them in the constitution in such a way that no lawyer, however cunning or astute, can possibly misinterpret their meaning. If we do not do so, we deserve to be, and will be, cheated again."[5]

Not only did the bogey of "black rule" fail to materialize: black delegates magnanimously led the way in urging that the political rights of former Confederates be restored, despite the fact that these gentry were heavily engaged in killing blacks who voted. A few voices called for the promised forty acres and a mule, but no convention resolved in favor of confiscation.

While Ole Massa was in no position to run the show, he did have his big foot in the door. Although white supremacists were in a minority among the delegates, their experience and expertise in governmental matters gave them power far beyond their numbers. In addition, they knew how to play skillfully upon whatever racial prejudices the Southern white Unionists and non-Southern white delegates might harbor.

Some white delegates wanted to put black voting on "hold" for five years, by stipulating that the state would fix qualifications for black voting come 1882. Others, with a view to keeping black officeholding to a minimum, proposed to make most state offices appointive rather than elective. So disgusted with this sort of thing was the African Methodist Episcopal Church that it urged that the conventions be called off and the South kept under military rule indefinitely. It is not too much to say that, had it not been for the countervening presence of black power, whites would have seen to it that few substantive changes were made in the old order.

The overall performance of the black delegates has been done justice by W. E. B. Du Bois in his *Black Reconstruction* and by a few other historians.[6] Even at the time, some Southern white observers felt obliged to make such comments as this one from Florida: "Now, I have never been known as a Negro-worshipper, but I must say I do not see any cause for alarm or want of intelligence in their faces or conversation. Fifteen of them are former slaves, wellbred gentlemen, and eloquent speakers."[7]

The Road to Reunion

When the constitutional conventions had done their work, the Southern states plunged into the next phase of the struggle: ratification of the proposed constitutions, and the election of new state governments and representatives to Congress. Once again Ole Massa made a halfhearted bid for black support and, when it was not forthcoming, once again resorted to economic lynching and terrorism. The Klan was in the forefront of this. In Alabama the occupation commander "outlawed" the Klan (to no avail),[8] and General Meade organized patrols to intercept the night riders, forbade the publication of Klan announcements, and asked Washington to send in reinforcements.[9]

In Mississippi, the terrorists succeeded in keeping enough blacks from the polls to enable whites to vote down the proposed new constitution—thereby barring the state from readmission to the Union and taking part in the presidential election. In South Carolina the terror concentrated, successfully, upon the capture of local governments by white supremacists. In Georgia, Democrats won over a number of white Republicans

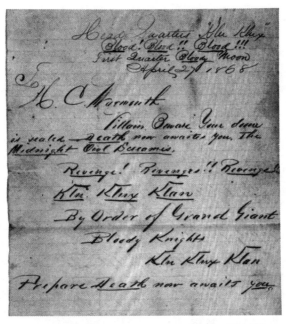

Klan message to Louisiana governor Henry Clay War-
mouth, 1868: "Villain Beware Your Doom is sealed—
Death now awaits you" (Southern Historical Collection,
University of North Carolina).

to defeat the election of equal-rights Republicans to the U.S. Senate. Although Republicans emerged with majorities in all of the legislatures,
white supremacist Democrats had substantial minority representation,
and in some instances came close to wielding a balance of power. The
proportion of black legislators ranged from a low of 1 percent in North
Carolina to a high of 40 percent in Mississippi.[10]

When seven of these legislatures had ratified the Fourteenth Amendment, Congress was satisfied that they were on the way to establishing a
republican form of government and so were fit to be readmitted to the
Union. The Arkansas Act, which became law on June 22 over Johnson's
veto, admitted that state on the condition that no class of its citizens then
enfranchised would ever be disfranchised. Three days later, on June 25,
an Omnibus Bill following this same formula, and again adopted over
presidential veto, finalized the readmission of the other six states, leaving
only Virginia, Texas, and Mississippi outside the fold. Before adjourning
on July 27, Congress seated the delegations of the seven states, declared

the Fourteenth Amendment to be ratified, and called upon Secretary of State William H. Seward to see to its implementation.

Reactions to this new state of affairs were not long in coming. Such Democratic journals as the *New York World* and *Chicago Times* seized upon the occasion to opine that, as reunion was at last a largely accomplished fact, black voting and the South's form of government were no longer legitimate concerns of the federal government or the rest of the nation.[11]

Readmission to statehood in fact represented a restoration of states' rights as set forth in the Constitution, the return of "home rule," and an end to military occupation. In the seven states concerned, the U.S. commanders lost little time in handing over power to the civil authorities—and white supremacists proceeded to make the most of it. Though "bound" by their new state constitutions and the Fourteenth Amendment to respect black political rights, it was soon evident that white supremacists regarded these as mere scraps of paper that they had pretended to accept for the sole purpose of ridding their borders of federal troops. The absence of those troops created a power vacuum that "Big D" Democrats were quick to exploit, to the disadvantage of Republican believers in democracy.

Elect and Eject

In Georgia, for example, Congress had no sooner adjourned than the white supremacists in the state legislature voted to expel all black members of that body on the grounds that nothing in Georgia's new constitution specifically asserted any right of "persons of African descent" to hold public office. The state's three black senators were given one hour in which to defend themselves; one resigned, and the other two were expelled by a vote of twenty-four to eleven. In the Georgia house, twenty-nine blacks had been elected to seats. Henry M. Turner, a black elected from Bibb County, took the floor to excoriate some of his brethren who had sought to placate the whites, saying they reminded him of "slaves begging under the lash."

"The scene presented in this house, today, is one unparalleled in the history of the world," Turner declared. "Never before . . . has a man been arraigned . . . charged with the offense of being a darker hue than his fellowmen . . . The Anglo-Saxon race, Sir, is a most surprising one. No man has ever been more deceived in that race than I have been . . . The treachery which has been exhibited . . . by gentlemen belonging to that race has shaken my confidence more than anything that has come under my observation from the day of my birth."[12]

Of Georgia's twenty-nine black legislators, only four escaped expulsion, and those did so only because they looked white. White runners-up were then appointed to fill the vacant seats. The expelled legislators appealed to the Georgia supreme court, which upheld them, but no one dared to enforce the ruling. In the other six rehabilitated states, racist assaults upon the new regimes were somewhat less frontal than in Georgia, but nonetheless widespread and ferocious. Ole Massa, assessing his prospects, gleefully concluded that he could live with the Fourteenth Amendment by ignoring it, whereas the presence of federal troops had cramped his style no end.

Party Lines

One reason that the Congress had resorted to the quick fix of the Omnibus Bill was the urgent need for adjournment to enable Republican members to attend their party's presidential nominating convention in Chicago. Grant had long since emerged as the Republicans' favorite, despite persistent attempts by the Democratic *New York World* to discredit him by publishing various "go slow" admonitions relative to black rights uttered by him in the wake of Appomattox.[13] But Grant's staunch support for black rights in the years that had followed was more than enough to win him the nomination.

The platform adopted along with Grant declared that, while voting rights for blacks was a matter the Northern states were entitled to resolve for themselves, the safety of the nation required that Southern blacks be allowed to vote without delay. Republican state conventions in New York, New Jersey, Ohio, and Wisconsin did in fact fail to renew their black suffrage planks, and Pennsylvania Republicans voted against holding a referendum on the subject.

The Democrats met in Philadelphia in July. Johnson was out of the picture as a potential candidate, having come to be regarded as a popular hero of white supremacy but one whose efforts had generally turned out to be counterproductive. Appreciating the fact that Grant, as the hero of Appomattox, would be hard to beat, Democrats knew that their choice of a standard-bearer would be crucial to any possibility of success. For a time, Chief Justice Salmon P. Chase (who had reported to Lincoln right after Appomattox that the white South would go along with black voting) was in the forefront of those under consideration. But when financier August Belmont sought to persuade Chase to back off from his advocacy of votes for blacks, all Chase would say was that he favored votes for ex-Confederates too. Chase did go on to say that he was opposed to military occupation, but this was not enough for the Democratic Party, which had made the cause of white rule its very own.

The top contenders who emerged were Horatio Seymour, wartime governor of New York, and Francis P. Blair, Jr., of Missouri, who had served as a Union general during the war but was nonetheless an avid white supremacist. On the eve of the convention, Blair saw fit to dispatch a letter to another Missouri delegate, one James Brodhead, which found its way into the press. In this letter, Blair declared that it would be the duty of a Democratic president, whoever he might be, to declare the Reconstruction Acts invalid, dissolve the state and local governments created under them, and leave Southern whites free to govern their states as they saw fit.[14]

When the Democratic convention was called to order, the ex–Confederate presence was very much in evidence. Even Georgia's Robert Toombs—who before the war had been one of the most outspoken champions of slavery—broke his voluntary exile in Europe to attend the convention and proclaim: "I regret nothing in the past but the dead and the failure. I am ready today to use the best means I can command to establish the principles for which we fought!"[15]

Also among those present were Confederate General Forrest, who by this time had become imperial wizard of the Ku Klux Klan, and his grand dragon for the South Carolina realm of the Klan's Invisible Empire, Confederate General Wade Hampton.

The nomination went to Seymour, whom editorialist Horace Greeley described as "the embodiment of copperheadism," the label applied by Lincoln to Northern opponents of the Union war effort. As for Blair, his racist letter netted him the vice presidential spot on the ticket. Confederate General Hampton and William Preston of Kentucky made the nomination, and when New York seconded, all other aspirants withdrew.

The presidential campaign of 1868 offered certain possibilities for an alignment of ideological forces on a national basis, such as had not existed since the firing upon Fort Sumter. Instead of an amorphous "South" arrayed against an equally amorphous "North," or Confederacy against the Union, it was at last possible for believers in white supremacy, North and South, to rally under one standard (that of the Democratic Party), and for advocates of equal rights, wherever they might be, to unite under the banner of the Republican Party. Although the boundary between these two camps was not as clear-cut as the foregoing might suggest, it was decidedly more precise than the Mason-Dixon line had been.

Klan notice served upon Alabama Republicans—"scalawag" Noah B. Gloud and "carpetbagger" A. S. Haskin (from Ohio)— illustrating the fate awaiting them in the event of a Republican victory in the 1868 presidential election (*Tuscaloosa* [Ala.] *Independent Monitor*, September 1, 1868).

In many respects—including rhetoric and the resort to force—the 1868 presidential campaign represented something of an echo of the Civil War. In the North, Union veterans staged reunions where they resolved to "fall in behind our old commander, and vote as we shot."[16] In the South, blacks and their white allies—banded together in the Union League, Loyal League, and Lincoln Brotherhood—posted sentries to protect their meetings from night riders and shouted such slogans as "Votes! Bread! Wages! Schools!"[17]

Democrats charged that Grant was a drunkard, an anti-Semite, a wartime trafficker in cotton, and a general whose ineptness had cost the lives of thousands of Union soldiers. If elected, they direly predicted that he would impose a military dictatorship not only upon the South but the entire nation. Republicans countered that a Democratic victory would mean that the Civil War would have to be fought all over again.

Open Season on Blacks

With Johnson still in the White House, much depended upon what he might do or not do to curb terrorism and otherwise protect the right of Southern blacks to vote. On the basis of his prior record, the prospect looked grim indeed. In those Southern states that would be taking part in the election, the federal military presence had been withdrawn. And since Johnson had already denounced the Reconstruction governments

Campaign flyer distributed by the Democratic party in support of its 1868 ticket, Horatio Seymour for president and Frank Blair for vice-president.

in those states as "illegitimate and of no validity whatever," he could hardly be expected to respond favorably to any appeals from them for troops or even for arms with which to defend themselves and uphold the law.

Such apprehensions proved to be more than justified. Without waiting for such appeals to come in, Johnson as early as July proceeded to replace some of the remaining occupation commanders whom he felt had been too supportive of congressional Reconstruction. Then on August 25 he dispatched a letter to all of the commanders, citing an opinion by his attorney general that U.S. marshals could only call for troop assistance to carry out some specific task (not anything so general as coping with terrorism or preventing intimidation at the polls).[18]

Thus obliged to look to their own defenses, Reconstruction governments appealed to the War Department for arms with which they could establish state militias. Johnson's man, Secretary Seward, turned them down on the grounds that the law passed by Congress the previous year to prevent the all-white regimes from forming militias without congressional approval applied to the new black and white regimes as well. Congress promptly convened itself to deal with the matter—but then could not muster the courage to do so. Instead, it decided to adjourn and take up the matter again when it next met, which was to be October 16—less than three weeks before the election. After all its travail in enfranchising Southern blacks and supervising the election of democratic governments, the Congress thus abandoned both to the nonexistent mercies of the racist terrorists.

Ole Massa Smells Blood

Figuratively and literally, Ole Massa smelled blood. A group of former Confederate generals, including Lee, were so excited by the new state of affairs that they got off a letter to U.S. General William S. Rosecrans, assuring the North that the South had no desire to reenslave blacks or otherwise "oppress" them and stood ready to resume its peaceful place in the Union, provided its "Constitutional rights" were respected.[19]

In the exercise of what it conceived to be such rights, the Southern Democratic press, less diplomatic than the generals, did not hesitate to proclaim black suffrage to be a "curse and inconceivable calamity" that justified "annihilation" of the black race if need be (*Memphis Appeal*). White supremacists should stand firm and fear not, it was said, secure in the knowledge that the president, Supreme Court, and Democratic Party stood behind them.[20]

Congress having abdicated its responsibilities, the struggle for the South did indeed promise to be an uneven contest. As the latter-day adage has it, power comes out of the mouth of a gun, and the Reconstruction governments had not any to speak of. About all that they had going for them were the new state constitutions and the new Fourteenth Amendment. In such circumstances the terrorists didn't really need guns —the bullwhip, mutilation knife, torch, and lynch rope being entirely adequate for their purposes. Besides, the camp of white supremacy still had the land, the jobs, the money, and the force of their traditional status as unchallenged rulers.

By this time Ole Massa's own right to vote and hold office had been fully restored in Florida, North Carolina, and Georgia, and in Louisiana all he had to do was pledge that in the future he would "support the political equality of all men." This he was reluctant to do, until reminded by his peers that such a pledge would be binding only so long as the Reconstruction constitutions remained in effect, which they assured him would not be for very long.[21]

Briefly, Old Massa made another pitch for the black vote. In South Carolina he went so far as to promise black folks that they could go on voting forever, provided they voted for white folks only. When this failed to work, unfettered terrorism again became the order of the day.

Statehood meant that not only the federal troops but also the military courts for dealing with civil rights offenses were gone. Not even the memory of the Northern backlash caused by the 1866 New Orleans and Memphis massacres served to inhibit the terrorists.

The Klan's Ultimatum

That the Klan's Invisible Empire now represented the real power in the South was made abundantly clear by Wizard Forrest in an interview by the *Cincinnati Commercial*. This interview, published August 28, 1868, revealed that the Confederate underground was fully prepared to come out into the light of day and wage open warfare against any force that dared to challenge its right to terrorize citizens by night. The interview read in part:

> "General Forrest, I came especially to learn your views in regard to the condition of civil and political affairs in the State of Tennessee, and in the South generally," I stated.
>
> "I have not now," he replied, "and never have had, any opinion on any public or political subject which I would object to having published. I mean what I say, honestly and earnestly, and only object to being misrepresented."
>
> I replied: "Sir, I will publish only what you say, and then you cannot possibly be misrepresented."
>
> "A few weeks ago," he said, "I was called to Nashville to counsel with other gentlemen who had been prominently identified with the cause of the Confederacy, and we then offered pledges which we thought would be satisfactory to Governor [W.G. "Parson"] Brownlow and his legislature, and we told them that, if they would not call out the militia, we would agree to preserve order and see that the laws were enforced . . . I never have recognized the present government in Tennessee as having any legal existence, yet I was willing to submit to it for a time, with the hope that the wrongs might be righted peaceably."
>
> "In the event of Governor Brownlow's calling out the militia, do you think there will be any resistance offered to their acts?" I asked.
>
> "That will depend upon circumstances. If the militia are simply called out, and do not interfere with or molest anyone, I do not think there will be any fight. If, on the contrary, they do what I believe they will do, commit outrages, or even one outrage, upon the

people, they and Mr. Brownlow's government will be swept out of existence; not a Radical will be left alive. If the militia are called out, we cannot but look upon it as a declaration of war, because Mr. Brownlow has already issued his proclamation directing them to shoot down the Ku Klux wherever they find them; and he calls all Southern men Ku Klux."

"Why General, we people up North have regarded the Ku Klux Klan as an organization which existed only in the frightened imaginations of a few politicians!"

"Well, Sir, there is such an organization, not only in Tennessee but all over the South, and its numbers have not been exaggerated!"

"What are its numbers, General?"

"In Tennessee there are forty thousand; in all the Southern states about five hundred and fifty thousand men."

"What is the character of the organization, may I enquire?"

"Yes, Sir. It is a protective, political, military organization. I am willing to show any man the constitution of the society. Its objects originally were protection against Loyal Leagues and the Grand Army of the Republic; but after it became more general it was found that political matters and interests would best be promoted within it, and it was then made a political organization, giving its support, of course, to the Democratic Party."

"But is the organization connected throughout the State?"

"Yes, it is. In each voting precinct there is a captain, who, in addition to his other duties, is required to make out a list of names of men in his precinct, giving all the Radicals and all the Democrats who are positively known, and showing also the doubtful on both sides and of both colors. This list is forwarded to the Grand Commander of the State, who is thus enabled to know who are friends and who are not."

"Can you, or are you at liberty, to give me the name of the commanding officer of this State?"

"No; it would be impolitic."

"I suppose that there can be no doubt of a conflict if the militia interferes with the people—is that your view?"

"Yes, Sir. If they attempt to carry out Governor Brownlow's proclamation, by shooting down Ku Klux—for he calls all Southern men Ku Klux—there will be war, and a bloodier one than we have ever witnessed. I have told these Radicals here what they might expect in such an event. I have no powder to burn killing

Negroes. I intend to kill the Radicals. I have told them this and more. There is not a Radical leader in this town but is a marked man; and if trouble should break out, not one of them would be left alive. I have told them that they were trying to create a disturbance and then slip out and leave the consequences to fall upon the Negro; but they can't do it. Their houses are picketed, and when this fight comes, we don't intend for one of them to get out of the country alive. But I want it distinctly understood that I am opposed to any war, and will fight only in self-defense. If the militia attacks us, we will resist to the last. If necessary, I think I could raise forty thousand men in five days, ready for the field."

"Do you think, General, that the Ku Klux have been of any benefit to the State?"

"No doubt of it. Since its organization the Loyal Leagues have quit killing and murdering our people. There were some foolish young men who put masks on their faces and rode over the country frightening Negroes; but orders have been issued to stop that, and it has ceased. You may say further that three members of the Ku Klux have been court-martialed and shot for violations of the orders not to disturb or molest people."

"Are you a member of the Ku Klux, General?"

"I am not; but I am in sympathy and will cooperate with them. I know they are charged with many crimes that they are not guilty of. A case in point is the killing of Bierfield at Franklin, a few days ago. I sent a man up there especially to investigate the case, and report to me, and I have his letter here now, in which he states that they had nothing to do with it as an organization."

"What do you think of Negro suffrage?"

"I am opposed to it under any and all circumstances . . . here I want you to understand distinctly I am not an enemy to the Negro. We want him here among us; he is the only laboring class we have; and more than that, I would sooner trust him than the white Scalawag or Carpetbagger . . . But there is a limit beyond which men cannot be driven, and I am ready to die sooner than sacrifice my honor. This thing must have an end, and it is now about time for that end to come."

The wizard's position was that the South's traditional ruling class, backed by a white yeomany convinced by appeals to racist vanity, did not acknowledge any right of the newborn democratic regimes to exist. So secure was he in the knowledge that real power in the South was in the hands of the Confederate underground, in the form of the Invisible Empire of the Ku Klux Klan, that he felt free to challenge openly the elected authorities exercising their police powers in upholding the equal rights provisions of the new state constitutions and the Fourteenth Amendment. Significantly, the wizard did not feel it necessary to challenge federal authority, for the very good reason that no federal authority was being brought to bear. With the president and the president's secretary of war and attorney general explicitly in agreement with the wizard as to the illegitimacy of the Reconstruction governments, and with federal troops gone, Congress on vacation, and Grant campaigning, it was truly open season down South on blacks and every other sort of equal rights advocate.

The racist terrorists made the most of the situation. Their victims, black and white alike, literally had no place to turn for succor. Just as Uncle Sam had earlier liberated the slaves and left them without a leg to stand on or a spot of ground to lie upon, he now abandoned to the wolves of white supremacy the infant democracies he had brought into being.

Savage as Rattlesnakes

In this extremity the victims could do no better than address their appeals to Republican Party leaders. From all over the South, the message was the same. "The Rebels are thoroughly organized and are using every means to intimidate and prevent loyal people black and white from a free expression & exercise of their political rights," a Florida Republican wrote the party's national chairman, William F. Chandler. "It is evident that the Rebels intend to take forcible possession of these state governments."[22]

In South Carolina, the state Republican chairman, a black man who was also a state senator, was assassinated in Abbeville County by a band of unmasked whites.[23] "Three members of the General Assembly and one member of the late constitutional convention have been murdered secretly," a South Carolina congressman further reported.[24]

The national Republican Party sent a special agent, John M. Morris, to investigate conditions in that state. "The rich Rebels coax with one breath and threaten with the next," Morris reported. "It is not safe for me to go alone unarmed into the up-country here. Negroes are daily shot dead or wounded. Nobody is convicted because no adequate testimony is found or the magistrates don't prosecute . . . I fear that thousands of voters will be kept away or driven from the polls."[25]

Skull and crossbones and the legend "2 × 6" signify death and the size of the coffin awaiting the recipient; the Klan mailed these handbills to black and white prospective Republican voters in New Orleans.

In Georgia, after going through the motions of electing a democratic government in order to regain statehood, the racists were so bold as to stage a palace putsch driving black delegates from the halls of the legislature. The struggle to reestablish the *ancien régime* there was out in the open. "There is . . . a reign of terror and violence in some parts of the State, and Republicans cannot hold meetings and discuss the questions involved in the canvass without actual violence or such threats of it as to drive off the timid from the meetings," former Governor Joseph E. Brown reported.[26] That these were not empty words was demonstrated when Georgia blacks, en route to a rally at Camilla, were slain by whites when they refused to surrender arms they were carrying for self-defense.[27]

"Our enemies here are as savage as rattlesnakes," a Republican observer wrote from Savannah. Another, writing from Augusta, reported that the Democrats thereabouts were speaking confidently "of the near day when all the Yanks & white niggers will have to leave the South."[28]

"There are parties of Rebels now going about through the state murdering loyal citizens in their houses at night and shooting them from bushes during the day," reported another observer of the Georgia scene. "These murdering parties are said to be chiefly composed of slave-holders' sons."[29]

"The present Rebellious spirit is greater here now than it was before the late war," came word from Dalton. "Congress has been too lenient toward the Rebels. Active measures must be enacted or we are Butchered up and law & Constitution trampled under foot."[30]

The Congress in question reconvened October 16 as planned, and again turned a deaf ear to all such pleas for arms in order that the Southern state governments might defend themselves and enforce law and order.

As for the victimized citizenry looking to its own defenses, there were some instances in which a show of weapons was made, resulting in retreat or compromise by the marauders.[31] But calls for organized armed resistance to the terror were turned down, not through any lack of courage, but rather in recognition of what the end result was likely to be.

"I have always told them that this would not do—that the white South would then come against us and kill us off, as the Indians have been killed off," was the way a Georgia black preacher, the Reverend Charles Ennis, put it.[32]

The Negro Hunt

And so during the few remaining weeks before the November 3 election the southwide "Negro hunt" continued apace. In Louisiana alone, such hunts took more than 2,000 lives.[33] In a two-day hunt through the woods and swamps of St. Landry Parish the Klan killed or wounded some 200 Republicans, most of whom were black. A pile of 25 half-buried bodies was found in the woods. In Bossier Parish, 125 bodies were recovered from the Red River.[34]

"For ten days prior to the election, the streets of New Orleans were filled with men carrying shotguns, pistols, and knives," it is recorded in E. P. Oberholtzer's *History of the United States Since the Civil War.* "A band called 'The Innocents' . . . roamed the city hunting for Negroes. Soon none could be found on the streets. Then the ruffians entered the houses to drive out the blacks, shooting them like rabbits as they ran. A colored man feared to sleep two nights in the same place."

Out of the Holocaust

All such as this and much more came to pass, be it remembered, in the very same year that Southern blacks—protected at first by a U.S. military presence—voted for the first time, the year when most of the former slave states adopted constitutions affirming the equal political rights of all males, the year when the Fourteenth Amendment "guaranteeing" the equal rights of American citizens was added to the Constitution, the year when the United States were united once again.

Despite all this laborious paperwork and the incumbency of white and black democratically elected regimes in the Southern states, the election of 1868, far from being free, was turned into a manhunt by the terrorists. The newborn democracy of the South, forsaken by the Congress that gave it birth, fell victim to infanticide.

On the national level, Grant was elected president with 214 electoral votes to Horatio Seymour's 80. In terms of popular vote, however, he received only 52.7 percent, less than the 55 percent that had gone to Lincoln in 1864 on the eve of Appomattox (albeit without, of course, the Southern vote). But while Republicans captured the White House, they lost their two-thirds majority in the House. There the white supremacist Democratic Party gained 25 seats, 16 of them going to former Confederate states. A portent of things to come was to be seen in the outcome in New York, New Jersey, and some other Northern states, where Democrats, using the same scare tactics of "black rule" and "social equality" as their Southern brethren, won major victories.

In the South the white supremacists regained control over Georgia and Louisiana. Just how much the untrammeled Negro hunts had to do with this is indicated by the fact that, in St. Landry Parish where one of the most sanguinary hunts was conducted, all 4,787 of the votes cast were claimed by the Democrats, despite the fact that the Republicans had 1,071 more registered voters in the parish than did the Democrats.[35]

Far from reaffirming the verdict of Appomattox, this first national election to be conducted by the re-United States provided much new hope for the eventual triumph of the modified war aims of the Confederate underground, not in the South alone but throughout the nation. After four years of defiance, chicanery, psychological warfare, and terrorism, Appomattox was well on its way to being reversed.

The political will of Southern blacks and other believers in democracy was still far from being broken, but it had been severely battered. The events of 1868 had brought about many a shift in the power struggle. Four years of executive sabotage of the legislative will had come to an end; but on the other hand, to a critical degree, so had the legislative will. The U.S. Army of occupation, whose courts and bayonets had stood guard over the Southern democracy aborning, was no longer the major factor it had been.

Ole Massa, back on the throne in two of the ex-Confederate states, and his hand immeasurably strengthened in the others, had good reason to believe that the star of white supremacy was on the ascendancy and that the Nation as a whole was destined to return to its traditional path of racism. For one thing, they reasoned, former Confederates could not much longer be barred from the polls and public office, whereas blacks could.

The Klan Plays 'Possum

The substantial success of the Southern terrorists in deterring blacks from voting and the failure of Congress to do anything about it suggested to the regents of the Klan's Invisible Empire that certain modifications of strategy and tactics were in order. With only undermanned and under-armed state militias to contend with, the Confederate underground was in a position to become a Confederate aboveground. In many areas, the covert reign of terror could now be replaced with an overt reign of ter-ror. Instead of riding by night in disguise, the terrorists felt increasingly free to do their work in the full light of day. Obviously, the counterrev-olution whose aim it was to overthrow democratic republicanism and re-store the racist oligarchy had entered into a new and prefinal phase.

It was with such "positive" considerations as these in mind—as well as such "negative" ones as an apprehension that the Justice Department might seek conspiracy indictments against the Klan hierarchy—that Wiz-ard Forrest in January of 1869 issued the following edict: "The Invisible Empire has accomplished the purpose for which it was organized. Civil law now affords ample protection to life, liberty, and property; robbery and lawlessness are no longer unrebuked; the better elements of society are no longer in dread for the safety of their property, their persons, and their families. The Grand Wizard, being invested with power to deter-mine questions of paramount importance, in the exercise of the power so conferred, now declares the Invisible Empire and all the subdivisions thereof dissolved and disbanded forever."[36]

This bit of wizardry did not have the effect of dampening Klan activ-ity in the least, nor was it intended to do so. Klansmen had a keen sense of appreciation for the Ku Klux brand of chicanery, and they recognized it when they saw it. Consequently they went about their business as usual, without having to be told by anyone that the only real intent of the edict was to con the nation into believing that the Southern "trou-bles" were over, and that a Fifteenth Amendment specifically asserting the political rights of blacks (then being debated in Congress) was not re-ally necessary.

Hand in hand with an actual intensification of orthodox Klan activity there was a certain proliferation of Klan "front groups," operating under a variety of names and garb. In some sections, most notably in South Carolina, the white robes of the Klan were put aside in favor of "the red shirt badge of Southern manhood." In short, the old familiar wine of racist terrorism began to appear in new bottles.

In a matter of weeks after the Invisible Empire issued its edict proclaiming that all was well on the Southern front, the U.S. Congress—knowing full well that all was not well (owing in good measure to its own failure to provide arms for its protégé democracies in their hour of need) —floated another piece of paper. Launched on February 26, it proposed adoption of a Fifteenth Amendment to the Constitution, to read as follows: "The right of citizens of the United States to vote shall not be denied or abridged by the United States or by any state on account of race, color, or previous condition of servitude."

Though somewhat disappointed by this turn of events, the Confederate aboveground was pleased to note that the amendment as proposed forbade only *state* action that interfered with black voting, leaving the *private* sector—such as the Klan and individual terrorists—a free hand. This omission, sad to say, was by no means inadvertent; rather, the loophole was deliberately adopted after long and frank discussion. The Soft Peace ultimately to be concluded with the Confederacy in the Deal of '76 was already taking shape.

Johnson Packs His Bags

While the Congress was making ready for the Grant ascension, scheduled for April 5, and the Klan was making ready by playing 'possum, the po-white who still occupied the White House busied himself striking a few more blows on behalf of white supremacy. Already, on Christmas Day of 1868, Johnson had declared a general amnesty for all Confederates against whom charges were still pending. This served to free, among others, the former president of the Confederacy, Jefferson Davis. Davis was in fact nominally free, having been granted bail in the amount of $100,000 in May of 1867. Among those providing for his surety had been Cornelius Vanderbilt, Horace Greeley, and Gerrit Smith (the latter once a militant abolitionist who helped finance John Brown's raid on Harper's Ferry).[37]

According to a diary kept by Interior Secretary Orville Browning, Johnson's cabinet during its final days in office was beset with reports of "anarchy . . . murders, assassinations, burnings, and general insecurity" in the South.[38] In the view of those latter-day historians J. G. Randall and David Donald, this "spectacle of carpetbaggers appealing to President

Johnson's administration for troops to protect them from the hostility of Southern whites" was "one of the exquisite ironies of reconstruction."

The "exquisite irony" came to an end on April 4, when, 'tis said, Johnson and his men labored "long past the hour of twelve" putting finishing touches on their escutcheon by such gestures as returning to General Lee's wife family relics captured at Mount Vernon.

On the day following they presumably rested, as none were in attendance at Grant's inaugural.

✠

CHAPTER 8

✠

When Ulysses S. Grant moved into the White House he was more determined than ever that the nation's wartime sacrifices not prove to have been in vain. In his bid for the presidency he had raised the slogan "Let us have peace." But peace was nowhere in sight. His four years of military campaigning had not really produced it at Appomattox, nor had his armies of occupation been able to pacify the region during the four years that had followed.

As general of the armies both before and after Appomattox, Grant had had a pretty fair idea what was required of him. But as president of the United States and commander in chief of its armed forces, the nature of his task was less clear-cut. It may be that he felt he had a better handle on the South while occupying it than he did while occupying the White House.

The South was not, of course, the only problem confronting his administration. While the question of whether the South was to have a republican form of government or white rule (a question that also had a direct bearing upon the future prospects of the national Republican Party), there were other grave issues, such as the state of the economy, which cried out for attention. Not least of these was the national debt, which by the end of the year was to total what was then the appalling sum of $2,453,000. Most of this was owed to the Eastern financial establishment, which during the war had purchased government bonds with paper money that had been worth substantially less then than it was at maturation. These gentry, however, were not only demanding repayment at face value; they wanted it in gold. So intense was the opposition of Western agrarians that an East/West civil war was bruited about as a distinct possibility.

A scant two weeks after Grant took office, Congress passed an "Act to Strengthen the Public Credit." In reality the act was a victory for the Eastern establishment—and a portent of the "Black Friday" market crash that was to come six months later, on September 24. But the severe economic depression that plagued the nation during Grant's administrations had been chronicled by others; suffice it to recall here that it was to prove a major factor leading American business, agriculture, and labor to worry less about the plight of Southern blacks and more about their own predicament.

As for the struggle for power in the South, it had a dynamic all its own. Ironically, Grant was still up against many of the old adversaries he had faced on the field of battle. Whatever the relative merits of Grant and the Confederate generals as military commanders may have been, the latter had, in serving as the high command of the Confederate Underground in the wake of Appomattox, proven themselves to be past-masters in the arts of psychological warfare, terrorism, and political chicanery. Besides, there was a whole coterie of them, and only one of him.

The task presented by Appomattox was a very special one. It was not as though some new territory had been conquered and annexed. Nor was it as though a portion of the national territory had been liberated from some foreign invader, with the populace rejoicing at reunion with the motherland. Rather, Appomattox marked the putting down of armed rebellion, and the forced reincorporation of territory that had seceded and did not want to be reincorporated. To be sure, Appomattox did represent liberation of sorts for the enslaved black people of the South. But black liberation, if carried to completion, would entail by definition a democratic restructuring of the South's economic, political, and social life—and Ole Massa had sworn he would "die first."

With white supremacist Johnson out, and the hero of Appomattox in, reconstructionists looked forward confidently to cooperation between White House and Congress and to relatively smooth sailing for the remainder of the course that had been set. On paper, Reconstruction ap-

U. S. soldiers modeling captured Klan robes in Huntsville, Alabama (*Harper's Weekly,* December 19, 1868).

peared to have a lot going for it: the Thirteenth Amendment abolishing slavery, the Fourteenth asserting the equal rights of all U.S. citizens, and the Fifteenth forbidding states to restrict voting on grounds of race. To back up these new basic laws of the land there were federal civil rights acts and the brand new U.S. Department of Justice. What was more, the fixed price tag on readmission to the Union was that the former Confederate states commit themselves to equal rights in new state constitutions of their own. With such rules of the game and referees in place, what more could believers in free elections and free institutions ask?

There was but one problem, but it was twofold: Ole Massa had no intention of abiding by the rules, and Uncle Sam lacked the will to enforce them.

Although the paperwork battles appeared to have all been won by the champions of freedom and equality, the South's white supremacists continued to hold an absolute monopoly on all the real instruments of power: land, money, credit, education, expertise, tradition, juries, shotguns, pistols, and horses. From their point of view, the regaining of statehood—

despite its cost in ostensible compromise of principle—actually tilted the balance of power in their favor. What had been a four-year post-Appomattox struggle to mop up racist resistance was fast turning into a struggle to mop up republican resistance. Regaining the upper hand, Ole Massa was to prove far more efficient at mopping up than Uncle Sam had been. Indeed, Pacification had always been Ole Massa's middle name.

Both camps, despite opposing agendas, were anxious to bring to completion the process of restoring the Union. Uncle Sam fancied this would represent a return to normalcy, while Ole Massa reckoned he could get his way easier within the Union than without it. The identification, isolation, encirclement, and mop-up of pockets of republican resistance did not await this eventuality, however, but proceeded apace—albeit at a faster pace where the federal presence had come to an end than where it had not.

Although Georgia had nominally been readmitted by the Omnibus Act of June 25, 1868, the temerity of its white supremacist legislators in forcibly ejecting black legislators and replacing them with proscribed ex-Confederates had kept that state out of the Union. The other three outsiders—Mississippi, Texas, and Virginia—had balked at adopting proposed new state constitutions that incorporated Fourteenth Amendment barriers to certain categories of ex-Confederates voting and holding office. Although the white supremacists in these states evidently felt they could somehow live with *federal* impositions of that nature if they had to, they would be damned if they would write such a thing into their *own* constitutions.

Intent upon rapprochement at almost any cost, the Congress and the president let these holdout states off the hook by permitting them again to put their proposed constitutions to referendum vote, this time with an opportunity to vote separately on the bar against ex-Confederates. And this time around the voters in those states, black as well as white, voted almost unanimously in favor of equal rights constitutions and against depriving former Confederates of political rights. The blacks who magnanimously went along with this were soon to regret it, for most of the men their votes enfranchised were soon hard at work seeking to deny them any rights worth mentioning.

Dixie Raises the White (Man's) Flag

Grant's initial year in office witnessed yet another attempt on the part of the South's white supremacists to "persuade" Southern blacks to accept the role of being "just voters." This proffer was not made with any view toward power sharing or a pluralistic political structure in the South but rather required that blacks cast their votes for candidates who were not only white-skinned but also dedicated to the doctrine of white supremacy in all its manifold ramifications. Although subject peoples in many parts of the world have long been forced to perform parliamentary charades purporting to ratify their rulers, the South's blacks would have none of it.

This decision was as fraught with consequences for the black man as the decision of the red man not to be a slave of the white had been for him. In opting not to accept the modified slavery that becoming "just voters" would have entailed, blacks let themselves in for a veritable holocaust, complete with threats of a "final solution."

For one thing, the resolve of blacks to exercise full political rights or none led to a resolve on the part of whites that it would have to be the latter. And so, in this first year of Grant's tenure in office, the rigid color line that had ever characterized Southern society, only to be bent out of shape by Appomattox, was redrawn.

"We have given the negro a fair trial," was the way the *Columbus* (Miss.) *Index* put it in December of 1869. "He has voted solidly against us, and we hoist, from this day, the white man's flag, and will never take it down so long as we have a voice in the government of the state."[1]

In that state, the "white man's flag" took the form of an emblem, adopted by the Democratic Party and emblazoned upon every Democratic ballot (where it was to remain until the middle of the next century), of a crowing cock and the slogan "White Supremacy—For the Right!"[2]

Not to be outdone by the defiant standard-raising of the *Columbus Index,* the *Columbus Democrat* proceeded to spell out the political ideology that was destined to reign supreme over the South for nearly a hundred years:

> Its leading ideas are, that white men shall govern, that niggers are not rightly entitled to vote, and that when it [white supremacy] gets into power, niggers will be placed upon the same footing with white minors who do not vote or hold office.
>
> There are professed Democrats who do not understand Democratic principles, that want the party mongrelized, thinking that the less difference between the two parties will give them a better chance for the spoils. They are willing for the niggers to vote, but not to hold office.
>
> Nigger voting, holding office, and sitting in the jury box, are all wrong, and against the sentiment of the country. There is nothing more certain to occur than that these outrages upon justice and

good government will soon be removed, and the unprincipled men who are now their advocates will sink lower in the social scale than the niggers themselves.[3]

The new outbreak of rebel fever spread rapidly across the South, erupting in a host of virtual declarations of independence from the newly adopted equal rights provisions of the U.S. and state constitutions. Johnny Reb was not exactly seceding again, but he was with equal ferocity proclaiming his intent to rule the Southern roost subject to no law but his own and to countenance no opposition from within or without.

Typical of the rebel yells that this second secession brought forth was that heard from the *Fairfield* (S.C.) *Herald,* which denounced: "the hell-born policy, which has trampled the fairest and noblest of our great sisterhood beneath the unholy hoofs of African savages and shoulder-strapped brigands, [giving] the rule to gibbering, louse-eaten, devil-worshipping barbarians from the jungles of Dahomey, and peripatetic buccaneers from Cape Cod Hell and Boston."[4]

Some of those who busied themselves forging new chains to replace the old got so carried away as to proclaim that, in addition to barring blacks from almost everything else, they should also be barred from practicing the Christian faith, even on an apartheid basis. The dictum of the Klan, that "blacks have no rights which whites are bound to respect," was made the cornerstone of the neo-Confederacy. And once again it was the *Columbus Democrat* that came forth with a rationale, invoking divine sanction for the proposition:

> A negro preacher is an *error loci*. God Almighty, in farming out his privileges to mankind, drew a line as to qualifications. He never exacted from a nation or tribe an impossibility. Does any sane man believe the negro capable of comprehending the ten commandments? The miraculous conception and the birth of our Savior? The high moral precepts taught from the temple on the mount?
>
> Every effort to inculcate these great truths but tends to bestialize his nature, and by obfuscating his little brain unfits him for the duties assigned him as a hewer-of-wood and drawer-of-water. The effort makes him a demon of wild, fanatical destruction, and consigns him to the fatal shot of the white man.[5]

Private Sector Terrorism

Grant's second year in office, 1870, was to witness the return to the Union of those four remaining seceders that, as the year began, were still on the outside. All having at length complied (with many a tongue in white cheek) with the congressional mandate that they adopt equal rights state constitutions and ratify the Fourteenth and Fifteenth Amendments, Virginia was readmitted on January 26, Mississippi on February 23, Texas on March 30, and Georgia—last of the recalcitrant lot—on July 15. Five years after Appomattox, restoration of the Union was at last an accomplished fact.

But far from having the tranquilizing effect upon regional and racial conflict for which Unionists had hoped, reunion actually brought with it an intensification of the power struggle in the South. And so, although 1870 was a year of reunion, it was also a year that saw the enactment of the first of a series of Enforcement Acts—"Force Bills," Ole Massa called them at the time (as have his apologists ever since). In reality, of course, the Congress was simply fulfilling its duty to provide enforcement legislation, as called for in the amendments themselves. Ole Massa, while not at all averse to using extralegal force to deprive blacks of rights assured by the amendments, was very much opposed to Uncle Sam using legal force to stop him from doing so—hence the appelation "Force Bills."

The first Enforcement Act was adopted by Congress on March 31— the very next day after the Fifteenth Amendment was declared to be in effect. The act made it a crime, punishable by a fine of up to five thousand dollars or imprisonment up to ten years, to "prevent any person guaranteed the right to vote under the 15th Amendment from voting by means of bribery, threats of depriving such person of employment, or ejecting such persons from a rented house . . . or by threats of violence to such a person and his family." Anticipating with good reason that the Department of Justice and the federal courts might be unable to cope with the scope of racist resistance, Congress empowered the president to bring the U.S. Army and Navy to bear if necessary.

White supremacists were dismayed—though far from daunted—by the fact that the act threatened to cramp their style in economic as well as physical lynching. Whereas the Fifteenth Amendment itself only forbade *states* to discriminate against black voters, this Enforcement Act went on to proscribe such actions by *private* individuals or bands. From the racists' point of view, the thing was in violation of the "Gentlemen's Agreement of '66," whereby they understood that if they would forego use of the *public* sector to discriminate against blacks, the North would look the other way when they employed the *private* sector (KKK, et al.) to the same end.[6]

This fond notion was based upon the indubitable fact that the origi-

Liberty's admonishment: "Halt! This is not the way to
'repress corruption and to initiate the Negroes onto the
ways of honest and orderly government.'" Cartoon by
Thomas Nast (*Harper's Weekly*, courtesy of the Florida
State Photo Archive).

nal Constitution left to the respective states exclusive jurisdiction over
the entire gamut of "ordinary crimes"—such as assault, battery, vandalism, arson, robbery, murder, mayhem, et cetera. A no less indubitable
fact, however, was that ever since Appomattox virtually the entire white
South was linked in a criminal conspiracy to commit all of these "ordinary crimes" against blacks as such (individually and en masse), not for
any of the ordinary reasons, but for the express reason of depriving them
of rights now assured them by the Constitution.

In order for federal authority to assert jurisdiction over the prosecution of such "ordinary crimes," all that was really necessary was a showing that the real motive was to violate federal law. In the circumstances of the time, this was not difficult.

At first the newly created Department of Justice prosecuted private practitioners of terrorism with vigor, and at first federal courts backed up the prosecutors. In Alabama and Ohio, U.S. Circuit Courts upheld the validity of Section 6 of the Enforcement Act forbidding private acts of terrorism aimed at the deprivation of Constitutional rights. In the Alabama case, armed and mounted whites had broken up a black political rally, and Supreme Court Justice William B. Woods held this to be a violation of the rights of free speech and assembly that were privileges and immunities of American citizenship now secured to blacks by the Constitution.[7] The Ohio case involved an act by a state official, but, in supporting the circuit court's decision, Supreme Court Justice William Strong went out of his way to assert that the Fourteenth and Fifteenth Amendments gave Congress power to protect the rights of U.S. citizenship against infringement by any source whatever.[8]

Some Five Thousand Atrocities

The Invisible Empire took note of all this, but its night riders rode on as though nothing had happened. In Georgia the terror became so rampant that Grant sent U.S. troops back in. In Virginia, Republicans of both races appealed to the White House for similar protection. As the year 1870 drew to a close, Grant on December 5 sent Congress a special message declaring that "the free exercise of the franchise has by violence and intimidation been denied to citizens in several of the states lately in rebellion . . . A condition of affairs now exists rendering life and property insecure." The situation called urgently for more stringent action by Congress, the president said.

Congress asked for proof, and on January 13, 1871, Grant sent it a documented report of over five thousand cases of floggings, lynchings, and other acts of terrorism. In transmitting this evidence, Grant declared that if he was to curb the terror effectively Congress would have to enlarge his emergency powers.[9]

By way of response to Grant's appeal, Congress in February adopted a Second Enforcement Act, providing for federal jurisdiction over and supervision of the election process when federal offices were involved. No more deterred by the Second Enforcement Act than it had been by the First, the Klan during March rode roughshod over prorepublic citizens in Georgia, Alabama, Mississippi, and South Carolina, as well as in

Cartoon by Thomas Nast (*Harper's Weekly;* courtesy of the Florida State Photo Archive).

other Southern states. What was needed, Grant told the Congress, was for it to give him the power to suspend habeas corpus in areas where he deemed that to be necessary.

Congress Sends in a Committee

As though Grant's list of five thousand terrorist atrocities was not enough, Congress on April 7 proceeded to appoint its own bipartisan "Joint Committee to Investigate the Condition of Affairs in the Late Insurrectionary States." The committee was comprised of thirteen Republicans and eight Democrats. Four were Southerners, and all twenty-one were white.

This done, Congress resumed debate on what was to become known as the Third Enforcement Act, or, more commonly, the "Ku-Klux Act." Introduced by Congressman Samuel Shellabarger of Ohio in May, this bill in its original form would have punished any two or more private parties who conspired to violate constitutional rights by committing any of a list (called "intolerably long" by racist historians)[10] of such crimes as assault, battery, murder, arson, as well as crimes not listed but committed for the same political/intimidatory purpose. Another section provided that when "domestic violence" (as terrorism was often politely referred to) prevented the upholding of federal law, or when state and local officials could not or would not protect the rights of U.S. citizenship, then the president was authorized, upon his own initiative and without invitation from a state legislature or governor, to suspend habeas corpus and send in the military.

In debate over the bill Democratic congressmen invoked the "Congressional Understanding of '66," with the result that, with the aid of some Republicans, they were able largely to confine the act, as finally adopted April 20, to state action. Anyone purporting to act under cloak of authority, law, *custom,* or *usage* came under the purview of the act, as well as anyone interfering with the ability of public officials to uphold federal law. In addition, the act gave Grant the power to suspend habeas corpus, and he promptly did so in nine South Carolina counties, and dispatched troops to some other sectors of the South where the terror was most prevalent.

TESTIMONIALS

✠

CHAPTER 9

✠

The Joint Committee began its deliberations in June of 1871. In advance of its scheduled hearings the committee sent out handbills urging (surviving) victims of the terror to come in and testify, "under the protection of the United States Government."[1]

The government of the Invisible Empire countered with an order-of-the-day to all Klan dens: "Death to all witnesses!"[2] To insure that as few as possible escaped, the Klan posted sentries—men who could recognize most of the people in the surrounding territory—outside the committee's hearing places.

With and without faith in the ability of the U.S. government to protect them, the victims—black and white—came in to tell their tales of the terror that rode by night. Many were felled along the way, coming and going, but the words of those who got through the gauntlet were faithfully recorded by the committee's stenographers.

Hearings were held in Washington, D.C., during June, July, and August (with witnesses being brought in from the South), and subcommittees were sent South, where they held hearings in Florida, Georgia, Tennessee, North Carolina, South Carolina, and Alabama, from July through November.

When the testimony was all in, transcribed and printed, it comprised thirteen bulky volumes.[3] So damning was the irrefutable record that those intent upon foisting the Big Lie upon the nation felt obliged to obliterate it. A systematic cover-up campaign to destroy the printed transcripts was launched, with such success that only two complete sets are known to have survived—one in the Library of Congress, and the other in the Schomburg Center for the Study of Black Culture at the New York Public Library.

All thirteen volumes have been painstakingly mined and thirty-three testimonials selected to comprise the body of this book. As the "condition of affairs" described by the victims was by and large endemic to the entire South, no attempt has been made to include here testimonials from every section of the region. Rather, there has been a deliberate concentration upon some states and locales in order to provide, in microcosm, a multifaceted view of the forces at work.

In making the selections, care has been taken to see to it that the role of the terror as the ultimate weapon for achieving each of the neo-Confederacy's modified war aims is exemplified: the prevention of blacks from voting, holding office, bearing arms, sitting on juries, attending schools, acquiring good land or jobs, and fraternizing with whites or associating with them in places of public accommodation. Whites, whether Southern or Northern, who gave aid or encouragement to blacks in any of these forbidden activities were, as their testimony reveals, meted out equal or even more severe punishment.

Many of the testimonials go on to reveal that ultimately the terrorists' hit list came to include everyone, of whatever race, who dared vote Republican. The new order of white supremacy did not propose to tolerate any dissidents, and to this end it resolved to drive the Republican Party out of office and out of the political arena.

In marked contrast to some of the concoctions of historians based upon interpretation, insight, hindsight, and bias, these first-person accounts by people who actually lived through Reconstruction and its forcible overthrow have the unmistakable ring of truth.

Theirs is not, of course, the whole story of Reconstruction. That story, as has been indicated, involved every institution of white Southern society in a general conspiracy to keep blacks subjugated. Terrorism was simply the indispensable ingredient without which—given the determination and fortitude of the blacks and their allies—the conspiracy might not have succeeded. Segregating, discriminating, preaching, jailing, and even economic lynching might not have prevailed had not the terrorists been there to intimidate, flagellate, castrate, and assassinate any-

"The same old pirate afloat again." Cartoon by Thomas Nast (*Harper's Weekly*, April 29, 1871; courtesy of the Florida State Photo Archive).

one and everyone who, despite those other forms of oppression, dared to challenge some prerogative of white supremacy.

It is the author's hope that, by resurrecting such as these to tell in their own words how it was, we can gain a clearer picture of what kind of people they were, what it was that they were trying to do, and how they were stopped from doing it.

Freedmen: "No Use for Blood Nohow"

"My name is Augustus Blair. Until last December I was living on Major Floyd's plantation, in Limestone County, Alabama. I had a son who was living with me—the only son I had—about 18 years old—very well grown—as big as I was.

"He went out on a Monday night over to what they called Allen's Ford, hog killing, and Jim Henry Cox, Bunk Hinds and Pony Hinds— three white fellows—were there, and they got into a fight, but he throwed up his hands, and some colored people prevented it. Cox said, 'You fight now, but you will not fight when the Ku-Klux come:' And on the Tuesday night following, they came."

"State what they did."

"They came that night and knocked on my door. I got up and opened the door very quietly, and they came in. Sim Hudson and Pony Hinds walked in at the door, and just behind them came Hugh Hudson—Sim's father—and he took a chair and sat down by the fire, and they ordered me to light a candle. I took a candle from the mantlepiece and pulled a straw from the broom to light the candle. Dick Hinds had a little piece over his face, but I knew him. Me and him was raised together.

"I heard them breaking the door down in the room where my boy was, with my two grown daughters—they had been married, but their husbands died in the war. Sim Hudson said, 'Here he is, by God! Here he is!'

"I walked in and says to my daughter, 'Where's William?' and she says, 'There he is—see the blood running!' I stepped up with the candle, and as I looked two of them had his head drawn back, and two others were beating him in the face with a pistol.

"They started to carry him off, and Dick Hinds came up to me and said, 'Do you know me? Don't you tell me no lie!'

"I said, 'No.'

"He said, 'No, Goddamn you—you had better not know me! This time I have nothing against you. You are a hard-working old nigger. You stayed at home during the war and took care of the little children.'

"I stepped in and put on my boots and slipped out through the stable, and as they went through the yard I went through the orchard and got over where there were hogweeds as high as my head, and came up and heard their conversation as they were going up the hill with my boy. They had stripped him naked. I heard him say, 'Oh, gentlemen, you–all carrying me along, and here are two men stabbing me with a knife!'

"They said, 'It's a damned lie! Nobody is sticking you!'

"He says, 'Oh, yes—I feel the blood running down my pants.'

"They says, 'Goddamn you, you will have no use for blood nohow mighty soon!'

"He went up the hill with them, and they were punching and cutting him. When they got up there they took him down and beat on his head. I crept right around behind a patch of briars and laid there. He never hollered but once, but I could hear him wheezing as they were choking him. Others were cutting him with a knife as they held him there, and some of the rest were going backwards and forwards to the other company. The night was mighty cold, and they made up a fire just a piece off. By and by, when they were cutting at him one of them says, 'The Captain says you have done enough.'

"They said to the boy, 'You feel here and see how you like these gashes. Do you reckon they will do you?' He went back to the Captain and told him, and the Captain hollered, 'I told you to spare life!' And then one says, 'Get up, get up, Goddamn you!'

The boy was so weak that when he went to get up he was staggering, and just then one hauled off and struck him, and then jumped onto him and stamped on him, and they shot off their pistols then and got on their horses and rode away.

"I was scrambling around in the bushes trying to find him, when I heard the girls cry out, 'Oh, Lord! Lord! Here's Billy cut to pieces with a knife! Come, sister, help me put him in the house!'

"I struck and ran home, and there he was standing with nothing on him but his shirt, and trembling all over and bloody, and I says, 'Oh, what's the matter? Can't you tell me nothing, my boy?' And he says, 'No, no,' and they took him in and I drew the bed before the fire and sent the little boy off as fast as he could go for the doctor, but the doctor sent word he was going to Huntsville and could not come. The next morning before day I put the little boy on a horse and sent for the doctor again. Doctor Frank Blair sent word he couldn't come, but he would send his father, old Doctor John Blair, the man that raised me. He never came until 8 or 9 o'clock that morning. Then he walked in.

"He looked at the boy and says, 'I don't think I can do him any good.'

"Says I, 'Are you going off without trying to do him any good, doctor?'

"He says, 'Have you got any tallow?'

"I told him I had.

"He says, 'Have you got any castile soap?'

"I said, 'Yes,' I had.

"Says he, 'Have you got any tar?' I told him we had.

"Then he turned in and made a poultice—a salve—and dressed his wounds. I heard him tell it in Huntsville afterwards that it took him two hours to dress the boy's wounds. You couldn't touch him anywhere from his shoulders down to the tips of his big toes."

"Why could you not touch him?"

"Because he was cut to pieces with a knife. The calves of his legs were split up and across, and his thighs were split open and cut across, and his knee looked like they had tried to take the cap off, and all his hands and arms were cut and slit up too."

"Did you say his feet were cut?"

"The bottom of his feet were slit open and the bottom of his heel split."

"Was he carried here before the grand jury?"

"Yes, sir, he was carried in on a litter."

"How long did he live?"

"He lived a year. I hired a wagon and fetched him here, but directly he came here he was taken down with a hemorrhage that came from stamping him on the stomach and breast. In two weeks after he was examined in the courtroom he died. Everybody that saw him said he couldn't live, and they were surprised that he lived so long. I had the doctors to tend him. I owe forty or fifty dollars to Doctor Henry Benfore; he asked me for the money on Saturday.

"Directly after the cutting took place, I came here and made complaint—I knew every one of them who had done it. Mr. Wager assisted me, and Jim Common and Mr. Lentz took the boy in the room and examined him. He says to me, 'Gus, he can't live.' At that time his legs were more than double the natural size.

"I had a good deal of property down there. They looked for me to go back. I left my wife and young child there. I didn't want to go away. I hadn't done anything, but I believe they would have treated me just the same way as they did my boy, so I went away. I left thirty head of hogs and one good milk cow; four bales of cotton and my corn in the field. When I went down there all my things were gone."

"Have these men been arrested?"

"Yes, sir, but they done run off."

"Did they forfeit their bonds?"

"Yes, sir. But I have lost my boy and my land and everything else I had. The night of the cutting, they told my wife, 'Tell Gus he has been here two years, and it is as long as we intend he shall be here. White folks wants to work this land!' I had six hundred acres cleared. Part of it I rented out to a white man named Mr. Wallace. He told my wife to tell me that inside of two weeks I must not be caught there. He said, 'He has got to get away, crop or no crop.' I never even got a chair—everything was destroyed and taken."

"You say you had two sons-in-law in the Union army during the war?"

"Yes, sir."

"Did they return?"

"No, sir, they died. Anderson Blair was my daughter Eliza's husband. She made affidavit for her widow's pension a good many times, but the government man always said she didn't make the right kind of proof, so she never got any pension."

"Did you have any arms about your house at the time of this occurrence?"

"No, sir, not a thing. I was living there just as quiet and peaceable as any neighbor or citizen could live. No black person but me lived in that section. They had run all the rest of them away, but I didn't think anybody would ever interfere with me any."

"Have you heard of any more disturbances of this kind down there? Did you hear of black people being whipped?"

"Yes, sir, and white men too. Mr. Harrison, who is Mr. Wallace's brother-in-law—a white man and a Union man—was taken out and whipped badly and treated awfully and then told to get away. He didn't go, and two weeks before they came to my house they came on him again, tied him to a persimmon tree, and shot him."

"Did you hear of any other case?"

"Just a while before they killed Mr. Harrison they went over to Benfield's, and they also had some big persecution and whipping of people over at Rodgersville."

"Black people?"

"Yes, sir. They took one man there and treated him pretty much as they had treated my Billy."

"Did you hear of other places where disguised men took people out?"

"Yes, sir—all through Tennessee. Mr. Hamilton, just a while before this happened, was up in Tennessee hunting a mule, and he said to me, 'I saw the awfullest sight day before yesterday that I ever saw in my life.' I asked him what it was. He said, 'I saw a man tied to a tree and shot six times through the head, and his head just laid back, his mouth open, and grinning dead, and it was the awfullest sight I ever saw.' "

"Did you ever hear the doctor say what was the cause of your son's death?"

"I heard him say, down there in the courthouse, that it was the cutting and stamping that had killed him. Mr. Joe Petty—a white neighbor man that ginned my cotton—was standing at my door and asked about it, and when I began to tell him he ran off to the gin and says, 'I can't stand to hear of a human being cut up in that way. I can't bear to hear that now; let me study on it a while and get my mind settled to hear it.'

"He went off, and came next day and asked to hear it, and I told him."

"Not a Praying Man"

"My name is Elias Thomson. I live up on Tiger River, on Mrs. Vernon's plantation, near Spartanburg, South Carolina."

"What do you follow?"

"Farming. I have rented about fifty acres."

"How long have you been living there?"

"Ever since the surrender—I never left home."

"Have you ever been disturbed any up there?"

"Yes, sir."

"How?"

"There came a parcel of gentlemen—or men—to my house one night. My wife was sick. I was lying on a pallet with my feet to the door. They ran against it and hallooed to me, 'Open the door, quick, quick, quick!'

"I threw the door open immediately—right wide open. I said, 'Come in, gentlemen.'

"One of them says, 'Do we look like gentlemen?'

"I says, 'You look like men of some description—walk in.'

"One says, 'Come out here! Are you prepared to die?'

"I told him I was not prepared to die.

" ' Well,' says he, 'your time is short—commence praying!'

"I told him I was not a praying man much, and hardly ever prayed; only a very few times; never did pray much.

"They led me off to a pine tree. There were three or four of them behind me, it appeared, and one on each side, and one in front. The gentlemen who questioned me was the only man I could see. Every time I tried to look around they would touch me with a pistol on the other side.

"The next question was, 'Who did you vote for?'

"I told them I voted for Mr. Turner—Claudius Turner, a gentleman in the neighborhood who ran for the legislature on the Radical ticket.

" 'What did you do that for?' they said.

"Says I, 'Because I thought it was right.'

"They said, 'You thought it was right? It was right wrong!'

"I said, 'I never do anything hardly if I think it is wrong; if it was wrong I did not know it. That was my opinion at the time, and I thought every man ought to vote according to his notions.'

"One of them said, 'Have you got a chisel here I could get?'

"I told him I hadn't, but I reckoned I could knock one out, and I sort of laughed.

"He said, 'What in hell are you laughing at? This is no laughing time!'

"I told him it sort of tickled me, and I thought I would laugh.

" 'Old man,' says one, 'have you got a rope here, or a plowline, or something of the sort?'

"I told him, 'Yes, I have one hanging on the corn-crib.'

"He said, 'Let us have it! String him up to this pine tree, and we will get all out of him!'

"I says, 'I can't tell you anything more than I have told.'

"Another then came up and said, 'Old man, we are just from hell—some of us have been dead ever since the Revolutionary War. We have heard your conversation for the last six months. I came up under your kitchen floor just this night and I have heard your conversation a good while.'

"I said, 'You have been through a right smart of experience. If I had been in hell I would not want to go back.'

"One says, "Have you heard a wild goose holler lately?'

"I said, 'I heard one the other night.'

"Said he, 'That was us coming over and looking down to see what you have been doing.'

"I said, 'You must fly, then.'

"He says, 'When we start we can go a long ways.' And then said, 'We have got to go to Spartanburg tonight, and from there to Asheville before daylight.' It was then about 2 o'clock.

"I says, 'You have a long trip,' and laughed.

"He says, 'What in hell are you laughing at?'

" 'Why,' said I, 'by your going on such a trip.'

"He says, 'This is no laughing time.'

"I says, 'If anything tickles me I always laugh, no matter how it is.'

"I told him I could do it.

"He said, 'Just let us hear of this thing, and when we come back we will not leave a piece of you!' That was the end of it. They left then, and got on their horses and went away."

"Had you not heard of these Ku-Klux operations before?"

"Yes, sir."

"And yet during all that interview you were not seriously alarmed?"

"Everybody was afraid of them."

"How has it been since?"

"They did not ride for a week or two after that. But it broke out again, and now we expect them at any time, and have been fearing them."

"Have any other colored men been whipped in that neighborhood?"

"They all reported here. You have their names, I think."

"A Negro Is Not to Preach"

"My name is Dennis Rice. I used to live in Unionville, South Carolina, but I left there on the 20th of March last."

"Have you a brother who is or was a preacher?"

"Yes, sir."

"What was his name?"

"Lewis Thomson."

"Do you know whether he is alive?"

"I have no idea that he is alive. I have heard by almost everybody that comes from Union that he is dead, but yet I have not seen him."

"Is it your information that he died a natural death?"

"No, sir. My information is that he was taken out by some disguised men and killed. On the 16th of June, I believe."

"State whether you have any knowledge of any threats made against him."

"I saw a paper with his coffin marked on it."

"When and where did you see it?"

"He brought it to me, some time in February, and he said, 'Here is the coffin that they have marked out for me if I preach in Goshen Hill Township.' "

"Describe the paper."

"It was a wide paper with a mark in the shape of a coffin, and in the mark was, 'Lewis Thomson, if you preach any more.' Then three K's—*Kill, Kill, Kill,* it was taken to mean."

"Was that all?"

"It said, 'You are not to preach here; a colored man is not to preach in this township,' as well as I can recollect."

"Do you know whether he did preach there again?"

"Yes, sir. He preached there that very day."

"Has he preached there since?"

"No, sir. He went back there on the day before he was taken out that night, and he asked some of the white people could he preach there. They told him they reckoned so, but gave him very cold satisfaction, and that night he was taken out."

"What church did he belong to?"

"To the Zion Methodist Church."

"How do you know he was taken?"

"That is what they told me."

"Who knows that the Ku-Klux called on him at all?"

"The ones out of whose house he was taken sent me word. His clothes were all there, lying in the chair just like he pulled them off. They laid there two or three days . . ."

"Did not anybody in the house know the Ku-Klux called on him?"

"Yes, sir, the family in the house knew it—William Tucker and his wife."

"Have you seen them?"

"No, sir. They sent me word then, here, that he was taken out by the Ku-Klux."

"Did they say what was done with him?"

"They didn't. They said the Ku-Klux took him off and killed him, but they didn't say they saw that. They only saw him taken and tied at the door."

"Who found the body in the river?"

"The hands that worked on the plantation that the river runs through."

"What did they do with the body?"

"I suppose they attempted to bury it, or sent word to his mother and brother to go and bury it. However, they saw a notice, or heard somebody say that the Ku-Klux forbade them to bury him, and they were scared from burying him."

"Have you heard whether the body was buried?"

"I have heard it was not buried. Those that come from there have told me so."

"And the whole people there, white and black, refused to give the body burial because, as was supposed, the Ku-Klux had given them notice not to do it?"

"Yes, sir. That is the last report I have."

"For all you know the body is there yet?"

"Yes, sir. It is my opinion that the body is there yet unburied."

"Did you hear in what condition the body was found?"

"Yes, sir. Stabbed—cut open. They said his privates were cut off, and his body was dragged along the road and stabbed—cut all about with stabs in the body."

"Have you been up there to see if these things are true?"

"No, sir, I have not."

"Why do you not go?"

"I am afraid to go. I have two brothers in that county, and a father and mother, and if his body could have been buried they would have done it."

"Did you hear what the Ku-Klux said when they came to the house?"

"When they came to the house he went up in a little loft, but they made up a light, and looked up and saw him.

"They said, 'Yonder is the black rascal—the black son of a bitch!' And they told him to come down.

"He didn't hesitate, and came down immediately. They told him if he didn't come down they would kill him immediately. As soon as he came down, they gathered and tied him right at the door.

"When they came upon him the woman—she was a member of the church—says, 'Thomson, look to the Lord!' and Thomson said, 'Lord, have mercy on me!' and they said, 'It's too late to pray now, for the Devil has got you!' "

"Don't Sass White Ladies!"

"My name is Caroline Smith, and I expect I am about thirty-five years old. I now live in Walton County, Georgia."

"When did you come to Atlanta?"

"I left home on Thursday before the second Sunday in October."

"What did you leave home for?"

"The Ku-Klux came there."

"Tell us all about that."

"They came to my house on Thursday night, and took us out and whipped us. That is about all that it was."

"Who came there?"

"A great many of them—twenty-five or thirty, perhaps more. Ten of them whipped me, five licks apiece. I do not know but two of them, Mr. Felkner and Mr. Rich."

"At what time was it?"

"Late in the night, I do not know what time. They caught my husband first, and beat him as much as they wanted to, and then they came in and said, 'Make up a light!'

"I made up a light, and then Mr. Rich came to me and said, 'Who is this?'

"I said, 'Caroline.'

"He said, 'H'm, h'm, come out here.'

"I went out, and they made me get down on my knees.

"He said, 'Who is in the other house?'

"I said, 'Sarah Ann.'

"Felkner says to some of them, 'Fetch her out here!'

"Felkner then said, 'Take off this,' pointing to my dress. He whipped me some, and then he made me take my bodi' off, which I wore under my dress. He gave fifty more licks, and then said, 'Go and get some water, and don't let's hear any more big talk from you, and don't sass any white ladies!' "

"Who was this Sarah Ann?"

"She was my sister-in-law, who lived with us."

"What did they do to her?"

"They beat her, and kicked her in her back, and she has not got over it yet. They hit her on the head with a pistol, and they made her strip."

"What do you mean by that?"

"They made her pull her clothes off, like they did me."

"Did they give any reason why they whipped your husband?"

"He said to them, 'Just hold on a minute, if you please—what are you whipping me for?'

"They said, 'Never mind that; so we whip you.' That was all the satisfaction they gave him."

"What did they whip Sarah Ann for?"

"They told her pretty much about the same they did me—not to sass white ladies. The colored people dare not dress up themselves and fix up, like they thought anything of themselves, for fear they would whip us. I have been humble and obedient to them, a heap more so than I was to my master, who raised me in slave days, and yet that is the way they treat us. After they had whipped all three of us, Felkner looked in and said, 'Do you know any of us?'

"I said, 'No, I don't.'

"He said, 'Do you suspicion who we are?'

"I said, 'No.' I told them a lie, for I knew them well enough, but I knew they would kill me if I said I did.

"Said he, 'Are you going to watch us when we go to leave?'

"I said, 'No, sir, I am not.'

"He said, 'I will leave two or three of these wild men to watch you, to see if you watch us. Shut the doors, and don't open them!' "

"Do you know of any other colored people or white people who have been whipped besides your own folks?"

"I know a heap that they whipped, but I cannot think of all of them now. They rode once a night every week. They made a scatterment of the darkies when they came through there. I talked to Mr. Moore about it. He said, 'If you will stay here and work my land, you shall not be pestered any more.'

"My husband had done run off, after their first raid, but I sent for him and told him what Mr. Moore said, and got him back. But just as we got our crop done, and had pulled all the upland fodder, and were going over the cotton the first time, they came again. We then had to leave any-how—I could not stand it any longer."

"What became of your crop?"

"We had to leave it behind."

"Was Mr. Moore friendly to the Ku-Klux—do you suppose he wanted them to treat you in this way?"

"Well, I could say, but then I do not know it. I hate to say anything about a man without I knowed it. He said that he was in favor of the Ku-Klux before we came there to work for him, but after we came there, and it did as it did, he said he was not in favor of it. He told me this: that he did not know what they did it for, for he liked us as well as he did any colored people.

"I said, 'Mr. Moore, Mr. Willis Gilbert is a man who owned a heap of darkies in slavery times, and he has lots on his plantation yet, and he says no Ku-Klux can come on his premises without he says so; and he is a man of good understanding.' Mr. Moore did not say anything more to me."

"You say they made a general scattering of the darkies once before?"

"Yes, sir."

"What reason did they give for that?"

"They said we should not have any schools, and that white people should not countenance us, and they intended to whip every last one. That's what they said."

"Why did they not want you to have schools?"

"Schools! They would not let us have schools. We allowed last Fall that we would build ourselves a schoolhouse in every district, and the colored men started them. But the Ku-Klux came and said they would whip every man who sent a scholar there. And so we have a schoolhouse, but no scholars. They went to a colored man there, whose son had been teaching school, and they took every book they had and threw them into the fire; and they said they would just dare any other nigger to have a book in his house."

"What had these disguised men been doing that they were afraid of being found out?"

"Nothing, only going about whipping us black ones."

"Trying to Get at the Ballot-Box"

"My name is Larry White, and I reckon I am about forty. I was born in Georgia, and now live in Jackson County, Florida."

"Can you tell us whether there are any people in Jackson County that they call Ku-Klux?"

"Well, sir, for to know it myself, I don't know; but there is great talk of them, and I can see a heap of sign of people that they say the Ku-Klux has been afoul of."

"Did you ever hear anybody say they belonged to it?"

"No, sir."

"You say you saw a great deal of sign; what sign?"

"I have seen people killed, some run off, and some that were shot at. I take it it was done by Ku-Klux, but nobody would ever own it."

"How many do you suppose have been killed in that county?"

"It is out of my knowledge to tell how many. If I was to say a hundred or a hundred and fifty, I do not suppose I would tell a story. I have seen as many as three lying dead in one pile."

"How do you stand on political questions?"

"I am all right. But you have asked for the truth, and I will have to tell it. I had to deny voting Radical to save myself. I said I would not do it anymore; and after I said that, they seemed to excuse me, and said, 'Old Larry is a good nigger, they should all do like him.' "

"What induced you to do that?"

"I saw so many stabbed and knocked down on election day, and a great many shot at, that I thought I would take the easiest way I could. When I went up to vote I made believe I was going to throw the Democratic ticket in, but at the last minute I slipped the Radical ticket in, and then I tore up the other."

"How many were there that were stabbed and shot at, and otherwise maltreated?"

"I recollect that there were one or two black men who were stabbed right in the thick part of the butt, and several were knocked over the head until the blood ran. How many, I cannot tell."

"What were these colored men doing?"

"Trying to get at the ballot-box."

"How is it when anybody commits a crime there? Can he be punished?"

"It is according to who he is."

"What do you mean by that?"

"I mean whether he be a white man or a black man. If he is a white man, they don't punish him; but if he is a black man, they punish him."

"Does not the sheriff try to arrest white men too?"

"They will not let him."

"How do they prevent it?"

"They tell him that he shall not arrest a white man for a damned nigger. If the sheriff is an honest man he will quit his office and go home, and some other man will take it."

"Do you think a colored man would be safe to vote the Radical ticket in that county now?"

"No, sir; he better not vote it any more. He better have nothing to do with it, because if he does they will kill him certain; he will die sure!"

"To whom do your people look to protect them?"

"We look to the Government to protect us, but they are so slow to do it that we are all afraid to go back."

"What Government? The government of Florida, or the Government of the United States?"

"The Government of the United States. The government of Florida is very shallow; we have no confidence in it."

"That has not given you much help?"

"We sent to the Governor of Florida when they were killing us like dogs, but we never received any assistance from him."

"In what way do you think the Government of the United States can help you?"

"I do not know. I thought they could help us—maybe through my ignorance."

"I would like to have your opinion."

"It seems to me if I was Governor all over the State, and the people were to get wrong in the State, I would send men right there and stop it."

"How do you think the United States Government could help you?"

"About the same way."

"You think they should send men there?"

"Yes, sir, and stop it, because we voted for them."

"What sort of men would you send—soldiers?"

"I would not care who they were—soldiers or officers—just so they stopped the Ku-Klux from killing."

"Somebody to take hold of them?"

"Yes, sir, right along. I have never offered to kill any man and I do not want any man to kill me. I felt mighty lonesome—mighty dissatisfied—when they were doing it."

"Their Business is to Kill and Murder"

"My name is Richard Pousser, and I am the constable of Jackson County, Florida."

"Have you any people in your county that are called Ku-Klux?"

"Yes, sir."

"What do they do?"

"Well, sir, they just make it their business to kill and murder. I am now toting their bullet in my right shoulder."

"State the circumstances under which you were shot."

"It was done at night. As I got home some person shot me right as I got to my door."

"Have you any knowledge or belief of what they had against you, that they should want to kill you?"

"Because I am a strong Republican."

"Was anybody ever punished for it?"

"No one at all."

"Has any other injury ever been inflicted upon you?"

"I have been stripped and pistols have been put in my face since I have been in office. Last week my mouth was abused because I was in office; an officer cannot carry out his duty in Jackson."

"By whom was this done?"

"It was done by a man of the name of Tom Barnes; some call him Sergeant Barnes."

"Tell us how it happened."

"I had some prisoners in charge by order of Judge Plantz, and I had my pistol buckled to me.

"Barnes said, 'What are you doing with that pistol buckled to you?'

"I said, 'I have a prisoner in charge.'

"He said, 'I have a mind to blow your Goddamned brains out, you Goddamned Radical son-of-a-bitch! You look pretty having a pistol buckled to you as a Goddamned officer!'

"I said, 'I am a lawful officer, and by order of Judge Plantz I am taking charge of these prisoners.'

"He said, 'If you say that word again I will blow your Goddamned brains out right now!' He then walked up and took a stick and struck me in the mouth."

"Why have you not prosecuted him?"

"There is no use in it; you cannot get justice there."

"Why not?"

"There is no use to try it, because they will make it appear that a colored man is a liar; and he cannot get justice. In fact, a colored man is afraid to try for it."

"Suppose you were to prosecute this man?"

"If the United States Government will give us assistance we will come out and do it. We cannot get protection unless we have assistance from the Government—the United States Government."

"What has been the condition of things there since Dickinson, the county clerk, was killed, so far as the colored people are concerned? Has it been better or worse than it was before?"

"It has been worse; there is no better about it."

"Who are the men—what people are they—who do this mischief?"

"We cannot tell exactly. They disguise themselves at night, and just go to your house and call you out, or if they do not call you out they will just open the door and come right in and kill you."

"How many people have been treated in that way in your county?"

"There have been ninety or a hundred, if I could remember them all."

"Were any of these men you speak of as having been murdered white Democrats or colored Democrats?"

"Not one of them. As to murdering, I cannot tell the end of the murdering since we were free."

"Do you never go to the white people there—you have good white people there, have you not?"

"They say it is not their business—that the Government did not put them in control, and they are not going to have anything to do with it."

"What is the feeling of the Democrats there toward the Government and in regard to the law?"

"Well, sir, they have an idea that they are not going to be controlled by the law—that it is all 'nigger law,' and they do not intend to abide by it. They say they did not vote for President Grant, and did not vote for Governor Reed, but they will have things their own way."

"Did you know Mr. Dickinson?"

"He was one of my particular friends."

"It has been testified to here before this Committee that Mr. Dickinson was killed by a man of your own color, because Dickinson had been living with a colored woman."

"That is not so. Mr. Dickinson was not killed by a colored man, he was killed by a white man."

"Did the white men there, especially the Democrats, charge it upon this colored man?"

"Yes, sir; they put the charge on him."

"Who do you think was the white man who killed Dickinson?"

"There was something about the tax on lands. I was Mr. Dickinson's bailiff, and he ordered me to take a bell and go around in the streets and ring it, and state that a sale of lands would be held at 11 o'clock.

"This man, John R. Ely, told Mr. Dickinson, 'If you sell my land I will whip or kill you!'

"Mr. Dickinson said, 'I will sell the land at the risk of my life. I have the right to sell it, and the authority to sell it. You may take it for granted what I tell you, for I am a man, too.'

"I went around and rung the bell, and I met Ely within twenty-five yards of the courthouse door. He said, 'What are you ringing that bell for?'

"I said, 'Mr. Dickinson ordered me to ring it for the sale of the land.'

"He said, 'You Goddamned Radical son-of-a-bitch, put that bell down, or I will kill you!'

"I let the bell fall.

"He went to Mr. Dickinson then and said, 'Now I am going to have satisfaction!' He told Mr. Dickinson that if he did not take that advertisement out of the paper about selling land, he would have him killed. Mr. Dickinson would not promise to do it."

"How long after that was Mr. Dickinson killed?"

"That was on Wednesday, and he was killed on Monday."

"This man Ely insisted that he had paid his taxes?"

"Yes, sir; and Mr. Dickinson said he had not—that the papers were there to show."

"If he had paid his tax, he could very easily have instituted proceedings in court and stopped the sale?"

"Yes, sir; but he said he did not intend to honor Dickinson that much."

"You think people were hostile to Dickinson anyhow?"

"They walked on him; they spit in his face, and he took it all. Colonel Coker took his fist and knocked Dickinson's hat off his head."

"Who is Colonel Coker?"

"He is a man of property, a very wealthy man."

"What had Mr. Dickinson done to him?"

"That was on the day of election. He asked Mr. Dickinson what he was doing with all those 'Goddamned niggers' in his office. Coker told Mr. Dickinson that if he did not come out of the office he would kick him out.

"Mr. Dickinson told him that the office was his.

"Coker's answer was that the 'Goddamned niggers' gave Dickinson that office, but that the whites did not intend for him to stay in it much longer. He then walked up to Mr. Dickinson and knocked his hat off his head. Coker said, 'I have a mind to put your eyes and mouth into one, you Goddamned nigger-loving son-of-a-bitch!' "

"Did you hear anybody express joy or satisfaction when Dickinson was killed?"

"Well, the Democrats all said that the last leading Radical was gone, and they did not intend to have any other carpetbaggers come there, and they would be damned if they would have any."

"There has been a great deal of complaint made here about Major Purman and Mr. Hamilton of the Freedmen's Bureau, that they behaved very badly in your county."

"They did not."

"It is represented that they treated the colored men very badly, that they tore up their labor contracts, and made new ones, and charged them for it, and all that."

"They did not do it! I would swear it on a pack of Bibles as high as from here to Heaven! The colored people appreciated Mr. Purman and Mr. Hamilton, because they treated us like gentlemen, and told us how to get along and how to manage. We would go to Mr. Hamilton and Mr. Purman for advice—that is what the whites objected to. If a man jumped on me and beat me, I would go to them for protection, and if they gave me protection, then Mr. Hamilton and Mr. Purman were regarded as just devils out of torment.

"The colored men have been falling back ever since Purman and Hamilton left; before they left we were living like gentlemen, going on as beautiful as any people in Florida. But as things are now, we cannot stay in Jackson County. If the United States does not give us aid and help us, we may just as well take our wives and children and move out."

"The Night Assassins Raided Me"

"My name is Henry Reed. I am about thirty-seven years old. Up to two years ago last month I lived in Jackson County, Florida."

"Why did you leave there?"

"The night assassins, or Ku-Klux, raided me so that I could not stay. I was doing very well there on a place I bought. They knew my principles—that I was a Republican, and always have been.

"One night I was sick, as I am now, but a little worse. I had been to a doctor and got some medicine, and he told me to go home and take it and rest quietly that night. But at 1 o'clock in the night there came a crowd of men there. They knocked, and told me to open the door. First they said that Mr. Dickinson, the Freedmen's Bureau agent, wanted me at the courthouse.

"I said, 'Gentlemen, I am not able to walk down there. Please tell him to wait until morning.'

"They said, 'Come out here! You have got to go now!'

"My wife got up, and I was going to make up a light in the house. One of them said, 'Don't make up a light!'

"I was somewhat excited from the alarm, and being very feeble and sick, I said, 'Let me get my coat and hat.'

"They said, 'You won't need any coat and hat! Come out!'

"My son, who is about fifteen years old, hoisted the window and jumped out. They shot at him one gun as he ran through my garden gate, and they put fifteen buckshot into the gate in a place the size of my hand. I cracked the door open a very small crack, and just as I could discern the men, I saw one standing at the corner of the house, with a double-barreled gun pointed right at my head. I shut the door.

"They said, 'If you don't come out of that house, Goddamn you, we will go back and get the balance of our company, and tear your house down, and blow your Goddamned brains out!'

"I did not know what to do. Nobody had anything against me—I was apparently as square with the citizens as any man in the world.

"At that time my wife came out, hollering, 'My son is dead, and they want to kill my husband!'

"The man at the gate got on his horse, and apparently went back for the rest of his company. I went back of the chimney to the kitchen part, and jumped out of the window. I went over to a rich neighbor of mine, and laid down there until 4 o'clock, the next day. Then some friends came there and called me. I would not answer them until I recognized their voices. They took me to a gentleman's house, and there I stayed, I suppose, about three or four days. He then took me in his hack, and fetched me and my wife and children to Quincy, and I have not been back there since. I had just bought a place, paid out a great deal of money for it, and had it fixed up real nice and comfortable, everything growing nicely, and ready for good living. They deprived me of everything I

"Dam Your Soul. The Horrible *Sepulchre* and Bloody Moon has at last arrived. Some live to-day to-morrow "*Die.*" We the undersigned understand through our Grand "*Cyclops*" that you have recommended a big Black Nigger for Male agent on our nu rode; wel, sir, Jest you understand in time if he gets on the rode you can make up your mind to pull roape. If you have anything to say in regard to the Matter, meet the Grand Cyclops and Conclave at Den No. 4 at 12 o'clock midnight, Oct. 1st, 1871. When you were in Calera we warned you to hold your tounge and not speak so much with your mouth or otherwise you will be taken on supprise and led out by the Klan and learnt to stretch hemp. Beware. Beware. Beware. Beware. (Signed) "PHILLIP ISENBAUM, *Grand Cyclops.* "JOHN BANKSTOWN. "ESAU DAVES. "MARCUS THOMAS. "You know who. And all others of the Klan." "BLOODY BONES.

Klan message to a U. S. postal official threatening his death if he carried out his proposed appointment of a black man as mail agent on a newly opened railroad (attached as an exhibit to the report of the Joint Congressional Committee investigating the Klan, 1872).

owned there in the world, and I have not had five cents from it. I hear very little, indeed, and it seems that I cannot hear from there.

"Where did your son go that night?"

"He went to a white gentleman's house he used to wait on. He went there and knocked on the door, and they took him into the house. I thought the Ku-Klux had killed him. I ran over there, and expected to find him dead; but only one shot had struck him, in the ear."

"Did you know any of the men that came to your house?"

"I could not say positively. I might have an idea, but that would not do. They had been seen frequently around there at night. When we came to church, there were men there with old black gowns on, and with old sunbonnets like women. One came into church and took a seat in the back part, but when one of us went close up to see who he was, he got up and went out."

"Had there been any persons molested or interfered with in the county before you left there?"

"Yes, sir; numbers of them. Just about that time you could go into the woods and find two or three dead there. I knew a family—they carried the son and father first, and then the wife went after them, and they killed them all."

"What were their names?"

"Matt Nichols, Maria Nichols, and young Matt Nichols. I suppose if I were to say fifty or a hundred were mistreated right at that time, I do not think I would say any too many at all."

"In what way mistreated?"

"By shooting at them and trying to cut their throats. In going to church at night they would stand behind a tree and shoot your brains out. They would go to a minister's house and make him come out and preach."

"What minister?"

"Caesar Ely was one; then another man named Reuben Wiggins. They went there, took all his family out, and ate everything and threw everything away. They took and led him about all night, and disturbed his family a great deal. Ah, gentlemen, it was as terrible a place at that time as ever there was in the world!"

"Has anybody been arrested and tried by the law for doing these acts of cruelty and violence?"

"O, no, sir! We never could get at them to do that in the world! They pretend that they never could find out anything about it. They appeared to be anxious to know, but it appeared to me that if they were very anxious the head men about that place could find out."

"Were these other people who were injured also Republicans?"

"O, yes, sir; they never bothered any other kind. Anyone on their side could stay there and do well."

"Were there white Republicans as well as colored in the county?"

"I suppose there were about twenty or thirty scattered about. But those who were there were almost afraid to own it, for fear they could not stay there. They were just merely on the balance. It got so there that they would not give a Republican any work, and if they went to sell a Republican anything they would charge him double price. When I left there the truth was that a true Republican could not stay in peace four and twenty hours."

"Was it ever ascertained by whom the Nichols you have named were killed?"

"Yes, sir. Their names were young Billy Coker and Peter Altman."

"How did they kill those people?"

"The woman's throat was cut from ear to ear, and her hair all torn up by the roots. The rest had their throats cut too."

"You have spoken of other persons——?"

"Oscar Nichols, a brother to that same Matt Nichols, was killed."

"Who killed him?"

"That same Peter Altman. He took Oscar out with him and appeared to be hunting, and when he came back his coat was spattered all over with brains, and I heard him say, 'Somebody has killed Oscar.'

"Then there was a colored sheriff that we had there, named Calvin Rogers—a good man and as true a man as ever there was in the world. They did not like him because he held office. They had him under bond—"

"Was that an act of oppression?"

"I suppose it was. They said they were going to put him in jail if he could not give bond for $1,500. I and some more men stood it. After a time this same young Coker and his father got after him to kill him, and he ran off. Since I left there I heard that they came up on him somewhere and killed him."

"Whom did you ever hear say that the leading Republicans should leave the country?"

"Jimmy Coker for one. He said that the Conservatives were going to carry the next election or kill the very last damned Republican in the place."

"I Expected My Days Were Few"

"My name is Emanuel Fortune. I am going on thirty-nine years old. I was born in Jackson County, Florida, and now live in Jacksonville. I am a common laborer—not much more."

"When did you leave Jackson County, and why?"

"In May, 1869. There got to be such a state of lawlessness and outrage that I expected that my life was in danger at all times, and I left on that account. In fact I got, indirectly, information very often that I would be missing some day and no one would know where I was, on account of my being a leading man in politics."

"Do you know anything about the Ku-Klux organization there?"

"I have never seen them, but I believe they are there as much as I believe anything. There is a man who saw two disguised men there about eight feet high, in the moonlight, sitting in a place where they finally killed a man."

"Who was it that they killed?"

"Calvin Rogers."

"Had there been any other men killed before you left?"

"Yes, sir. Dr. Finlayson was killed for one, and Major Furman was shot at the same time. Three men were called out of their doors and shot.

Some were shot through the cracks of their houses, and others as they were going into their houses. There were a great many cases of that kind. I was told by my friends that there were men staying around my place as though for no good purpose. I expected that my days were very few, and I thought I would leave for a while. I did not expect to move away for good when I left, but it kept getting worse. My parents wrote to me not to come back."

"Did you ever get any written notice to leave?"

"Yes, sir. It was addressed to 'Major Purman & Co.', and I considered myself included."

"Did you ever hold any official position?"

"In 1868 I was a member of the constitutional convention, and I was a member of the legislature."

"Who were your colleagues from Jackson County in the legislature?"

"Major Furman, Jesse Robinson, and Mr. McMillan."

"Were they colored people?"

"Robinson and myself were colored; the other two were white men."

"Where did Major Purman and Mr. McMillan come from?"

"McMillan is an old citizen of Jackson County; I think he was born in Alabama. Major Purman is from Pennsylvania; he came here since the war."

"Was Dr. Finlayson a man respected and esteemed?"

"Yes, sir. His relatives had been very highly thought of; he was from the first class of people. After he joined the Republican Party he was tried to be cried down and made small. They said he was a rogue, and all this, that, and the other, just as they do all the Republicans generally."

"You have said that Major Purman came here since the war—is that made any objection to him?"

"I suppose that was one objection. The great objection was that he was a prominent Republican and a leader of the people there. They said they 'never could do anything with the damned niggers as long as Purman was there.' It has been spoken of very often that 'we have plenty of men of our own to rule our government, without having men to come here to do it for us.' I have had a great many arguments on that. I said I thought that an American citizen was a resident wherever he stopped long enough to become a voter."

"Do they make a distinction between Northern men and Southern men?"

"They make no distinction about men who joined the Republican Party. A Northern man was a 'damned Yankee who came here to rule us;' and a Southern man who joined the Republican Party was a 'damned Scalawag, and there is no honesty about him—he was a traitor to his country and his race.' "

"Did you ever hear any threats from any quarter going to show that you or your race was in danger?"

"I have heard that 'those damned politicians should be got rid of.' It was a kind of indirect expression made by the crackers, etc."

"What language would they use?"

" 'The damned Republican Party has put niggers to rule us and we will not suffer it;' 'intelligence shall rule the country instead of the majority'; and all such as that. They always said that this was a 'white man's government,' and that 'the colored men had no rights that white men are bound to respect.' I heard it used privately, and I also heard the public speakers use it."

"Did they say colored men?"

"No, sir, they said 'niggers.' "

"What was the feeling in Jackson County in regard to your people being given their freedom?"

"At first there was a very strong feeling of opposition, but then that feeling seemed to have died out. The white planters adopted their bogus constitution, and had everything they wanted and became reconciled. But after the reorganization of the state under the Congressional Reconstruction Acts they became very much opposed to the rights of suffrage for colored people—giving us the vote seemed to make them very bitter."

"How do they regard your people getting land and owning it for themselves?"

"They will not sell us land. We have to purchase land from the Government, or from the state—otherwise we cannot get it. They will sell us a lot now and then in a town, but no farm land of any importance."

"Can you not buy all the good lands you want for ten or fifteen dollars an acre?"

"Very poor people cannot afford that."

"You can get it if you have the money?"

"They will not sell it to us in small quantities. I would have bought forty acres there if the man would have sold me less than a one hundred acre tract. They hold it in that way so that colored people cannot buy it."

"Have you heard people use any language to indicate an indisposition to sell land to colored people?"

"I do not know that I have ever heard anything *said* against selling us land, but it is my opinion that that is the general understanding among them."

"Is there not plenty of other land to buy?"

"Not that is worth anything. I do not know of any Government land that will raise cotton. The lands available for homesteading are of no account at all—very poor."

"Had you been a slave?"

"I was."

"How much education have you?"

"None, only what I have got by my own perseverance. I learned to read before the war; since the war I have learned to write."

"What is the feeling in regard to colored schools?"

"At the outset, after freedom, they disturbed our schools a great deal. They were mistreating our children, stoning them, and talked about mobbing the teachers, and all such as that. We complained to the United States Marshal several times, but he did not do anything. We had only such teachers as we could get."

"Of your own color, mostly?"

"No, sir, they were white. We had a man from New Orleans, but he did not stay long. After that several companies detailed soldiers to teach for us while they had nothing else to do in their quarters. We never had any public schools, only private schools such as we could get up for ourselves. The government has not done anything for us in the way of schools. I got after the state superintendent of schools to go into Jackson County, but he did not go. I suppose he was afraid. It was such a bad place that they naturally didn't want to go there."

"Have you ever known of anybody being punished for any of these crimes?"

"Not one."

"Why has it not been done?"

"The crimes were always a done in such a way that no one could state who did it. As a general thing if we suspicioned a man, the Ku-Klux would always arrange the testimony so as to prove that he was at such-and-such a place at the very time the thing was done. They are perfectly organized."

"What is the purpose of that organization which commits these killings, do you suppose?"

"Well, the object of it is to kill out the leading men of the Republican Party. Captain Dickinson said to me a year ago, 'Fortune, you could go back to Jackson County and live if you would—you would not be hurt.'

"I said, 'Could I go back there and be a free man, to use freedom of speech and act in politics as any man would want with his own people—could I do that?'

"He said, 'No, you could not—you would have to abandon all that if you went back.' "

"This Land Is Ours"

"My name is Samuel Tutson. As near as I can come at it, I am between fifty-three and fifty-four years old. I was born in Virginia, and I now live in Clay County in Florida."

"Are there any people in your county that they call Ku-Klux?"

"They called themselves Ku-Klux that whipped me that night."

"What night was that?"

"I do not know exactly what night it was; but they whipped me like the mischief. It was in May."

"Were they disguised?"

"They had blacked their hands and blacked their faces."

"Tell us what they did when they came, and all that was done."

"They came to my house, and my dog barked a time or two, and I went out but could see nobody. My wife went out and could see nobody at all. We had not more than got back into the house and got into bed, when they came.

"My wife said, "Who's that?'

"Five of them swung onto me, and four to my wife. They dragged my feet from under me and flung me down across a cellar door and near broke my back. They dragged me over the fence, and broke down five or six panels, and took me away down the hill on the side of a hammock, and tied me to a pine and whipped me."

"How many licks did they strike you?"

"I cannot tell you—they hit me a whole parcel of times. Dave Donley struck me over the eye before I got to the place where they tied me, and they stamped on me and kicked me. Cabell Winn struck me with a pistol and choked me, and run my head up against the tree, and told me that if it was not for sin, he would 'blow my God-damned brains out!'

"He said that I pulled down my fence and let other people's stock in my fields and then killed them.

"I said, 'You can't prove it.'

"He said, 'I can prove it on your God-damned back!'

"They stripped me just as naked as your hand. They took every rag off of me, and took my shirt and tore it up, and took a piece and blindfolded me, and then took another piece and twisted it up, and put it into my mouth, like a bridlebit, so that I could not holler. They made me hug a tree and then tied my hands together around it. They said they were going to whip us as long as they wanted to; and then they were going to tie us up by the thumbs and let us hang awhile; and then hang us by the neck until we were dead; and then fling us into Number Eleven Pond . . ."

"When they got through whipping you, what did they do?"

"They went and tore down my house. While they were tearing it down, my wife broke loose, and I got clear too."

"What did they whip you for?"

"Because I would not give my land to Mr. Winn. I bought a man's improvements, a man by the name of Free Thompson. After Thompson was gone with my money, Winn came there and said that it was his land. I asked him why he had not said nothing when I first came there, and he said he wanted me to do a heap of work there before he bothered me.

"I said, 'Are you going to give me anything at all for what I gave for the land?'

"He said, 'No.'

"I said, 'Are you going to give me anything for the crop in the ground?'

"He said, 'No.'

"I said, 'Are you going to give me anything at all for the improvements I have put on?'

"He said, 'No.'

"Then I said, 'Is there any law here for kinky-heads?'

"He said, 'Yes, there is.'

"I said, 'No, there isn't.'

"He said, 'Yes, there is as much law for you as for me.'

"I said, 'Then, if there is any law for kinky-heads, I will find it, if I have to go all the way to Tallahassee . . .' "

"My name is Hannah Tutson."

"Are you the wife of Samuel Tutson, the previous witness?"

"Yes, sir."

"Were you at home when he was whipped last Spring?"

"Yes, sir, I was at home."

"Tell us what took place—what was done, and how it was done."

"When they came to our house that night the dog barked twice, and the old man got up and went out of doors and then came back and lay down. She flew out again, and I got up and went out of doors. I knew the slut barked more than usual, but I could see nothing. I went back into the house, and just as I got into bed five men bulged right against the door, and it fell right in the middle of the floor, and they fell down.

"George McCrea was the first who got up. He went where I had left all the children—went circling around toward the children's bed. As I saw him coming, I took up the baby and held him.

"George McCrea said, 'Come in, True-Klux!'

"I started to scream, and he catched me right by the throat and choked me. I worried around and around, and he catched the little child by the foot and slinged it out of my arms. I screamed again, and he gathered me again. Then there were so many hold of me that they got me out of doors. I looked up and saw Jim Phillips, George McCrea, and Henry Baxter. I looked ahead of me and they had the old man, and they tore down the fence the same as if you saw people dragging hogs from the butcher-pen. And they went to another corner of the fence and jerked me over, just as if you were jerking a dumb beast.

"I said, 'Sam, give up! It is not worth while to do anything! They will try to kill us here!'

"They said, 'O, God damn you, we will kill you!'

"I said, 'I will go with you.'

"George McCrea said, 'Come right along!'

"I said, 'Yes, I am coming; I will come right along . . .'

"They took me down to the lower end of a field, and when they got there he said, 'Now, old lady, you pretend to be a good Christian; you had better pray right off!'

"I cast my eyes up to the elements and begged God to help me.

"George McCrea struck me over the head with a pistol, and said, 'God damn you, what are you making so much fuss for?'

"He said, 'Where is the ropes?' They said they had lost the ropes. They went off next to my field and came back with a handful of saddle-girths, with the buckles on them. They took and carried me to a pine, just as large as I could get my arms around, and tied my hands around it. They pulled off all my linen, tore it up so that I did not have a piece of rag on me as big as my hand.

"I said, 'Men, what are you going to do with me?'

"They said, 'God damn you, we will show you! You are living on another man's premises!'

"I said, 'No, I am living on my own premises. I gave $150 for it, and Captain Buddington and Mr. Mundy told me to stay here.'

"He said, 'God damn you, we will give them the same we are going to give you!'

"I quit talking to them then, only as they asked me anything. They whipped me for awhile, and then went off to where the saddles were, and came back and whipped me some more.

"Every time they would go off, George McCrea would stay behind, and act scandalously and ridiculously toward me, and treat me shamefully.

"He would make me squat down and say, 'What are you trembling for?'

"I would say that I was cold, and was afraid that I would freeze.

"He would get his knees between my legs and say, 'God damn you, open your legs!'

"I tell you men, that he did act ridiculously and shamefully, that same George McCrea.

"He sat down there and said, 'Old lady, if you don't let me have to do with you, I will kill you!'

"I said, 'No—do just what you are going to do.'

"He said, 'God damn you, I am going to kill you!' But then he saw the other men coming up again, and made me get up. They whipped me, and he asked me where was my ox. It was in the field, but I would not tell him; I said that my son-in-law had got my cart. They would go and hunt, and he would make me sit down while they were gone. Understand me, men, while they were gone to hunt for that ox, George McCrea would make me sit down there, and try to have me do with him right there. They came back and whipped me.

"I said, 'Yes, men, if you will stop whipping me, I will give way to you.' There were four men whipping me at once. That is the way they did me, and I had been working and washing for them very nearly three years.

"George McCrea said, 'We came to dispossess you once before, and you said you did not care if we did whip you.'

"I said, 'Stop, men, and let me see.'

"One of them said, 'Stop and let her get her breath.'

"Mr. Winn had always talked all kinds of nasty talk to me. I got so I did not count him any more than he counted me. I had told him just exactly three weeks before they whipped me that I did not care what they did to me, just so I saved my land.

"Said I, 'In the red times of slavery, how many times have they took me and turned my clothes over my head and whipped me? I do not care what they do to me—not if I can only save my land.'

"He asked me again if I had said that, and after a minute I said, 'Yes, I did say so.'

"He says, 'Yes, you damned bitch, you did say so!' "

"How many lashes did they give you in all?"

"I cannot tell you, for they whipped me from the crown of my head to the soles of my feet. I was just raw. The blood oozed out through my frock all around my waist, clean through, by the time I broke away from them, and went to Captain Buddington's. But first I ran to my house. My house was torn down. I went in and felt where my bed was. It had been dragged out in the middle of the floor. I went to the other corner of the house and felt for my little children. I could not see one, and their bed was standing on end in one corner and is hitched there now. I could not feel my little children and I could not see them.

"I said, 'Lord, my little children are dead!'

"I went to the box where I kept my things, and I picked up a dress I had there, but I went five miles before I put it on my back. I cannot read, and I have got no clock, but as near as I can get to it, I got away from there an hour to day, and I went twelve miles by sunrise. I could not bear my clothes fastened on me. I went through to Mr. Montgomery's house, and hollered 'Murder!' and he heard me.

"I said, 'Give me a light. I expect my husband is dead, and I want to go back and look for my children.'

"I went back, but I could hear nothing. I went to Mr. Ashley's, and went in there. I turned up my clothes, and let Mr. Ashley see how I was whipped. I had on nothing but a frock, and I could not fasten it.

"He said, 'Woman, go back home and hunt for your husband and children. If he is dead, don't stand to bury him, but go right on to Whitesville!'

"It was 12 o'clock when I finally found them. My husband had laid out in the field, and my children too. They said that when they got away they went out into the field, and my little daughter said that as the baby cried she would reach out and pick some gooseberries and put them in its little mouth. When she could hear none of them any more she went up to a log-heap and stayed there the rest of the night and morning with her brother and the baby."

"Did the baby get hurt?"

"Yes, sir, in one of its hips. Every time you would stand it up it would scream. But I rubbed it and rubbed it, and it looks like it is outgrowing it now."

"Who was it who came there to try to dispossess you before?"

"George McCrea, and old Mr. Sullivan, and Dave Donley, and Mr. Hagan, and Jake Winn. Mr. Hagan came back and wanted to give me some advice. He told me it was from Judge Buddington and Barney Crocker. I said I did not believe it, because they had told me that this was my land.

"I said, 'I am going to die on this land!'

"Hagan said, 'You'd better give it up!'

"Mrs. Lane sent for me to come and wash for her one day in a week, but they made me mad Saturday about driving me from my place, so I did not go to her house the first day of the week. I had to go through Jake Winn's yard to go to her house. My son was working there, and I went in and saw Mrs. Winn and told her good morning.

"She says, 'Hannah, I thought you were gone.'

"I said, 'Gone where?'

"She said, 'Off the place.'

"I said, 'No, I am not going off the place. No law is going to move me from here except Tallahassee law.' Then I said, 'What are they going to do to me, Mrs. Winn?'

"She said, 'They are going to whip you.'

"I said, 'I wish they would whip me,' and I went off.

"I told Mrs. Lane about it, and she said, 'I have nothing to do with it. It is your land; you ought to have your land.'

"Then on Friday while I was eating my breakfast, with nobody there but me and my little children, old man Byrd Sullivan came up to the house and said, 'Aunty, these people are devilish people; they are determined to put you off this land. Now, pay good attention to what I say. When you get your hand into a lion's mouth you pull it out just as easy as you can. You can tell your old man to give it up, or in a month's time—or such a matter—they will come here, and the lot will push him out of doors and let you eat this green grass!'

"I began to cry, and finally he said, 'You will stop this grieving and crying. Tell your old man to keep on writing to Tallahassee, and when he gets the papers for his land tell him to come to me and he will have his land back.' "

"You spoke of one of these men 'wanting to do with you,' as you expressed it. Did you give way to him?"

"No, sir. But he was so bad, and I was stark naked. I tell you, men, he pulled my womb down so that sometimes now I can hardly walk."

"What does McCrea follow for a living?"

"He was a deputy sheriff when he came and whipped me."

"Did you go with your husband when he made the complaint before the United States lawyer?"

"Yes, sir."

"To whom did you tell it?"

"I cannot tell you; there are so many people here that I cannot tell who it was."

"Was there any suit by this man who claimed your land? Did he ever go into court there against you?"

"No, sir."

"You do not know enough about courts to know what was done?"

"Sir, it never has been in court."

"Did they get out a writ for this man McCrea?"

"They got out a writ, and they served it; but it did not read like I had said—there was a difference. They put me in jail and said that I swore false."

"What did they do with your old man?"

"They put him in, too."

"Who got you out?"

"Mr. Bennett paid me out, and he has my ox and cart now; I had to put it in pawn."

"You have told us all you know about it?"

"Yes, sir, and just as straight as I could tell it. I have told it straighter today than I did before, because when we had a trial here the other week they stopped me almost every word, and I missed some I told here to-day."

"They Wanted to Skin Me"

"My name is Robert Fullerlove, and I live in Choctaw County, Alabama. I have been principally raised there."

"When did you leave there to come to Livingston to testify before us?"

"I left there Monday about 10 o'clock."

"Had you any subpoena with you to testify before this Committee?"

"I had, but a young gentleman took it away from me."

"Who took it away from you?"

"The men who arrested me—at four o'clock this morning, before day."

"Who arrested you?"

"A gentleman named Charlie Brand and a gentleman by the name of Morris Dunn."

"What did they say they arrested you for?"

"They asked me where I was going, and I said to York Station.

"They said, 'What for?'

"I said, 'To carry a letter, but who to I don't know.'

"They said, 'Who did you get it from?'

"I told them a colored man gave it to me.

"He says, 'Let me see it!' I handed it to him and he took it and read it."

"Who was the letter from?"

"It was from here."

"Was it a paper calling for witnesses to come here and testify before this Committee?"

"Yes, sir."

"What did he do with it?"

"Put it in his pocket. They handed the envelope back to me. They punished me a great deal, but I begged them off from killing me. They knocked me down with a gun and took my stirrup-leather which had a buckle on the end, and whipped me with it."

"What did they say they were whipping you for?"

"They said I was a Radical."

"How did these young men know you had this paper?"

"Well, sir, it happened like this. I came to the house at Black's Bluff. I had got lost. I was in a strange land. I found four or five strange gentlemen there, white people. I didn't know them.

"I said, 'Can you tell me the road from here to York Station?'

"One gentleman, I knew his voice when he spoke, was in the house. 'Who is that?' he called out.

"The gentleman I was enquiring of says, 'I don't know.'

"Then this gentleman inside says, 'Is that Bob Fullerlove?'

"I says, 'Yes.'

" 'What are you going to York Station for?'

"I says, 'To carry a letter.' Then I said to them, 'I'll go on . . .'

"But I had no more than got started good on my mule when they overtook me. They rode up, and before I thought a thing about it, one on each side, they grabbed me, and both put guns in my ribs, and one says, 'Who's this?'

"I said, 'It's Bob.'

" 'Weren't you at Black's Bluff tonight?'

"I says, 'I don't know. I was at a house.' He hauled away, then, with his gun and knocked me off my mule.

"And he says, 'You are the very scoundrel who was at Black's Bluff! I would kill you, if you were the last nigger in God Almighty's world! Run down that hill!'

"Says I, 'Gentlemen, I will not run to be killed. If you want to kill me, kill me. I will stand and receive it like a man. I will not run.'

"Then one of them drawed back his gun and hit me, and I fended it off with that hand; and the other cocked his gun and said, 'Did you fend that lick?'

"I said, 'Yes, of course.'

"He said, 'You don't fend another!'

"He run his gun in my side, and pushed me down; and the other cotched my pantaloons and jerked them off, and got on me; and the other got the stirrup, and they beat me scandalous with it."

"Did they inflict those blows on your naked flesh?"

"Yes, sir. They whipped me until they broke off a piece of the stirrup-leather about a foot long. They took a pair of new kidskin gloves from me too."

"Did they tell you not to come to Livingston?"

"No, sir; they didn't know I was coming here. They couldn't make out the subpoena where I was coming to."

"Were they not able to read?"

"No, sir, they could not."

"Where did they think you were going?"

"I had told them the letter was for Mr. Gilmore, at York Station."

"Is he a Radical?"

"Yes, sir."

"A known Radical?"

"Yes, sir."

"Are there many white Radicals living in Choctaw County?"

"You can't find them. If *you* were there, they might tell you, privately; but they won't tell anybody else."

"You may state to this Committee, now, whether you have ever been interfered with before by bands of men in disguise."

"I have been interfered with twice. It was the same class of men, I reckon, who came to my gate and fired into my house with a double-barreled shotgun."

"You do not know what they came and fired for?"

"No, sir. And the second time they came and shot fifteen balls into my house, and set it afire. They shot twice at my wife, and she hollered for life and mercy, and made all the alarm she could. They had the house surrounded, and the house was in a blaze nearly to the roof. A large place is there now to show to anybody upstairs, and every ball is there to show, sticking in the wall. They shot at my son in the room where he was staying, and the ball cut his pantaloons in two right across the top part of his thigh."

"How did you put the fire out?"

"My wife came out and put it out. They were there, all around the house, and she begged them and made all the apologies she could in the world not to burn her and her children in the house alive. They cursed her and rebuked her. She hollered and cried when she saw the house burning up, and she said, 'If you want to kill me, kill me!' And she took a bucket of water and began to put out the fire. They aimed two balls at me, and one stuck in the window sill and another in the wall. By that time somebody else hollered, and they run off, and my wife got the house and saved it, and our two children also.' "

"What has ever been done with them for these attacks?"

"Nothing at all."

"Did you make complaint to anybody of your bad usage?"

"I never made any complaint at all, for I knew it would be of no use."

"Why? Did you think you would not obtain any redress?"

"Well, they would have brought it before a grand jury, but the grand jury would never indict anybody."

"Have you been molested since?"

"Not until last night. They have made several threats . . ."

"What kind of threats?"

"They said they were going to kill me and skin me."

"Who told you that?"

"White men told me that, and told me to leave there. They pretended to be my friends. I told them I wouldn't leave; I wasn't guilty of any bad acts; I was at home and would stay there, and if they wanted to kill me they could."

"On whose plantation was this?"

"It was my own land."

"How much land do you own there?"

"Four hundred acres; but now I never expect to set my foot on it no more . . ."

"Why not?"

"Well, I can't. I have been there, and I have been imposed on. I have been pestered, and sleeping out-of-doors instead of sleeping in the house. I have a good house, but is it of any use for me to go in it, but not go to bed?"

"How long have you lived out-of-doors?"

"Ever since April, when they almost burned me out."

"Where did you go at night?"

"Under the house, and down by the garden palings, and around the cribs, and in the corner of the fences; me in one place, and my wife and children in another. What is the use of a man trying to live in this world in that condition?"

"What do you suppose is the cause of this conduct of those white men toward you?"

"I can't tell—really, I can't tell. They told me after my house was attacked the last time, if I would come over to the Democratic side they would stop this and protect me in every way; and if I didn't do it, I would be a dead man."

"Do you know of any other colored people that have been shot or their homes fired into?"

"I know of as many as four that has been killed."

"Do you know of any Negro schools being broken up?"

"I can't really say, sir; we don't have any."

"What other property have you?"

"Besides the land, I have about twenty head of cattle. I have an ox-team. I have corn, and fodder, and hogs. I had a very fine crop of cotton planted, when this last raid came, and I lost my crop. It isn't worth-while, gentlemen, for me to stay. I am a hard-working man, and I love what I have worked and earned, but I declare I can't stay with no satisfaction."

"Do the other colored people down there feel as you do?"

"I believe all the people in the neighborhood are fixing to go."

"Are they afraid to stay there?"

"Yes, sir. There is no peace in the neighborhood—no, not a bit. They can't stay in peace."

"You are afraid now, having testified, to go back, after having stated what you have stated here?"

"If I go home tonight or tomorrow, or next day, when they hear I am at home some of the men will be shooting at me, killing me for what— for my rights."

"Are these disguised men out every night?"

"No, sir, the Ku-Klux are not out every night, but the colored people lie out all the time, for we never know when they will come."

"You are out on the watch?"

"Yes, sir; out on the watch, and we have done got tired of it. It's coming cold weather now, and I tell you we just can't stand it another Winter. I am going to leave. If I can't live honest and just and right here, I am going where I can, if I go naked in the world."

"I Chose Castration"

"My name is Henry Lowther, and I will be forty-one years on the 4th day of next February. I was born in Newton County, Georgia, but live in Wilkinson County when I am at home."

"Have you been in jail recently?"

"Well, yes, I was in jail in Wilkinson County. The charge was that I had a company of men to take a colored man out and try to kill him."

"Go on now, and state everything that happened to you after you were put in jail."

"I was put in jail Saturday evening, the 2nd day of September last. I asked Captain Thomas to turn me out, for I was in there for nothing. He said I could not get out without a trial.

"I said, 'Captain, I want a trial.'

"He said, 'If you want one, you must have it; but today is Sunday, and if you will take my advice you will put it off until tomorrow. Monday morning I will take you out early and give you a fair trial.'

"Monday morning came. They went around and arrested about sixteen persons. They carried them to the courthouse and examined about half of them. They did not take me out of jail at all. They dealt with them all, either by making them pay $2.70 costs, or giving bonds for appearance in court. Of course they gave the $2.70.

"My son came to me in jail and said, 'Father, Rack Bell says he is satisfied you did not have this company of men to take him out and try to kill him. They say it is left with him whether you get out of jail or not.'

"I said, 'You go tell Rack Bell to come here to the jail.'

"He came, and I said to him, 'What does this mean? We have ate together, and we have helped each other.'

"He said, 'Captain Eli Cummins and Lewis Peacock say you cannot get out of jail.'

"I said, 'Tell Captain Cummins to come here.'

"Captain Cummins came and sat down and talked with me about an hour, but there was nothing he said that I thought had any substance in it, only when he went to leave he said, 'Harry, are you willing to give up your stones to save your life?'

"I sat there for a moment, and then I told him, 'Yes.'

"Said he, 'If they come for you will you make fight?'

"I said, 'No.'

"That was about an hour by sun. I lay right down then and went to sleep, and did not wake up until 2 o'clock in the morning. Then I saw one Ku-Klux in jail with a light. I raised up, and he caught my arm and told me to come out. I came out and looked around, and the whole town was covered with them. They tied me up and carried me off into a swamp about two miles. They went for a rope, and I was satisfied they were going to hang me. I begged for my life.

"After some conversation, every man cocked his gun and pointed it right at me. I thought they were going to shoot me, and leave me right there. They asked me whether I preferred to be altered or killed. I said I preferred to be altered . . .

"After laying me down and getting through they said, 'Now, as soon as you are able to leave do it, or we will kill you next time!'

"I asked how long it would take me to get well, and they said five or six weeks. I was naked and bleeding very much. It was two miles and a quarter to a doctor's. The first man's house I got to was the jailer's. I called him and asked him to go to the jail-house and get my clothes. He said he could not go. I said, 'You must! I am naked and nearly froze to death!'

"That was about 3 o'clock in the night. He had a light in the house, and there was a party of men standing in the door. I said I wanted him to come out and give me some attention. He said he could not come. I could hardly walk then.

"I went right on and got up to a store. There were a great many men sitting along on the store piazza. I knew some of them, but I did not look at them much. They asked me what I wanted; I said I wanted a doctor. They told me to go on home and lie down. I had then to stop and hold on to the side of the house to keep from falling. I stayed there a few minutes, and then went on to a doctor's house, about a quarter of a mile, and called him aloud twice. He did not answer me.

"The next thing I knew I was lying on the sidewalk in the street— seemed to have just waked up out of a sleep. I wanted some water. I had to go about a quarter of a mile to get some water. I was getting short of breath, but the water helped me considerably.

"I went to a house about fifty yards further. I called to a colored woman to wake my wife up, but she had already gone into town. I found my son, and he went back for the doctor. When he got there the doctor answered the first time he called. The reason he had not answered me was that he was off on this raid. I asked the doctor where he was when I was at his house, and he said he was asleep.

"After that, men kept coming to see me and saying that I did not get to the doctor's house, but I said that I did. After two or three times I took the hint, and said nothing more about that. But I told my son the next morning to go there and see if there was not a large puddle of blood at the doctor's gate. They would not let him go. But some colored women came to see me and told me that the blood was all over town—at the doctor's gate and everywhere else. It was running a stream all the time I was trying to find the doctor, and I thought I would bleed to death. My son tended me until I got so I could travel.

"Doctor Cummins came there to my house on Tuesday evening, between sunset and dark, and said, 'I am told you say the reason I did not come to you was that I was out on the raid with the Ku-Klux.'

"I said, 'I did not say so.'

"He said, 'That is what I heard,' and he seemed to be mad about it. He said, 'I am a practicing physician, and am liable to be called at night, and must go. I was in my horse-lot then.'

"He talked a long while, and then he said he was in his stable. He kept talking, and after awhile he said he was in his drug-store. So I never knew where he was.

"In a day or two he came to my house again and said, 'The white people have got up a story here, and say I am the man who castrated you. Now, this talk must stop!'

"I said, 'Doctor, I can't help it. I don't know who did it. I didn't start the story.'

"In a few days his brother, Captain Cummins—the man who first came to me in jail and asked if I would give up my stones—came in and said, 'Harry, I am told you make a threat of what you are going to do when you get well.'

"I said, 'What can I do?'

"He shook his head.

"I then said, 'Do you think the Ku-Klux will bother me any more?'

"He said, 'If this talk dies out, I do not think they will pester you any more.'

"I was not able to walk, but I was uneasy, and after I lay there about twenty-one days, I left."

"What reason did the Ku-Klux give for wanting to get hold of you?"

"They said that no such man as me should live there, white or black. They said they were going to kill out all the leading Republican men, both white and black. I worked for my money and carried on a shop. When some of these white men did not pay me after I gave them credit, I sued them."

"Who were the men who castrated you?"

"I knew the two who had me by the arms, and one who was walking in front of me with his gun. There were three I would swear to. One of them I would as lief swear against my brother at him. He was a man I thought a heap of. I did not think he would be in such a place. One was Bob Hyman, another Henry Hyman, and the other Andrew Porter."

"Who is the sheriff of Wilkinson County?"

"They do not have any sheriff—he was killed about three days before they came on me. His name was Mr. Mat Deason. He was a white man, and had been living with a colored woman a long time—since before the war. He had five children by her. He had a white woman for a wife, but she was deranged and in the asylum. They killed him and the colored woman at the same time. There were five bullet holes in his head, and the back of his head was mashed in with a club. After they killed them they tied a heavy bar of iron to each one and threw them both into the same hole of water."

"Were they in bed together at the time?"

"No, sir—they were just fixing to go to bed."

"Do you know of any other persons in your neighborhood who have been injured in any way by the Ku-Klux?"

"Yes, sir. On the first day of September a colored man named George Meadows was killed, and Joel Bease, a white man, was shot three weeks ago last Saturday. Boston Fulward, a colored man, was shot two months ago; and they whipped a great many around there."

"How many have they whipped?"

"They whipped John Lavender, Fred Dease, Henry Winn, and John Winn, and Lije Dease, and they also broke his jawbone with a stick. And they whipped his mother, a very old lady I did not know her name. They whipped Bill Brigan. The way they did him was, they tied him down on a log and took a buggy-trace to him, and whipped one of his seeds entirely out and the other very nearly out. Before I came away Doctor Smith said he thought he could save one of them."

"Was anything of the sort done before that time?"

"Last Fall a year ago a couple of young men were hung by the Ku-Klux; and a white man was castrated in an adjoining county—his name was Register."

"Who is in charge of the jailhouse?"

"Mr. Lewis Peacock was bailiff; he had charge of it."

"Was he there when these people took you away that night?"

"I do not think so. I looked around when they led me out of the jail-house to see if I could see him or Captain Cummins there, but I could not see either one of them, though he must have given them the keys. After they took me out and locked the doors they put the keys in the post office."

"Has your case been brought before the United States court?"

"No, sir."

"It is not before the grand jury here in Atlanta?"

"No, sir."

"Where have you lodged complaint?"

"In Macon, before Mr. Fitzpatrick, a magistrate. I went there and stayed ten days. I wrote a letter back to my wife, and the Ku-Klux got hold of the letter and read it and found out where I was. Five of them came to Macon and stayed a week, hunting for me; and I left there."

"Do you know whether Mr. Fitzpatrick has jurisdiction to have these people arrested?"

"I think not, for this reason: Captain Cummins came to Macon and wanted to know who I had accused, as he had heard that his name was among them. Mr. Fitzpatrick said it was. Captain Cummins said, 'When are you going to arrest me?'

"Mr. Fitzpatrick said, 'That is not my business; I cannot tell when you will be arrested.'

"Have you made any complaint to anybody here in Atlanta of this great wrong upon you?"

"I sat down and talked a little with Judge Pope. He told me to stay until this Committee came here."

"He is District Attorney here for the United States?"

"Yes, sir."

"Had there been any complaint against you for anything wrong before this thing happened? I mean any offense against the law, any breach of the peace, any insult to any white woman, or anything of that kind?"

"No, sir, I never insulted any white woman."

"I asked you if there had been any charge against you?"

"They did not make any particular charge against me, only they said that no such man as me should live there, white or black."

"I Chose Africa"

"My name is Elias Hill, and I live in Clay Hill precinct in York County, South Carolina. I was born belonging to the Hills, and I am now about fifty years old."

"How long have you been in your present crippled condition?"

"I was afflicted and became disabled from walking when I was seven years of age. I continued to get gradually worse from that time until the present. The doctor said it was rheumatism."

"How were you maintained?"

"My father bought himself some thirty-odd years ago, by paying $150 to the estate of the Hills, and that made him free. When my people were sold, he bought my mother, and as I was a cripple, they compelled him in the contract to take me."

"Can you read and write?"

"Yes, sir, I learned that gradually, between the years 1830 and 1845, from the white school children, and catching it up as I could. Between those years I became so much of a scholar as I am. I am a teacher and a preacher. I have to be carried, but I can sit comfortably for three or four hours teaching or preaching."

"State whether at any time men in disguise have come to the place where you live, and, if so, what they did and said."

"On the night of the 5th of last May, after I heard a great deal of what they had done in that neighborhood, they came. It was between 12 and 1 o'clock at night, when I was awakened and heard the dogs barking, and something walking, very much like horses. As I had often laid awake listening for such persons, for they had been all through the neighborhood, and disturbed all men and many women, I supposed that it was the Ku-Klux.

"At last they came to my brother's house, which is in the same yard, and broke open the door and attacked his wife, and I heard her screaming and moaning. I could not understand what they said, for they talked in an outlandish and unnatural tone, which I had heard they generally used at a Negro's house. At last I heard them have her in the yard. She was crying, and the Ku-Klux were whipping her to make her tell where I lived. I heard her say, 'Yon is his house!'

"Someone then hit my door. It flew open. One ran in the house, and said, 'Who's here?'

"Then I knew they would take me, and I answered, 'I am here.'

"He shouted for joy, as it seemed, 'Here he is! Here he is! We have found him!' He threw the bedclothes off of me and caught me by one arm, while another man took me by the other and they carried me into the yard and put me on the ground.

"The first thing they asked me was, didn't I tell the black men to ravish all the white women. No, I answered them.

"They struck me again with their fists on my breast, and then they went on, 'When did you hold a night-meeting of the Union League, and who was the president?' I told them I had been the president, but that there had been no Union League meeting held at that place since away in the Fall. They hit me again.

"Said one, 'Didn't you preach against the Ku-Klux?' and 'Wasn't that what Mr. A. S. Wallace, in Congress, was writing to you about?'

" 'Not at all,' I said.

" 'Let me see the letter,' said he. 'What was it about?'

"I told them if they would take me back into the house, and lay me in the bed, which was close adjoining my books and papers, I would try and get it.

"They said I would never go back to that bed, for they were going to kill me—'Never expect to go back; tell us where the letters are!'

"I told them they were on the shelf somewhere—and I hoped they would not kill me. Two of them went into the house. My sister says that as quick as they went into the house they struck the clock at the foot of the bed. I heard it shatter.

"One of the four around me called out, 'Don't break any private property, gentlemen, if you please. We have got him we came for, and that's all we want.'

"They caught my leg—you see what it is—and pulled me over the yard and then left me there, knowing I could not walk nor crawl, and all six went in the house. I was chilled with the cold lying in the yard at that time of night.

"After they had stayed in the house for a considerable while, they came back to where I lay and asked if I wasn't afraid at all. They pointed pistols at me all around my head, telling me they were going to kill me, wasn't I ready to die; and willing to die? I told them that I was not exactly ready; that I would rather live; that I hoped they would not kill me that time. They said they would—I had better prepare. One caught me by the leg and hurt me, for my leg for forty years had been drawn each year, more and more year by year, and I made moan when it hurt so.

"One said, 'Goddamn it, hush!'

"He had a horsewhip, and he told me to pull up my shirt and he hit me. I made moan every time he cut me with the horsewhip. I reckon he struck me eight cuts right on the hip bone. It was almost the only place he could hit my body, my legs are so short—all my limbs drawn up and withered away with pain. I saw one of them standing over me motion to him to quit.

"One of them then took a strap and buckled it around my neck and said, 'Let's take him to the river and drown him!' After pulling the strap tight around my neck, he took it off and gave me a lick with it.

"One of them said, 'We've burned up that damned letter of Wallace's and all.' Then he brought out a little book and says, 'What's this for?'

"I told him to let me see with a light and I could read it. They brought me a lamp and I read it. It was a book in which I kept an account of the school. He asked if I had been paid for the scholars. I said no. He said I would now have to die. I was somewhat afraid, but one said not to kill me.

"They said, 'Look here! Will you put a card in the paper next week like June Moore and Sol Hill?' They had been prevailed on to put a card in the paper to renounce all Republicanism and never vote.

"I said, 'If I had the money to pay the expense, I could.' They said I could borrow, and gave me another lick.

"They asked me, 'Will you quit preaching? I told them I did not know. I said that to save my life.

"They said I must stop that Republican newspaper that was coming to me every week from Charleston. They said I must stop it, quit preaching, and put a card in the newspaper renouncing Republicanism, and they would not kill me; but if I did not they would come back the next week and kill me . . .

"With that one of them went into the house where my brother and sister-in-law lived, and brought her to pick me up. As she stooped down to pick me up one of them struck her, and as she was carrying me into the house another struck her with a strap. She carried me into the house and laid me on the bed. Then they gathered around and told me to pray for them. I tried to pray.

"They said, 'Don't you pray against Ku-Klux, but pray that God may forgive Ku-Klux. Pray that God may bless and save us.' I was so chilled with cold from lying out of doors so long and in such pain I could not speak to pray, but I tried to, and they said that would do very well, and all went out of the house."

"Who else was visited in your neighborhood by the Ku-Klux?"

"On the same night they were at June Moore's and Sol Hill's. I heard them. And at Jesse McGill's too, on widow Mary Watson's plantation; then down by Ross Watson's they came. He heard them coming and ran off. They threw his bed in the fire. Then they came on to me."

"State how many have been whipped, according to information which you believe to be true."

"They went on and whipped J. P. Hill's wife the same night they were at my house. And Julia, Miles Baron's wife—rumor says they committed a rape on her. Samuel Simrell's house was burned down that night."

"Do you know of anybody being whipped at any other time?"

"Yes, sir. Sam Simrell and Addison Woods, who live not far from me, and Jack Garrison, who is out here now, waiting to testify."

"What effect did this have on the colored people up there—were they alarmed?"

"Yes, sir—so alarmed that they did not sleep in their houses at night. During last Winter and Spring all slept out in the woods from the effect of this excitement and fear. Some women would sleep out with their husbands. The women would be so excited when their husbands left that they would go too, with the children, and one stayed in the rain-storm while her husband was fleeing for his life. There is June Moore—his wife went out with her little babe in the rain every night until late in the Spring, and many, many of them did the same."

"I see the following article in the *Yorkville Inquirer* of July 20, 1871," said the Chairman: " 'GOING TO LIBERIA—We learn that a large number of Negroes—comprising sixty or eighty families—in the vicinity of Clay Hill, have determined to emigrate to Liberia, and are now making their arrangements to embark in the vessel of the Colonization Society which will sail from Charleston or Baltimore early in November next. Rev. Elias Hill and June Moore (two colored men of this county) are at the head of the movement, and it is the intention of the emigrants to locate in that part of Liberia known as the North Carolina Colony.' "

"That did come out in last week's paper," said the witness. "It was because of the outrages of the Ku-Klux that I took the resolution and am making preparations, and others are doing the like. We all ascribe the same cause for this movement: We do not believe it possible, from the past history and present aspect of affairs, for our people to live in this country peaceably, and educate and elevate our children to that degree which we desire. I think so from reading history and from the present state of things around us."

"What is the feeling out there now among the colored people?"

"Those who are not arranging to go to Liberia have some hope that the operation of this Congressional Investigating Committee will pacify the whites, who will cast off the Ku-Klux. We hope for much through the operation of this Committee, and through the punishment of the Ku-Klux, so that the time will eventually come that those who want to go away now may stay, finding that they can live in peace."

"What is the temper of the white people—do they rejoice over these outrages?"

"They did, judging from what they said."

"What is their temper now?"

"I will tell you my impression: They are so afraid just now that, with the exception of one in a hundred, they cannot bear to see a Federal soldier coming out there; it frightens them. Not one in fifty of them now but is uneasy and trembling at the sight of an officer or a blue-coat, and staying out in the woods by day, and some by night, like we used to. Now the white men, the young men and boys, from fifteen to the gray-headed, are out, some by night and hunting by day, so that if a summons should come for them they would be absent. Some in my neighborhood have fled the state, and others are ready to go."

"What in your judgment, would be the condition of affairs if the United States troops were not here?"

"I would not then have come up here to report for anything in the world, for I would have expected to have been killed tonight if I had."

"Could you not emigrate to some state out West, instead of going to Liberia?"

"I have learned from papers and from pamphlets and speeches and from letters Mr. Wallace has sent me, that in some of the Western states these outrages are as bad as they are here. I saw that those Western states toward which I had looked are worse plagued than we are, if it is possible, and I did not know where to flee. I wrote to the Colonization Society at Washington, and they have been sending me papers and pamphlets for some time. In them I found that in Liberia there is greater encouragement and hope of finding peaceful living and free schools and rich land than in any place in the United States that I have read of. These things encourage us a great deal in our intention to move away to Africa. That is where my father came from."

"Do you think Africa is your only refuge now?"

"In a general way I do—that is, for general peace, abiding peace and prosperity for me and my race, and for the elevation of our people."

"You do not feel very kindly toward the white race?"

"I am afraid of them now. I have good-will, love, and affection toward them, but I fear them. I know it is my duty as a human being to respect all the human race, and also the grace of God teaches me to say so."

"When you get to preaching, do you not show up the wrongs and oppressions suffered from these white people?"

"Yes, sir."

"Is that what you generally preach about?"

"Yes, sir—love universal."

"You have the idea that these white people are determined to put you black people down?"

"Yes, sir, I have that idea very strongly. They are determined to keep us from using any influence for republican government, which we believe is God's will. I do believe that republican government comes nearer to God's will and universal love and friendship in this world than any other."

Scalawags: "They Gave Me 37 Hours"

"My name is Robert Forson. If I live to see the 27th day of next August I will be twenty-four years old. I live in Columbia County, Florida, where I am a farmer."

"Have you any people there they call Ku-Klux?"

"We have some there that call themselves Ku-Klux."

"State what you know about them."

"I know that they came to my father's house where I was living, and took me out in the yard."

"How many of them were there?"

"I cannot tell you precisely how many there were—I think there were about thirty."

"Had they any disguises on?"

"No, sir."

"Did you know any of them? If so, give the names."

"William Niblack, William Somers, Larkin Somers, Mr. Pregit, George Hancock, John William Niblack, James Taylor, Frederick Geer, James Cobb, John Kune, John Gumillion, Andrew Larkin, Joseph Talbot, Luther Snellgrove, Burt Sheely, Levi Haltermonger, Elhore Haltermonger, David Haltermonger, Ed Collins, and Jeff Callahan."

"You say they took you out—how did they get at you to get you out?"

"I had gone to bed and was asleep. I had a brother living in Suwanee County, near Live Oak, and he had written to us that he and his family were coming to spend the 4th of July holidays with us. When I heard someone hail at the gate, I thought it was my brother. I got up in my night clothes, and walked out to meet my brother, as I thought. When I got out there, there was a man on horseback and I soon found out it was not my brother. There were two men concealed behind the post of the gate, and they caught hold of me and told me that I was their prisoner."

"Did they whip you?"

"Yes, sir. I cannot tell how many blows—I think about eighty, as well as I can recollect."

"With what?"

"A leather strap. I strove against them at the gate, before they got me out of the yard. My sisters came out—it frightened them. They tore me loose from my sisters, and beat and knocked them down. They fired a great many guns over their heads and in front of their faces. They carried me off and put me on a horse. It was a bay horse; I knew it. The horse pitched with me and they could not do anything with him, so they jerked me off that horse and hurt my hip very badly. I have not had a good use of my hip since; it hurts me in walking. They put me on another horse behind a man, and then carried me about three-quarters of a mile, tied my hands around a tree, and there whipped me."

"Have you any idea what they had against you?"

"One of them asked me what I was doing there [at the hearing], and I told him 'Little or nothing.' He asked me what I had them dragged up there for, paying out court costs. I told him I had not done it—that I had not prosecuted any one of them. He told me that he would give me a piece of advice, and I might take it as a friend's advice, for me not to show myself in court another day, but to keep away from there and not appear against them."

"Did you appear against them?"

"Yes, sir."

"Did your sisters also appear?"

"Yes, sir. I appeared there the next day, but the day after that I stayed at home, for I saw that they meant to have a difficulty with me. Judge Bryson, I suppose it was, sent out an attachment for me and my sisters that day to come in, and we went in, and trial came on that day."

"What was the result of the trial?"

"They proved themselves clear."

"How did they prove themselves clear?"

"Some of them had alibi witnesses, and others got up and boldly swore themselves that they were at home that night. After the trial they told me that if I were not gone in thirty-seven hours they would come on me again."

"I Was Neighborly with Negroes"

"My name is William Champion, and my home is in Limestone Township, South Carolina. My business is farming and milling."

"Go on and state if, at any time, you have been visited by any men in disguise; and, if so, what they did and said to you, and all that occurred."

"Yes—but I hate to tell it . . . Sunday night before the last state election, I was visited by a crowd of disguised men. They were in my house, when I awoke, ripping, and tearing, and cursing and hollering, 'You damned radical son of a bitch!'

"There was a gentleman named Rufus Erwin staying all night with me. He woke first. I was awakened in time enough to speak. They were telling me to get up. He spoke and said he would get up and make a light. As he rose up in the bed, they shot him in the arm, through the left shoulder. As to the shooting, I don't know how much to tell you was done. Perhaps a hundred shots—it may be not so many—were fired in the house. They had me to get up. They suffered me to put on my shoes and hat. Mr. Erwin did not get his on.

"They took me about two miles. They then blindfolded me, and told me I had but a few minutes to live—I will not say how many, maybe it was five minutes; it was a very short time—and if I had any praying to do, to pray. They told me they were going to take me to the river and tie a rope to me, and roll us both together into the river.

"They then took down my shirt and breeches, and whipped me. I could not tell you how much—as much as I was able to bear. I think I was about to faint and they ceased whipping me.

"There were some Negroes they had there, but I had never seen them before. Well, they made me kiss the Negro man's posterior, and held it open and made me kiss it, and a Negro woman's too, and also her private parts. They asked me how I liked that for nigger equality. They also told me to have sexual connection with her. I told them they knew, of course, I could not do that. They struck me some more, and said if I voted the Radical ticket again they would kill me. Then they made me whip one of the Negro men some."

"How many lashes were laid on you?"

"A hundred, I reckon. They beat me about with their pistols and with sticks. Do you see my teeth? There is one knocked loose, and this is gone, and that one is loose, too."

"Was your back bruised?"

"Of course it was bruised. My shirt, when I took it off, was stiff with blood."

"Where did the blood come from?"

"From the beating and bruising—it just oozed through. It was black, and so sore that I could scarcely go anywhere for days. I could scarcely swallow, they choked me so."

"Had you had any quarrel, or given offense to any of your neighbors, to account for this proceeding?"

"I have never had a quarrel with a man in my life. I have been a man that has done this: Now the neighborhood I live in was Democratic, and I joined the Union League. I was convinced that that was the course we would have to pursue."

"State fully what you mean."

"I thought that would be the only safety—the Union and the Constitution—that we would have to be governed by the laws. We were sworn to protect the Constitution of the United States and the laws thereof."

"Had you been in the Rebel service?"

"No, sir. I had a sore leg, and never was mustered. I was a Union man in principle when the war came, and remained so."

"Did that lead to any difficulty between you and your neighbors?"

"Not that I know of."

"What has been the effect of these proceedings in your township, as regards the sense of security enjoyed by the people who are Republican?"

"It has thrown us into the woods at night, and we are afraid to be out in daytime. I have never laid in my bed from the time I was whipped until now. I am afraid of being visited again."

"To what extent does that feeling prevail in your part of the country? Are there other people who sleep out at night?"

"Yes, sir. I guess the whole Republican Party do."

"Do you mean by that white and colored?"

"Yes, sir, both white and colored, and they take the weather as it comes."

"Do you believe that this is a well-grounded fear?"

"I do. You can look at this letter, and see whether you think I am wrong in my feelings [the witness produces a letter].

> Headquarters Ku Klux Clan
> Algood, South Carolina
> Mr. Buster Champion: We have been told that our visit to you was not a sufficient hint. We now notify you to leave the country within thirty days from the reception of this notice, or abide the consequences.
> K. K. K.

"How did you come into possession of that paper?"

"I can't tell exactly how it was contrived to come to me. It had been left at the house, and my wife handed it to me."

"Have you any actual knowledge of any other person being whipped or injured in that vicinity by masked men?"

"Of course. I do not know who-all to tell you. It commenced with the Negroes a little before they whipped me. I was the first white man I have heard of their whipping, in this county. As to the Ku-Klux, I, of course, saw it in the paper and read it, but I could not think it would have any bearing at all. There was a gentleman, Mr. O. P. McArthur, who generally talked in favor of the Ku-Klux. I put it up to be a great bugaboo. We talked a great deal about it. I told him that as to the Ku-Klux, I would not be afraid of it. He contended that there were as good men as we had in society who were Ku-Klux. I told him we need not argue such a doctrine—that I know no Christian-hearted or civilized man would be a Ku-Klux."

"I will ask whether, before this trouble you had with these unknown parties, you had been a trial justice?"

"Yes, sir."

"How many cases before you were between white men and Negroes?"

"Not very many."

"Had you not been in the habit of pretending to read the law to the Negroes, saying that they were not bound to leave the land they were on when their terms expired, but were entitled to stay there under the law?"

"Well, I have had some such chat on that. I have read the law on that."

"Have you associated pretty generally with the Negroes there in your neighborhood?"

"I have associated this far: I was a Republican and it drew the Negroes to a person. I showed friendship to the Negroes. I have never visited their houses and I have not been in one since the surrender nor before more than two or three times, or if I have I don't know it; or if there is a time when I have eaten with one I don't know it."

"You say you united yourself with the Union League as their equal?"

"Yes, sir."

"Are the Union Leagues not made up of black men?"

"Yes, sir, but I am speaking of houses."

"You united yourself with the Union League, which was made up of Negroes?"

"Yes, sir, and a few whites."

"But a very few whites?"

"Yes, sir."

"Have you not endeavored to impress the Negroes' mind with the idea that they were the equals of the whites in social life?"

"No, I have never done that because I knew that this generation never could do that. I knew that this generation could bring social equality only this far: that we would associate with the Negro enough for his friend-ship—that is, we would neighbor with him and be friendly to him."

"I ask you whether, while telling them their political rights, you have not added that they were entitled to all social relations with the white people, and if this was not given to them they ought to fight for it?"

"No, sir."

"You deny that?"

"Yes, sir, I deny that."

"I Refused to Join the Ku-Klux"

"My name is John Neason, and I live in Sumter County, South Carolina. I have opened a commission business, and am also engaged in planting."

"How much did you invest in your plantation?"

"My plantation cost me about $17,000."

"Go on now and state whether, at any time, you have been visited by persons in disguise."

"Last October, the night Mr. Robertson's store was burned, they came to my house before they went to him."

"Who came?"

"The Ku-Klux—men in disguise. They had out patrols and guards on horses, and the party that came to me was armed with double-barreled shotguns. Some of them had calico dresses, others had on homespun dresses, paper hats, and so on. I came out in my night clothes; I had been in bed. I asked them if they would allow me to put on my clothes, and they said, 'Yes.' I put on my pantaloons and coat and came out.

"They said, 'Tell your wife we do not intend to harm you.'

"They walked me on to my store, and I said, 'Do you mean to burn my store?'

"They said, 'We don't intend to burn your building.'

"I asked them, 'What do you intend to do?'

"The answer was, 'Whip you!'

"I said, 'For what? Am I guilty of any crime?'

"The reply was, 'No, but you keep a country store, and you allow Republicans to hold their meetings and their barbecues there, and you have been the manager of elections for the last five or six years, and we intend to stop it. We give you ten days to close up your business, and then we will give you five more days in which to leave the country!' "

"Did they whip you?"

"No, sir, they did not. They let me off. I begged out of it, and they did not put the lash on me. I had built a schoolhouse on my place for the benefit of the colored children—nothing more than a shelter. They would not allow it to stay on the place, and burned it down."

"What had been your party politics before you went to Sumter County?"

"I went into the Confederate army quite young. I never meddled with politics. I established myself there at Sumter and tried to make an honest living there. But now I have to break up and go away from there."

"Did you extend credit to whites and colored men?"

"Yes, sir. I gave the colored people credit for from $15 to $150, and to the white people I gave credit up to $200. The colored people all paid me; the whites sent me bankrupt notices."

"Had you any difficulty with the people there on account of that fact the next year?"

"I could not give credit to these white parties again. In the first place, I got my supplies from Baltimore, New York, and other places, and I had to keep my own credit good."

"Was that fact, that you extended credit to the Negroes who paid you, and would not give it to the whites, who didn't pay you, given as a reason for your being obnoxious to the community?"

"Yes, sir."

"Do you feel at liberty now to go back to that county and resume your business, and take charge of your property?"

"I do not, without some protection is given me."

"What is the proportion of colored population in Sumter?"

"You can find a hundred blacks to one white person."

"Upon the Ku-Klux visit to you, how many persons were there in the raiding party?"

"At least twenty-five or thirty. When they took me out and told me they were going to whip me, I said, 'Gentlemen, if there is any honor about this party, I beg you, in the name of God, not to put the lash on my back! You can cock your guns and discharge their contents in my breast!'

"They said, 'If you say nothing about a whipping no one will know it.'

"I replied, 'I will know it.' I begged off in that way, and at last they let me off. After they had consented to let me off without whipping me, they commenced to dance around me, and poke their fingers at me this way and the other, and make all sorts of signs. Everything was done by signals and signs, and but one man was allowed to say a word. I thought I knew some of them, but I was afraid to say anything."

"Are these men of position?"

"They are young farmers there—young gentlemen there."

"Sons of the old planters in the neighborhood?"

"Yes, sir."

"Do you know of any other occurrences of that character in that neighborhood?"

"Yes, sir, an old gentleman of the name of Davy Andrews, sixty-five or seventy years of age, who had served in the Union army, and at the close of the war had gone there and bought a small place. He was doing very well there in business, and they closed him up. About four nights ago they took another man out and whipped him, about a mile from where I live, and took out a woman and tarred-and-feathered her."

"Did they state their purpose?"

"It was to put down all country stores because the Republican Party held their meetings there, and drive out all Republicans from the county."

"Can you, from your information, tell how these masked men operate?"

"Well, sir, I can tell you this much: Going home one night from church, between 10 and 11 o'clock, I saw them encamped on one side of a by-road running through a plantation. They met there, and as they saw anybody riding by they would whistle."

"Who met there—the Ku-Klux?"

"Yes, sir. My wife and my wife's cousin were in the buggy together, and I rode along behind on a mule. They whistled as I went by. Before I got to the end of the road, about a half a mile from there they overtook me, and took me back to where they were camped, and asked me if I wanted to join.

"I said, 'No, no—I do not propose to get out of my bed on a cold night for any such fun,' and they let me off."

"Would you say that nearly all the white men in the neighborhood belong to this organization?"

"That is my honest belief."

"Have any persons been tried in Sumter County for these offenses?"

"Yes, sir. After they burned the store of Mr. Robertson, he had some twenty-five or thirty of them arrested. The result was that there was no verdict against them."

"I Wanted a People's Government"

"My name is Walter Brooks, and I am about forty-three years old. I now reside in Haralson County, Georgia, where I am a lawyer and a farmer. For the past eight years I have been a member of the state senate. I was first elected during the war, but immediately after the election, I was imprisoned by the Confederate authorities."

"Were you arrested for crime, or as a conscript?"

"Well, they said I was disloyal to the Confederate Government."

"You were imprisoned because of your sentiments against the war?"

"They may have coupled with that that I owed service to the Confederate authorities. I was appointed to serve as a conscript officer, but I refused to act. My superior officer said he would make me do it; he pointed to the jailhouse and said that that was made to make men do what they ought to do. As soon as I gave up my appointment as recruiting officer, a company of state troops were sent down with instructions that I and perhaps some others were not as true to the Confederate states as we ought to be—that we were Union men."

"Was there any issue between the Union men and disunion men at that time?"

"Yes, sir, and I ran on the Union ticket. I was a Union man. I opposed secession, and was a candidate for the convention in opposition to secession, and was beaten in my county by only 53 votes. In the first election, in 1863, the issue was clearly made, and I was considered the leader of the Union Party. The Democrats sent a military force to every voting place in my county, with orders to arrest me or anybody who cast a vote for me. On the day of election, a guard of these men rode up to where I was, and I was taken prisoner and was put in jail."

"Have you been following along on that same general line ever since?"

"Yes, sir, in the regular channel all the time. I opposed secession, and when Congress settled down on the Reconstruction policy, I tried to search into its principles and ideas, and became convinced that it would be altogether best for us to accept the Reconstruction Acts, and therefore I was a Reconstructionist; that has been my political policy."

"State whether any unusual or improper efforts were made to affect the results of the recent election in your county."

"Ever since about the 1st of May, there has been an organization of men that has been riding over a large portion of my county, whipping the people there. And on the night previous to the election some Negroes were pretty cruelly treated—seized, stamped, kicked, whipped, and generally knocked about. My opinion is that the county today, if this thing of going about and whipping men was done away with, and every man could go up and cast his vote according to his desires, is 75 to 100 Republican majority. But as it is, it will not vote over 25 or 30 Republican votes."

"Can you mention any of the persons injured by the Ku-Klux?"

"Well, yes. A man by the name of Coley came to my house some two weeks after he had been whipped and hanged. He slipped up his pants and showed me where his legs had been whipped, and they then had black stripes on them. He offered to pull off his shirt and show me his back, but I said, 'Mr. Coley, I don't want to see it.'

"Mr. Joe Addison told me himself that he had been badly beaten. He was talking about leaving, and I said, 'Joe, you have a farm here and a family, and you ought not to leave.'

"He said, 'They notified me to leave in ten days, or they would kill me.'

"I said, 'Well you should risk it, anyhow.'

"He continued to work on his farm. I saw him along occasionally, and asked him how he was doing. Said he, 'I am lying out nights and working daytimes.'

"About a month after that he came to me a second time, and told me the Ku-Klux had come to his house in the open daytime. His dog barked, and he turned his head and looked out of the door, and just then his wife said, 'There are the Ku-Klux!' He jumped up and went out of the door, and there were three men on that side of the house with their guns and pistols cocked, and they ordered him to halt, and he did so. His wife told me they swore they were going to kill him, and she began to make a fuss, and told them not to kill her husband. She said one of them jabbed his pistol up against her breast, and said that if she did not shut her mouth he would kill her."

"Have you known any other parties to be abused?"

"Well, yes. I know a gentleman by the name of A. B. Martin, who came to me and told me that they had whipped him most cruelly. I am of the opinion that the old gentleman stated the truth."

"Did you hear of other cases?"

"A great many others. I sat down at one time and counted up the number who had been whipped since the 1st of last May. There have been betwixt twenty and thirty cases in Haralson County."

"Has there been any killing there?"

"There was one Negro killed—a man they called John Walthall."

"Have any of these parties you have spoken of been brought to punishment in your county, or any steps taken for that purpose?"

"So far as I know, not a single thing has been done. On the day the news came to the town of Buchanan that that Negro was shot, the people were perfectly terror-stricken. I did go so far as to tell some white men that if they would send for a physician, I would see that he was paid myself, for we heard the Negro man was shot and lying where he fell, in a bad condition. He lay there, and no one went to him; he got no medical aid at all. The people were afraid to do or say anything."

"What is the cause of this terror you speak of?"

"Well, sir, the cause is a Klan of men that are riding over my country there."

"Do you know Joseph Roe?"

"Yes, sir. Last Thursday a week ago a gentleman by the name of Daniel Dodson came to my house, and said to me that Joseph Roe had sent him to see me, to get me to use my influence to get him out of the difficulty that he expected he was in—that perhaps there was a bill of indictment against him in the United States court. Dodson went on to tell me that Joe Roe was a chief of the Ku-Klux. The next day he came back with Tom Roe, a brother of Joseph Roe. They said they had all three joined the organization so as to protect themselves."

"Did they mention any other persons who were members?"

"Tom said that a fellow by the name of N. J. McClung was the 'Night-Hawk' officer. He told me that William Fincher, Duncan Monroe, Tom Riddelsperger, Willliam Riddelsperger, John Ward and his son William Ward, Jim Newman, William Sides, William Longshore, Lafayette Morris, Daniel Head, and a great many others were members."

"Did they give any particulars about the Order?"

"Daniel Dodson gave me what he said were the signs of the Klan, their passwords, that I might know them. He told me that this Roe had told him to post me, and had also sent him over into Alabama to post the judge of the court of probate, William Mancock, whom the Ku-Klux had threatened. He said he had also been to Edwardsville, and had posted the Union folks there."

"So you could be on your guard and protect yourself against the Ku-Klux?"

"Yes, sir. Said he, 'I will post you.' "

"Can you repeat the signs and passwords now?"

"He said that supposing we were in a crowd, or in a house where there were a great many people together, and he wanted to know whether I belonged to the organization or not, he would put his foot on top of mine, and press on it, and say, 'I ask your pardon.' If I belonged to the Order, I would remark, 'It is granted.' Also, if I met with a gentleman and shook hands with him, or anything of that sort, and asked him how he was, if he belonged to the organization he would say, 'I am *well;* how are you?' He said, 'Well' was the word. That is about what he said to me. He said that one sign was to shut up the third and fourth fingers of the right hand, and put the thumb on them, and have the first and second fingers stretched out straight; and the answer would be in the same way with the left hand."

"Did he say anything about their lodges, or convocations, or whatever they call them?"

"Yes, sir. He went on to give the names of the Klans—he called them dens. He said that one den, known as 'Moccasin Den,' included a portion of Alabama and one of the districts in my county, and that Joe Roe was the presiding officer, or Cyclops. He gave me the name of another den, but I do not now recall it. He told me who was the officer who commanded it at one time."

"Who was he?"

"William Pound. He said they had recently turned him out of office. He said that each one had to pay his dollar initiation fee, or something of that sort, and they paid it to him, and he failed to account for it to General Nathan Bedford Forrest. He stated that General Forrest is at the head of the entire organization, and his money, or a part of it, was to be paid over in that direction."

"So far as you know, with what party do the men said to belong to this Klan associate and vote?"

"Well, sir, I tried to watch so as to be right about it. I have nothing at heart except the good of our country. I could not think people would be so bad. My honest opinion is that every man who belongs to the organization casts a Democratic vote."

"How with regard to their victims?"

"If there is any man or woman in my county who has been whipped, that does not belong to the Republican Party, I do not know it."

"What is the impression of the people with regard to this organization? Do they say much about it in any way?"

"Well, there is some talk about it. I find some Democrats who say it is wrong, and I think they are honest about it. But, upon the whole, I think that a very large majority of the Democratic Party are willing that the organization should continue. At one time we endeavored there to get a public meeting to condemn this thing, but we failed to do it. The Republican Party was afraid to go into the courthouse and pass resolutions condemning the matter, for fear they would be assassinated. The Democratic Party, who I thought ought to have taken hold of the question—for it was confined to their Party—would not do it. It passed off in that way without any public action in that direction at all."

"Are you conscious of considerable bitterness of feeling against the Democratic Party?"

"None in the world; all I want is a good government of the people."

"They Hanged Me by the Neck"

"My name is John Coley. I was born in South Carolina in 1821—or so my parents tell me. I now live in Haralson County, Georgia, and my occupation is that of a farmer."

"Have you been interrupted or in any way injured by any organized parties of disguised men?"

"I have, some."

"State the circumstances and manner of that occurrence."

"On the 25th day of February last there came to my dwelling a band of men. I did not notice the particular hour, but my wife informed me it was between 10 and 11 o'clock. She had laid down, but had not gone to sleep. I had worked all day pretty hard, and had laid down and gone to sleep earlier. They came up in haste. You know how the thing is—a man can hear, and understand, and know something, when he is not really good wide-awake, and yet he is awake enough to know that there is something about.

"With strange voices they hollered out 'Open your door, old man! Open the door quick!'

"Of course I waked up in a sort of fright, hearing the hasty words of unknown voices, and a quantity of men walking. I got up and opened the door, according to their direction. My dwelling is an old-fashioned, poor man's cabin, and the door was pinned with a pin, like old times. When I pulled out the pin and as I bent myself to look out, two men seized me by the left arm, and tried to jerk me out of doors. They jerked me so hasty it brought the door up and closed it. My wife was standing by, and, being a person of ready mind, she took the pin out of my hand and pinned the door.

"In the scuffle I had got pushed around sideways toward the wall of the house. It was a log wall sealed with a sealing-board, and the board was split. Somebody stabbed at me through the crack of the board—the fire shone on it, and showed that it was metal of some kind.

"By this time I became sort of roused, and called for an axe, intending to try to defend myself. While that was going on a gun was run in right by the side of the chimney, through another large crack, and presented directly at me, not more than five or six feet from me. The fellow swore that if I did not open the door he would 'shoot my Goddamned liver out.' Well, that brought to my mind the thought of a gun, and I called for one. The gun was handed to me, and I set the trigger, and presented the gun so that I thought I could shoot through the crack at that man. I told him to take his gun away from there, or I would shoot him dead. He left from that place, and there was an order from someone at the back of the chimney to break down the doors.

"They went to break down the doors, and in the tumult someone got by the side of the chimney, and said, 'Open the door or I'll burn your house!'

"He lit a match and held it in a crack to fire the house. I saw the place by the shine of the light, and it brought to my mind the notion that I could, perhaps, shoot him through that crack. While I was standing in that position they broke down the north door, and four men ran into the house. Two seized me, and two seized the gun.

"They ran out of doors with me, and as soon as they cleared the wall fairly, I looked up and saw a quantity of men. I saw they were generally disguised, so far as I could see.

"When I saw that, I said to them, 'Gentlemen, I am not afraid of you—you are Ku-Klux. I understand you now. Previous to this time I had not understood; I know now what you are. I am not afraid of you if you are the Ku-Klux.'

"One said, 'We are your friends. We are not going to hurt you. Was there not another man in the house?'

"I said, 'Yes, it was my wife's grandson.'

"They said, 'We don't want to hurt you or him either. We are your friends. We only want to talk to you. Let's go back to the house.'

"They turned right around and went back to the house. They held me by the arms all the while, for fear, I suppose, that I would make fight or do something.

"I said, 'Gentlemen, let me put on my clothes. I hate to be going about this way.' They let me put on my pants and coat.

"I called for my step-grandson. I could not get him up—could not find him. He had gone up into the loft and made his escape through the housetop and got away."

"Can you state more what they did, and less what was said? Tell what they did to you, and what led up to it."

"That is what I am endeavoring to do. I thought I would give the whole catalogue of it. They ransacked the house in such a way in search of him that things were pretty badly torn up. My wife was scared almost to death, and also this young man's wife. She just sank right down—it was enough to cause anybody to sink down. But I was not excited, from the fact that I considered that I had done nothing to be Ku-Kluxed for.

"When they took me out there were thirteen came into the house that I counted, and I concluded that there were as many more out where the horses were. At that place there were two men I noticed in particular. I think one was Enock Branham and the other was Dolph Beacham. They took me about seventy-five yards, and put a rope around my neck, and I began to be suspicious that they would abuse me, as all of you would have been. They took me to the west end of my plantation, and there they stopped me and whipped me.

"They said to me, 'What about this difficulty that took place between Jim Branham and Tom Martin, and this t'other fellow?'—referring to this step-grandson of mine.

"I said I had nothing in it, except to keep it down; and that I called for help to take away the knife from this step-grandson when Brown had a hand-spike striking at him. I said to the crowd, 'Gentlemen, stay with me, and do not let this difficulty go any further.' We got it sort of squashed there. The foremost turned round and cursed the crowd, and swore that he would bring the Ku-Klux on and have us every one killed. That was Thursday, and Saturday they came. I just told them this story as I tell it to you.

"They said, 'All right, that is enough.'

"Then they said, 'You stole two of this old man's hogs—Branham's hogs.'

"I said, 'If he will say so, and swear to it, I will pay for the hogs.'

"They said, 'We say so; we come from the moon. We are dead men, and come from the moon, and we have been taking cognizance of your conduct below here for many years.'

"They then said, 'What about the shooting done at this old man's dogs?'

"I said, 'I know nothing about it.'

"They took me to Jim Hill's, where I expected to make the proof that I was an innocent man. When I got there I could not find Jim Hill; he was not at home. I then proposed to go to Martin Brown's, the next house below. They would not suffer me to do it.

"They then took me out by the side of the road to a shade tree, where they hanged me up by the neck, pulled me up clear from the earth. The last thing I knew about myself or my actions I was trying to hold on to the rope. When I came to, to know anything, I was not holding on to the rope, but was standing on the ground with my hands by my side. How long I had been there I could not say, because they deadened me to that extent that I did not know anything.

"I said, 'Gentlemen, I am dying and I shall never see my friends nor my family again!'

"They led me forward in the direction of the big road, and said, 'Now, old man, if you have any more arrangements to make, make them! Your time is not long here! Are you a Radical? How do you vote?'

"I told them.

"They said, 'If you have any arrangements to make, make them quick!'

"I said, 'I have nothing. If you are going to execute me take me away from the house, and suffer me to make a prayer.'

"They said, 'Go on!'

"I knelt down in the big road, and I tried to pray. I got through and said, 'Amen!' As I got up they fastened on to my arms again and led me down in the direction of home. In the edge of the woods they halted me. I saw the man with the shrub come up again. They commenced hitting me. It hurt desperately.

"I said, 'Lord, have mercy on me!' for I saw that those people had no mercy.

"They gave me six licks over my shoulder, and across my back they gave me four. Then they set another person to whip me across the legs, but how many licks he gave me I do not know. I reasonably suppose that, first and last, in the three whippings they gave me that night, the very shortest was seventy-five licks; but it is only supposition.

"Then the commander, as it seemed to be, led me from that place to about the middle of the road, and looking me in the face with all the impudence in the world, said he, 'Don't you think you can find a home away from here?'

"I said, 'I cannot go. This is my place. I have earned it with my hands'—holding out my hands—'and I cannot leave it.'

"He said, 'We will kill you if you don't!'

"I said, 'How long before I must go?'

"He said, 'Fifteen days; and if you tell what we have done to you, or said to you, we will kill you!'

"He told me to run, and fired a pistol right near me. He fired a second pistol, and I left in a sort of slow trot and went back to my dwelling. Later on, I was informed by another man, who professed to have got knowledge of him, that this commander's name was Joseph Burrows, of Cleburne County, Alabama."

"Have you been disturbed since that time?"

"I have not stayed at my house. I stayed there eighteen days in the daytime, but at night I went into the woods and hid myself. About two or three weeks after that time, this same crowd came up there, and tore down the doors. There were the horses' track there."

"You say they asked you about being a Radical. Had you voted the Radical ticket?"

"Yes, sir."

"What reason had they for making this attack upon you, more than you have stated?"

"None in the world that I can tell."

"They Insisted on Blood"

"My name is Joseph Addison. I am about twenty-four years old, and live in Haralson County, Georgia, I have been living there ever since I was a little bit of a boy. I am a farmer."

"During the war which side were you on?"

"My feelings were on the side of what you call the Radical Party now. I was what you call a Union man then."

"Were your opinions well known?"

"Yes, sir, I reckon I am well known."

"Have you seen any people, or do you know of any, called Ku-Klux?"

"Yes, sir."

"Tell us what you know about them."

"I will tell you how they did me. They first came on a neighbor of mine, a brother-in-law, and they took both him and his son out and whipped them. They sent me word to leave where I was living. I said I should not do it. They said that if I did not leave they allowed to shoot me. I laid out then about three weeks. I then went into the house and laid there, I believe, two nights. The third night they came on to me, and took me out and hit me some ten or twelve licks with a hickory. After that they took me back to my house to talk to me, but one of them insisted they had not got any blood, and they ought to have blood. So they took me out and whipped me some more until they got it. They then told me they would give me ten days to get away in. I begged them to let me stay until I had made my crop; they said I should not do it.

"They said, 'Yes, I would rather do anything than to die.'

"That was in the last of March, the first time they came on me. I laid out then, and the next time they came on me was the last day in May, on a dark rainy evening, about a half an hour by sun. I had been to the store to sell some wheat and corn, so as to get some little things I wanted. My wife had been hoeing cotton, and asked me if I wanted dinner; she said there was cold victuals enough for dinner. I ate a cold snack. We then went on and hoed until it came up to rain. My wife then got supper, and I went in and sat down to supper. I got about half done eating when one of the dogs broke out barking powerfully.

"I said, 'What is that dog barking at?'

"My wife looked out and said, 'Lord have mercy! Joe, it's the Ku-Klux!'

"I jumped out of the door and ran. One then was right in the back yard, and he jabbed the top of his six-shooter against my head, and said, 'Halt, Goddamn you!'

"I said, 'I will give up.' I asked them what they were doing that for.

"They said, 'We gave you time once to get away, and, Goddam you, you have not gone; now, Goddamn you, you shall not go, for we allow to kill you!'

"I said, 'If you do not abuse me or whip me, I will go the next morning.'

"They said they would not abuse or whip me, but they would kill me.

"I said, 'Let me go and see my wife and children.'

"They said, 'No, Goddamn you!'

"I turned away from the man. He jammed his pistol in my face, and said, 'Goddamn you, go on, or I will kill you!'

"They took me about eighty or ninety yards from there into a little thicket. The man on my right stepped back, and said to the little fellow on my left, 'Old man, we have got him here now; do as you please with him!' They were all standing right around me with their guns pointing at me. Just as he turned around, I wheeled and run. Before I had run ten yards I heard a half a dozen caps bursted at me. I must have gone seventy or eighty yards, and then I heard what I thought was a pistol fired. I heard a bullet hit a tree. I run on eight or ten steps further, and then I heard a bullet hit a tree just before me. Every one of them took after me, and run me for a hundred and fifty yards. I ran down a little bluff and ran across a branch. When I got across there, I could not run any further, for my shoes were all muddy. I cut the strings off my old shoes, and left them there. I stopped to listen, but I never saw anything more of them. I then went around and climbed up on the fence, and sat there and watched until dark. I then went to the house and got some dry clothes, and went back where I had fixed a place in the woodshed to sleep in, and went to bed.

"My wife would not sleep at home by herself, but went to her sister-in-law's. The Ku-Klux came in on them on Sunday night, about two hours and half before day Monday morning. They abused her and cursed her powerfully, and tried to make her tell where I was. They said that if she did not tell them they would shoot her Goddamn brains out. I was laying out close by there, and I stood there and heard them. They shot five or six shots in the yard; some of them shot into the house. They scared my wife and sister-in-law so bad that they took the children and went into the woods and stayed there all night. Before the Ku-Klux left they told my wife that if they ever caught her or her sister-in-law back there again they would kill the last Goddamn one of them."

"Do you still stay there?"

"No, sir, I have done moved now. I moved off, and left my hogs and my crops and everything there, what little I made. I did not make much crop this year, for I was afraid to work, and now I am afraid to go back there to save anything."

"Where is your brother-in-law now?"

"He has done left and gone away over into the valley."

"Do you know any of the men that came either time?"

"I know two of them. One was Joe Roe, and the other man John Gilpin. I was raised up with Gilpin from a boy."

"What, is your opinion, was the reason that they persecuted you in this way?"

"I just think it was on account of politics—that it was because I was a Radical."

"State whether the Ku-Klux have been riding about Haralson County a great deal this Summer."

"Yes, sir. They have been doing a right smart of whipping. They have beat up lots of people powerfully, and they killed a black man there not long ago."

"Do you know any reason why they should make war upon the Radicals at this particular time?"

"It was just before the election, a short time back, that they made all their raids."

"Tell us about your brother-in-law being whipped."

"I have just his word for it."

"They gave him no reason why they whipped him?"

"No, sir, he said they never gave him any reason why."

"Death to All Witnesses"

"My name is James M. Justice. I am a native of North Carolina, and reside in the town of Rutherfordton."

"What is your business or occupation?"

"Till recently I have been a mechanic, but in 1868 I was elected to the legislature. Since that time I have been admitted to the bar, and I am at this time engaged in the practice of law in my town."

"Are you still a member of the legislature?"

"Yes, sir—I was re-elected last August."

"To what political party do you belong?"

"I claimed to belong, and I have belonged as well as I understood myself, to what we first called the Union Party, and since the war to the Republican Party."

"The particular object about which we wish to enquire is in regard to the condition of affairs in your state, so far as relates to its peace and order, or the contrary, and the enforcement of the laws."

"Well, sir, our state courts can enforce the laws as heretofore, with regard to ordinary crimes. But there is a class of crimes in that section of the country that is entirely above and beyond the reach of the civil authorities there."

"What class of crimes is it to which you refer?"

"A series of outrages that have been committed upon a great many people by persons who go about in disguise and in the night."

"Have these bands of disguised and armed men who commit these crimes come to have a name and designation in common parlance?"

"They are usually called Ku-Klux."

"Have you taken any pains to inform yourself about the doings of these bands of disguised and armed men?"

"I have seen a great many colored people, and some white men, who have come to the state capital and made known their troubles there."

"Did their persons exhibit the appearance of having been scourged, or of their having received gun and pistol-shot wounds?"

"Yes, sir. I remember to have seen one colored man whose body presented quite a mangled appearance. On his breast were two marks or wounds, which he said had been produced in this way: they jabbed him with the muzzle of a double-barreled gun, and his breast exhibited two small circular wounds. I think that in the last six months I have heard of sixty or eighty or a hundred cases of a similar character."

"In the course of our investigation heretofore there has been reference made, and questions have been asked, concerning rapes committed by Negroes on white women. Has there been any case of that kind in your county?"

"There has been but one case of rape, and that was the rape of a white girl by a white man."

"State what you have heard about other outrages."

"I was told by an old colored woman, and one entitled to credit—her word, I think, would be believed by everybody who knows her—that some of her kinfolk were in a great deal of trouble about things of that sort. She said that when the Ku-Klux had gone after a Negro man in some places they had attempted—and in other places they had actually committed—rape upon colored women in the presence of their husbands. This old woman told it to me as a secret, for she said she was afraid to have it known, for fear they would kill her. She said that her daughter, who was lately married, was about to be raped, and her husband begged them off. The woman said that he alleged reasons that ought to have deterred any man. I think that four or five, maybe ten, outrages are committed on Negroes in that way and not made known at all, to every one that becomes publicly known."

"When did you last go to the capital at Raleigh?"

"On Saturday, the 8th. On Sunday morning I received news of a very shocking outrage on Mr. Aaron Biggerstaff."

"State the substance of that transaction."

"Well, sir, Judge Logan had started to go to Cleveland County to hold court there. He was met at the edge of the county by the daughter of Mr. Biggerstaff, who told him that she thought her father had been murdered, that he would die of his wounds. He turned back to town with her, and she made a statement which caused him to issue a warrant and send for the sheriff to summon a posse of quite a number of men. I was summoned among others. I went to Mr. Biggerstaff's on Monday. He is a man about sixty or sixty-five years of age."

"Is he a white man?"

"Yes, sir. He is a farmer. I found him the most shamefully abused piece of human flesh I ever saw."

"Describe his appearance."

"From his face to his feet the surface of his body was literally cut to pieces. Some places on his back had the appearance—well, I do not know how it could have been done, but there were indentations in his flesh to some depth. His whole body was inflamed, and almost black with bruised and bleeding wounds. He said he thought two of his ribs were broken. I know that he had difficulty in breathing, and he was very much prostrated. He was not sitting up exactly, and he said he could not lie down. They had him propped up with pillows."

"Give the substance of his statement."

"He says they came about midnight. His daughter said the road seemed to be full of men and horses. They brought such a pressure against his door as to cause the hinges to give way. They found the old man in bed, and they dragged him out into the road, where they beat him with hickories and kicked him for a long time, and then brought him back into the house. They spoke about his politics—that he was a bad man, and all such as that.

"One of them said they had not given him enough, and they took him out a second time and beat him severely. He says they put a bottle or something on his head and applied fire to it, and it exploded with a noise like a gun. He said it produced a very painful feeling in his head; and I noticed that his hair was burned.

"They also whipped his daughter a great deal about the shoulders. She is the widow of a deceased soldier—her husband was killed in the Confederate Army. They told her they whipped her for being a witness against them, in a forcible trespass case, which has not yet been decided. They said their purpose was to kill Judge Logan, Mr. Carpenter, and myself."

"Is that the Mr. Carpenter who is the editor of a Republican paper in Rutherfordton?"

"Yes, sir—the *Rutherford Star.*"

"Some men were arrested for this, and a prosecution commenced?"

"Yes, sir. About twenty were arrested, I suppose. Judge Logan had them at the courthouse. He held them all to bail in a bond of $500 each, to re-appear before him, and also to keep the peace, and then they were discharged.

"Then another warrant was issued, on the application of Mrs. Norvill, the daughter of Biggerstaff; it was issued by United States Commissioner Shaffer, at Raleigh. The deputy U.S. marshal came up there with a small detachment of soldiers, eight or ten, and arrested some of the same parties over again. They started back by way of Cherryville. The marshal said he was going to carry the prisoners to Charlotte to be tried before the U.S. Commissioner there. He summoned Mr. Biggerstaff, his wife and daughter, to be at Cherryville the next day.

"They got into a wagon to go there, and took along with them a young Mr. Biggerstaff, and a Mr. Holland, who, I believe, is a son-in-law of Mr. Biggerstaff. They went on in their wagon until after dark, by which time they had got into Cleveland County. The soldiers and the prisoners had gone on ahead. Mr. Biggerstaff and his family stopped at a new cabin that was being built. The young lady, being very much frightened by the Ku-Klux, refused to stay at the camp, and she went off into the woods by herself.

"During the night a crowd came there, some in disguise, and surrounded the house and wagon. They went in the house then and struck Mr. Holland on the face with a gun, and he remained insensible for some time. They pulled old Biggerstaff out of the wagon and threw him on the ground, breaking his arm. They then took the rope he drove his mules with and tied it about his neck and made him run off with them into the woods, saying they were going to hang him, because he had promised them before that he would say nothing about what had been done to him.

"Holland was able to stand by this time, and they took him, and Mrs. Biggerstaff, and Biggerstaff out of the house—young Biggerstaff was a one-armed Confederate soldier, a brave man, not a coward by any means— they took them out and placed them in the road, as they said, to shoot them.

"About that time one of the mules became excited and commenced making a noise, and the men turned to look at him. As they were looking away, young Biggerstaff broke and ran. They fired at him, but they did not hit him, and he got away. Knowing that a witness was at large, they then ceased to abuse any of the party, but told them to go back to their homes, and not to say anything about all this, or they would all be killed. And so they returned to Rutherfordton, the old gentleman being very sick.

"Ever since, I have been home from the legislature, in consequence of the repeated threats—"

"Threats against yourself?"

"Yes, sir. One Sunday, as quiet a day about Rutherfordton as ever I saw in my life, I rode with my wife five miles into the country to church. We returned, and about sundown I heard the discharge of two guns, out east of town, in the direction the Ku-Klux usually came from. I have understood that firing a gun at sundown is a signal for a meeting of these men.

"I retired to bed very early that night. The next thing I recollect was being aroused by a violent crash at the door, and also a regular discharge of guns and pistols. I got out of bed intending to go across the room and get my gun and make the best defense I could. But it turned out that they split the panels of the door with an axe, and some men came into the room and passed between me and where my gun was.

"Matches were lighted, making the room perfectly light, as matches will. They stood there in the room, several of them, looking more like a man would imagine that devils would look, than you would ever suppose human beings would fix themselves up to look. The places where the eyeholes in their masks and also the mouths were cut, was bound around with some reddish stuff. And my idea is that there was either a white strip sewn on, and something painted, for a nose. Some had very long white beards—one that I have examined since, that I saw at Raleigh, was made of the tail of a cow. Some had horns which were erect. Others had horns which lopped over like a mule's ears, and their caps ran up to a point with tassels. One had a red suit out-and-out—a great deal like those I have seen on clowns in circuses. There were a number of strips on each arm—something bright like silver lace—like stripes on a sergeant's sleeves. There was something on the breast of one of them, something round, of circular form. He stood in full view of me, right before me."

"Was there any elegance in the manner in which he was gotten up?"

"Yes, sir. It appeared to be a neat concern, much neater than ever I supposed a Ku-Klux disguise would be got up. I could do nothing but look at them as they all stood there, after the matches were lit.

"Two of them came forward and said, 'Don't say a word; your time has come!'

"They struck me with a pistol—a very large pistol. You will see the scar on my forehead now. I fell down and became almost insensible. I then felt a pounding and beating in my side. My side is very badly bruised, from near the armpit down to the hip.

"The first thing I remember after that distinctly, I was in the street opposite my own gate. They commenced firing their pistols again, and made the most hideous screams of exultation, that they had got me at last, and were going to kill me, a damned scoundrel.

"They told me to run, and they pulled me along. I said it hurt my feet so much I wished they would not do that. They said I would not need my feet long. I was first asked what my profession was; I said I was a lawyer.

"One said, 'What kind of cases have you been trying lately?'

"I said, 'We have been trying some cases against the Ku-Klux.'

"'Yes,' said he, 'we know something about that; and you have been making some very strong speeches lately; you are in favor of hanging our leaders. Our party proposes to rid this country of this damned, infamous nigger government, and you propose to defeat us by hanging our leaders, you damned rascal! Now, you are a leader on the other side—what objection can you make to your being hung, as you advocate the doctrine of hanging leaders?'

"Well, I thought he was getting in on me pretty close, sure enough. He went on to say that I was a man they liked in everything but my political course, which was most infamous and troublesome to them—that I supported Negro suffrage and Negro supremacy.

"In reply I told them that I thought they ought not kill me for that; that the Negroes received their enfranchisement at the hands of our Government, and that I had supported it as I desired to support all the laws of the country in which I lived.

"They said, 'Damn such an infamous Government, that would put ignorant niggers to rule over and control white men! You are a white man, and are you not ashamed of yourself?'

"I became very sick. I asked the fellow to let me sit down; that my head was bleeding very much.

"He said, 'It's the damned nigger equality blood that is running out, and it will do you good!'

"Presently another crowd of them rode up, and a voice called for the prisoner. They led me to a little man, who told me he was the chief of that command. He then commenced telling me how mean I had been in advocating principles that gave Negroes the right to vote and hold office, and said they were going to kill all such men."

"Did he appear to be an educated man?"

"I think he was. He then said, 'What will you give if I discharge you without further injury?'

"I said, 'I have nothing out here, as you see, but my nightshirt.'

"Said he, 'Have you not your drawers on?'

"I said, 'No.'

"He said, 'I beg your pardon; I didn't know that.' He then said, 'Where is old Biggerstaff?'

"I said, 'I don't know where he is.'

"He said, 'I will tell you what I will do—if you will go and find old Biggerstaff and show him to me, I will turn you loose.'

"The others objected to that, and said that he had come there with orders to kill me, and that he should do it and let them be off. One of them said, 'Don't you turn the damn rascal loose! He says he don't know any of us, but if you turn him loose he will go right off and swear to every one of us! He will go off to Washington, in less than a week, and have the troops here and play hell with us, and have every one of us taken up! Damn him, kill him now we have got him!'

"The little man said, 'Remember our oath: justice and humanity.'

"They were loud and clamorous in their protestations against letting me go, and declared that I must be killed.

"The little man said to me, 'Do you know that our camps have lately all been assembled, and that we have taken a fresh oath to the effect that we will kill every man who swears against us in the United States courts? Now Biggerstaff has testified so, not only once but twice, and he has got some of our friends into a heap of trouble, and we will have to kill him. If he leaves this state and goes to another state, all we have to do is to send a decree to another camp there and they will kill him. So you may as well show us where he is, so that we can kill him, for we are bound to kill him anyhow.'

"I said, 'He has run off into the woods somewhere, and I wouldn't know how to find him if I tried.'

"At this the clamor was raised again to kill me, and some fellows poked their pistols into my face. One of them said, 'These are the tools we work on damned radicals with!'

"The little chief said to them, 'Damn you, take charge of your men! I was given this command, and I will be respected!'

"Gradually they went away, and when they were all out of sight, the chief said to me, 'These fellows want to kill you very badly, but I want to save you if I can. I have an absolute order to take your life tonight. But I will tell you something about our rules. We may be ordered to take a man's life, but if he behaves so as to justify us we may spare him. I think you ought to be spared, and I will do it if I can control these men, though they seem to very ambitious toward you. But let us have a clear under-standing—do you promise here and now henceforth be a true friend of the Southern Cause?'

"I was right smart in for a trade by then, and I answered in this way, which is the truth: I said, 'Yes, sir; I will hereafter be a true friend of "Southern men." ' " That was my answer. He said 'Southern Cause.' but I said 'Southern men,' which he accepted as an answer to his proposi-tion.

"He discharged me then, and I ran home as rapidly as possible."

"They Shall Never Change Me Any"

"My name is A. B. Martin, and I will be seventy-one years old on the 17th day of next January. I was born in Carolina, and now live in Har-alson County, Georgia. I keep a shop there, and farm too."

"On which side were you during the war?"

"I have been a Union man from my boyhood; I was not taught any-thing else by my parents."

"Are there any such people there in your county as are commonly called Ku-Klux?"

"There are a set of men there that are disguised people. They disguise themselves with calico, or anything, I do not know what all."

"How many times have you ever seen them?"

"I got to know them only one night. On the 7th of last May."

"What did they do?"

"I will tell you plainly how the circumstances took place. I lay in one room and my sister-in-law in another. I had just got to sleeping soundly, so I had to be shaken two or three times to wake me up. The first I knew she was shaking me, and said, 'Mr. Martin, get up! There are a hundred men coming here, I think!'

"I jumped right up, with my drawers on, and ran out and opened the front door, I peeped out, and it looked to me like a heap of women. My mind struck me that it was another runaway set wanting to be married. The Alabama line is right close by, and they run over on our side to be married. Such things had happened before, and I thought it was all right.

"I opened the door wide open, and said 'Come in!'

"I set the chairs as well as I could feel them, and said that I would put on my clothes and be out in a minute. I put on my pants over my drawers. As I went in, I told my sister-in-law to light the candle. She smelled a rat a little worse than I did. I got through, and when I went out they presented their guns at me. They took me and my step-son out and whipped us plenty. They whipped me so that I had to tote my drawers and pants in my hands to the house, and they whipped my step-son pretty considerably. I do not know what sort of people they were, whether Ku-Klux or not, but I am sensible that some of them are pretty close neighbors to me. They are mighty rigid Democrats, and I was as much the other way. Gentlemen, I will tell you just as it is. I am a Union man, certain!"

"How many blows did they strike you?"

"I cannot tell you. They struck me until I had no feeling; if they had whipped on until yet it would not have made much odds."

"Did they whip you standing up?"

"They made me lie down on my belly."

"Did they hold you down in any way?"

"No, sir. I tell you my principles are pretty strong, and I just thought I could bear anything."

"What did they whip you with?"

"I cannot tell you. It was something that flew off in the time of it. There came another man walking along, and spoke to him, and they went off, and, I think, fixed it again; and then he came back and whipped me another spell. They put a rope around my neck, and tried to draw me up to a post-oak sapling. And then they whipped me about the legs. My neck is swelled yet, and it was black for two months."

"I understand you to say that in your opinion those were Democrats who were whipping you, because you were a Radical and a Union man?"

"Yes, sir. I had been a notary public for some time, and I think they begrudged me the office. After they crossed the fence and got down into the big road, the first word any one of them said to me was, 'What is your politics?'

"I told them I was a Union man from my cradle.

"Another man said to me, 'Can you pray?'

"I had begun to see into the thing pretty plainly, and to know that something was going to take place. I said, 'I am not a praying man; but if I was, the prayers of the wicked avail nothing.' When I said that one of them took me with a gun across my head, and sort of staggered me."

"How many were there in the crowd?"

"I think there must have been sixty of them. They had some Negroes along with them, prisoners. They whipped them powerfully, and kept whipping them."

"In regard to the last election, did your people all vote?"

"I know of four of them who would not go in my precinct, and they advised me not to go. They advised me not to open the election, but I went up myself and opened the election. I am not afraid when I am in a good cause."

"How do you feel about going back to Haralson County?"

"I am not going back."

"Why not?"

"Because I am afraid to go among them now, after testifying. My wife and I have not slept in my house three nights since they came on us."

"You say you know of some Democrats whom you do not believe belong to the Ku-Klux, but who encourages them?"

"I am certain of that. Duncan Monroe is one—I am as certain of it as I can be of anything I do not positively know."

"What makes you think so?"

"I heard him tell a man there, about a man in the neighborhood, 'If he don't leave in three days, I will have him Ku-Kluxed,' and they went and did it. His name was Thomas Powell. They whipped him and his wife too."

"Did you know any of the parties who made assault on you?"

"Yes, sir."

"Did you give their names?"

"I did to the grand jury."

"What are their names?"

"James Casey, Thomas Casey, Jack Thomas, David Lowry, James Cox, and James Garner."

"You expect these men will be tried for that offense?"

"Well, I think they ought to be. But if a man was to shoot another there, and I should issue a warrant, I could not get a man to arrest him."

"Do you recollect what was the number of votes cast at your election?"

"I disremember now. I know a heap would have voted on our side, only they were afraid to go up and vote. The Ku-Klux have run it over us certainly, but they shall never change me any."

"White Outside, Black Inside"

"What is your name?"

"My registered paper is Lewis Perkins; my father's title is Lewis Wills. I live seven and a half miles north of Columbus, Mississippi, on the military road."

"State if a white man by the name of Mr. Farmer, a school teacher, boarded with you at the time he was teaching."

"Yes, sir."

"What, if anything, do you know about his being driven away and his school broken up?"

"Well, sir, I was taken very suddenly by—as well as I could state the amount—forty men arriving to my house, asking at the door, 'Where is that damned school teacher?'

"Mr. Farmer walked to the door. 'How are you, gentlemen?' says he.

" 'I understand, sir, you are teaching niggers and boarding with a nigger,' they said.

"Says he, 'I am boarding with old man Lewis Perkins, which, you all know, is a nice, quiet old gentleman.'

" 'I haven't been long in this country—I don't know old man Perkins. But,' they said, 'are you from Chicago, sir?'

" 'I am from New York, sir.'

"Says he, 'All-ways you are boarding with a nigger; why don't you board with your own color?'

" 'Gentlemen,' says he, 'I endeavored to do so, and I had not the opportunity to do so.'

"They said, 'How can you prove that?'

"Says he, 'I can go over to Mr. Whiteside's—I went there and tried to take board with them.'

"After that his reply was, says he, 'Why is the reason that they didn't board you?'

"Says he, 'Gentlemen, I don't know.'

" 'Who authorized you to come here to teach niggers?'

"Says he, 'Mr. Bishop and Mr. Simons and other authorities.'

" 'Well, Mr. Bishop is as black inside as that old nigger woman is outside!'

"Did they say that to him?"

"Yes, sir. And they went on to say, 'Mr. Eggerson is all about.' "

"You mean Mr. Eggerson, the tax assessor here?"

"I don't know what he is—but he is not far off. He says, 'He is all about;' that is to say, he is without principle. Then the remark was, 'Come here, Captain!' Two gentlemen rode around the house, and one says, 'We'll hang him, anyhow!'

" 'No,' says the other. 'Lieutenant, come here!'

"They rode around the house, came back and said, 'Sir, I give you ten days to get away from here, and if you don't be away from here in ten days I wouldn't give you anything for your head nor body!'

"Well, gentlemen, I think, as far as the United States oath is, I have delivered all I know with truth . . ."

"How long had Mr. Farmer been teaching school there?"

"As well as I could barely make a guess, I think about two months before he was troubled."

"Had he given satisfaction as a teacher?"

"O, beautiful! Columbus [Mississippi] itself couldn't touch him! It was the beautifulest thing I ever see in that section of the country or anywhere else."

"Was he a well-behaved good man?"

"I think as good as Almighty God ever made. He only labored to teach his children. And he was making himself so careful that he wouldn't interfere with no labor contracts; nothing but the true course of learning, and the history of the Bible."

"Do you know that he had tried to procure board with white families?"

"I can prove it tomorrow, in a minute. When he first came there, I says, 'Mr. Farmer, I will not set down to table with you. Not that I am not as good as you, but it's not the rule of our country. I'll give you a good meal till you get your house, and when you get your house up, I'll allow my wife to make your bed and cook your meals, but I can't sit at meals with you.'

"My wife go so much dissatisfied that she wasn't willing for him to stay there under the circumstances, so I went up to Mr. Presley's mill, and spoke to Mr. Presley for lumber to build Mr. Farmer a house outside of the African tribe."

"Did he quit teaching after the Ku-Klux visited him?"

"Yes, sir. He quit on those terms."

Carpetbaggers: "I Represented the Freedmen's Bureau"

"My name is W. J. Furman. I am thirty years of age, I was born in Pennsylvania, and now live in Marianna, Jackson County, Florida. I am a lawyer by profession."

"Are you connected in any way with the state government of Florida?"

"Yes, sir. With reference to my residence, I desire to say that, while I do not actually reside in Marianna, yet I have answered that I did, from the fact that I am unwillingly away from there at this time."

"Explain why you are unwillingly away from there."

"I am unwillingly away from there because I am not permitted to live there, in consequence of the murderous political opposition to me. My life would not be safe there for one hour; that is a sentiment publicly expressed by the leading men there."

"Have any attempts been made upon your life?"

"Yes, sir. In February, 1869. When I and the clerk of the court, Dr. Finlayson, were going home one evening from a public concert, about 10 o'clock at night, we were fired upon in the town, and Dr. Finlayson was killed, and I was shot through the neck.

"The condition of my health required that I should go North. On my return in September, when I got as far as Washington City, I was informed of the murdering and rioting going on in Marianna at that time. I came as far as Tallahassee, and the Governor of Florida, as well as all my other friends, would not permit me to go over to Marianna, in consequence of the danger and threats against me as a public man.

"I might here give a short history of what those murderings and riotings were at that time. On the 28th of September, 1869, the colored people had a picnic about two miles out of Marianna. While proceeding there peaceably in their carts and wagons, with their women and children, they were fired upon by unknown parties, and one man and one little boy were killed. A day or two afterward, J. P. Coker, Colonel McClellan, and Miss McClellan, and some others, were sitting on the piazza of the hotel; that party was fired into. Miss McClellan was killed and Colonel McClellan was wounded.

"Tremendous excitement prevailed. The chivalry assembled under arms—virtually put Marianna and all that section of the country under martial law, appointing their own provost marshal. They took Mr. Samuel Fleishman—a white man and a merchant of twenty years standing in that country—out of his store, ransacked his store, took away all the arms and ammunition there were there, carried him by force into the state of Georgia, and declared that if he put his foot into Jackson County again he would be killed. Fleishman came back a few days afterward and was killed a few miles outside of Marianna.

"Two men, by the name of Sullivan and Cox, while proceeding out of town on their way home, were both badly wounded; one was a white man and the other a colored man."

"These occurrences took place after you had been shot?"

"Yes, sir. I was shot in the February preceding, and these things took place in the September following. One year thereafter, in August, I, in company with Colonel Hamilton, member of Congress from this state, visited Marianna. I was then United States assessor for Florida. We arrived in Marianna, and it produced quite a consternation at once. Judging from the reports of fire-arms that took place during that day, they must have been cleaning out their pistols and shot-guns, and preparing for operations. We stopped with the sheriff and county clerk at their house.

"We were secretly informed that a raid would be made upon the house, and that we were all to be murdered. The first programme was to poison the watch-dogs, of which we had three. No attention was paid to this secret information, but on the next morning, when we woke up, we found the three watch-dogs lying stiff and stark, dead in the yard. We then believed there was a programme of that sort on foot, and the next night we were on guard.

"There was great excitement in town—running of horses, blowing of horns, and so on. About midnight a man on horseback approached the house, and surveyed it very leisurely, and then rode off. He happened to find that every window in the house was open, and probably he saw a man with a double-barreled shot-gun at every window. I suppose he reported that information, and there was no raid that night.

"On Saturday we had a public meeting of a political character, in the public square. At that meeting a great many men who lived in town were there on horseback, with blankets and overcoats strapped on their saddles behind, which in that country means being in the proper fix to 'go to Texas.' Others appeared in buggies, with double-barreled shotguns. Probably fifty or sixty men of that character were there, while none of the more peaceable citizens were there at all—showing a certain programme to be carried out. One or two speeches were made, but the danger was so great that the meeting was adjourned. They had three or four men there from Columbus, desperadoes, who were to commence the fight. They call them in that country 'twenty-dollar men,' who are known as assassins, and who will kill any man for twenty dollars.

"Immediately after the meeting adjourned, parties of men started out from Marianna—some parties with guns, giving out that they were going off on a hunting expedition. Other parties went out with fishing-rods, pretending to be going upon a fishing excursion. This was merely a pretext for the absence of different parties from town. We found upon investigation that every cross-road, by-path, every possible avenue of escape from that town was blockaded. At night, men were halted in every direction on the roads.

"To go back a little: This sheriff, at whose house we were staying, was a Southern man, and had a brother who was a planter. That brother came there and begged, with tears in his eyes, that the sheriff should go away from that house. They also attempted to get the sheriff drunk, and abduct him, and they almost succeeded.

"Finding that we could not leave Marianna when we wanted to, we called in some of the oldest citizens, men of standing, integrity, and property, and explained to them the condition of things. They pretended that such could not possibly be the case; that we must be mistaken. We assured them that it was the case, and that they really knew better; and they did know better.

"After staying there four or five days beyond our time, the sheriff issued a summons for a posse of five hundred armed men, with four days' rations, and at the head of that body of men we were going to march out of that county. When the older citizens found such was to be the programme, they immediately came to us, and begged, for God's sake, not to call out such a posse, saying their young men would not stand it—that war would take place right away at once.

"They said, 'Ask any means for your safety, and you shall have it!'

"Thereupon, we selected ten of the oldest and best citizens, and they promised to be there early the next morning, and to accompany us in the form of hostages, and as an escort out of the county.

"I desire to make one point right here. It was stipulated that the road the party should take should not be decided until after the party left town. Early the next morning the escort of old citizens arrived. With one or two exceptions they were all well armed. After proceeding three or four miles out of town, the party halted, and our escort, or hostages, determined the road we should take."

"Do you mean that these ten or twelve old men went out to answer with their lives for any assault upon you?"

"No, sir. I will explain what I mean, Mr. Senator. We have heard of Indians, who, when pursued, would interpose the women and children they may have kidnapped between the guns of their enemies and themselves. Had we been pursued in that way, we would have made a bulwark of those hostages. They came with us to give us protection; we relied upon them, and it was good for them that they did give us protection."

"They treated you in good faith?"

"Yes, sir, and when we got to Georgia we treated them gloriously to champagne."

"Have you been back there since that time?"

"No, sir, I have not. I was in charge of that portion of the country there—of six counties—as agent of the Freedmen's Bureau. It was a lawless country; murders were taking place constantly. I remember a conversation I had in the Spring of 1868 with the sheriff of Jackson County—a Conservative sheriff. In talking about a murder that had taken place a few days before, he said it was the sixtieth that had taken place in the county since the surrender."

"How many have occurred since that conversation?"

"Well, a great many. At least twenty or twenty-five—all of our prominent political men, our best men. Dr. Finlayson was a native of the place. He favored the Reconstruction of the state, and was clerk of the circuit court; or the prothonotary. Many threats were made constantly during those days against prominent Republicans."

"What was the character of the threats?"

"They said that we were incendiaries; that we set the colored people against the white people, stirring up the country; that we were damned Yankees, damned Radicals, and should be killed like dogs."

"Who were the people that made those threats?"

"The chivalry. That does not cover it exactly, however. It was not the poorer people by any means, but the better sort of people, mostly young men."

"What do you mean by the better sort of people?"

"I mean those contradistinguished from the poorer class—from those known as 'crackers.' "

"When you used the term 'chivalry,' you use it as a term of contempt, do you not?"

"No, sir. I used it to describe a certain class of men—a pistol-and-bowie-knife class of men."

"You mean to speak sneeringly of them?"

"It is a designation to be applied to a certain class of men in this country."

"I merely ask you in regard to the tone in which you used the term."

"I do not know in regard to the tone; I speak of a certain class of men. After these proceedings, these men met and dictated certain appointments to the Governor. When the Governor accepts recommendations of such men after such proceedings, it certainly must be a cowering before dictation. I am responsible for my own words there."

"I take it you are responsible for all your words?"

"I mean that is my construction of that proceeding."

"Are you conscious that you are speaking under very great excitement and prejudice against these people?"

"Well, I hope not."

"Are you conscious of that feeling?"

"I try to be perfectly conscious of what I am saying. I probably speak the truth in an emphatic manner, but I know whereof I speak."

"You are aiming to give a historical account of certain transactions?"

"Yes, sir."

"You may call it a historical account, but I would ask you if you are not giving suppositions, rather than statements of facts?"

"No, I am speaking of facts."

"What was the character generally of the colored men who were killed?"

"Prominent men among their race. They were our best colored men both in intelligence and industry."

"What is the voting population of Jackson County?"

"In a fair election there, I think there would be but few less than 1,400 black voters and 500 or 600 white voters."

"How many white Republicans are there in the county?"

"There were about sixty or seventy."

"How many are there now?"

"I judge there are none, for the last one has been killed."

"Do you think any white Republicans voted there at the last election?"

"I do not think there were any. The son of our late member of the legislature, Mr. McMillan, was shot through the face as he was taking a drink out of a bucket of water. All that is discouraging to the white Republicans there."

"You say that none of these men who have committed these assassinations have been brought to trial?"

"Do you want to know why they have not been arrested?"

"Yes, I want to know, and the reason is this: the machinery of this state government has been in the hands of members of your party. Now, why is it that, having the whole state bound hand and foot, under the control of your partisans, so far as office is concerned, your officials have not done their duty?"

"That is not the construction that should be put upon it. If the people, by general sentiment—to say nothing about conspiracy—are opposed to a certain government and all its officials, and combine knowingly or instinctively, as it were, to harass that government, and throw all impediments in its way, it is a very easy thing for murderers to escape, and for officers of the law to be prevented from pursuing."

"How is it possible that if there had been proper diligence, capacity, and honesty in your official circles there would not have been at least more attempts to arrest these people?"

"Let me illustrate, if you please, Mr. Senator. Colonel Dickinson, who was one of the best men who ever breathed the breath of life, intellectually and morally, was prevented by the people *en masse* from holding inquests over the dead bodies. He could not get anybody to serve on that inquest, and the people there dared him to hold it."

"That is the case, with a voting population of three to one in your favor, and with all the officers on your side?"

"Yes. Now take the conspiracy that exists—"

"What conspiracy do you refer to? Give it some specific name."

"You might call it Ku-Kluxism; I suppose that is it. Those men will combine to prevent the arrest of any man; they will spirit him away or protect and conceal him and make it dangerous for officers of the law to attempt to arrest him. It is not that officers of the law have not made exertions to arrest these men, for they have done so. But the men get away, or if they do stand trial, and any one of these conspirators is on the jury, he will hang the jury, and you cannot get a conviction against any of them."

"How can you state more than mere opinion upon that subject?"

"Well, I might state it as my opinion that it is the Spring of the year, because I see leaves springing from the trees and vegetation springing from the earth. In the same way I give it as my opinion that there is such an organization, and I base it upon facts as they show themselves to me. They may call themselves Invisible Empire, Ku-Klux, or anything else they choose, but they are a combination."

"You say the evidence of Spring is a matter of fact. Now, do you say, as a matter of fact, that there is a combination of these men? Have you seen them come and go, and do you know that there is such an organization?"

"I have seen them in their works, and I have felt them myself."

"Describe what you mean by 'their works.' "

"Their works are the murdering, scourging, whipping, and intimidating of a certain class of political men, and it all comes from the opposite class."

"There has been no one killed there since the murder of Dickinson?"

"No, sir, because they have killed off everybody there is any opposition to on their part. I have a friend here in Jacksonville, who comes from Jackson County. He received a letter from a Democratic friend of his out there, after the murder of Dickinson. He told me in a laughing, happy, rejoicing way, 'Well, Dick writes to me from Jackson County that they have things their own way there now; that there is not a damned nigger that dares to speak in Jackson County; that Purman dare not go back again; that Dickinson was the last leader among the Republicans there, and he being away, there were no more niggers to make speeches; no more white Republicans dare go there; and they are going to have a perfect elysium now.' "

"Mere Fiendishness"

"My name is A. Webster Shaffer. I live in Raleigh, North Carolina, where I am register in bankruptcy and United States Commissioner."

"When you went there, from where did you go?"

"From New York. I went to Raleigh in March, 1866, under an order from the Secretary of War, as an officer of the Army, and was mustered out in October, 1867."

"In the discharge of your duties as United States Commissioner, have you had occasion to inquire into the commission of acts of violence and lawlessness in any part of North Carolina?"

"I have since the Act of May 21, 1870. The warrants issued from my office have run into Johnson, Chatham, Harnett, and Moore Counties. The parties who made oath for the issue of the warrants testified that parties in disguise had come there in the night-time, assaulted their houses and persons, broken down their doors, and in most cases taken the inmates—men, women, and children—and whipped and mutilated them. Do you want the details of any particular case?"

"So far as you recollect individual cases that have been before you, proceed in order and given them."

"There are several cases that I never issued warrants upon, for the reason that while the outrages have been terrible, in some respects, there is no testimony upon them. One is the case of Frances Gilmore, a colored woman from Chatham. She came to my office and complained that disguised persons had visited her house in the night-time, laid her on the floor, taken her clothes off, and whipped her with a board; turned her over and whipped her again; then with matches burned the hair from her private parts, and stabbed her several times in the same place with a knife. She had been lying there about three weeks, unable to get to me before. I asked if she could identify any of the parties. She said she could not."

"What reasons were ascribed for such an act?"

"I could not ascertain any reason why they did it. She was not living with any white men. She was not doing anything, so far as I could ascertain, that would justify it at all. It appeared to be mere fiendishness."

"What political objectives were to be obtained by such proceedings?"

"The driving of the whole Negro race out of the country, I should suppose—the disorganization of the people, white and black."

"Would intimidation be produced by such an act?"

"I should suppose it would . . . Right after that there was another case in which another Frances Gilmore was involved—a white woman. She belonged to a party of contractors on the Chatham Railroad. The Ku-Klux came there in the nighttime, and entered the camp of these persons, firing right and left, hooting and hollering.

"They went to the house of this Mrs. Frances Gilmore and found two Negro men sleeping there on a pallet. They found one white man, named Gilmore, and four white women. The Ku-Klux took one Negro out and whipped him. They then undertook to take the other out, but he ran to get away, and they shot him dead. The women also were whipped, including a girl sixteen to eighteen years of age. They took her clothes off, whipped her very severely, and then lit a match and burned her hair off, and made her cut off herself the part that did not burn."

"Did the testimony disclose whether the men who committed this act gave as a reason for it the presence of these women of bad character?"

"They did not give any testimony as to the cause of it."

"Is there any information or public impression down there that there are frequently counterfeit Ku-Klux—that other parties assume masks to correct the morals of the people?"

"No, sir. No one has ever given any testimony of that character before me."

"Are there many private broils and much trouble among the Negro population themselves?"

"No, sir. The colored people are as orderly, quiet, respectful a people as I ever saw in my life anywhere."

"Do you say that the Negroes as a race are free from any disturbances among themselves?"

Captured Mississippi Klansmen (*Harper's Weekly,*
January 27, 1872).

"I have not heard of any broils or disturbances among them, or anything of that nature."

"Nothing that might induce any of *them* to assume masks and punish
disorders among themselves?"

"No, sir. Not even the Ku-Klux who have been called to testify before me have ever attempted to show that there were Negro Ku-Klux."

"What was there to explain this attack upon the camp of this railroad
contractor?"

"The contractor, a man by the name of Howle, was a particular friend
of Mr. Congressman Porter, who was then campaigning for another term
in office. Mr. Howle made some speeches in behalf of Congressman
Porter, and did some talking among the colored people working for him
in the railroad camp, advising them to vote for Porter. The Ku-Klux left
warnings at the camp, saying that Yankee contractors had to leave the
country—that this was a Southern country, and belonged to the Ku-
Klux, and they intended to govern it."

"From the investigations which you have made in these cases, is it
your impression that what is known as the Ku-Klux organization is still
in existence, and still continuing its operations?"

"I am abundantly satisfied of that."

"Is any effect upon these organizations perceptible since the passage of
the Act of Congress of last May?"

"I cannot say that there is. I have not seen any perceptible difference in their going about in disguise nor in their outrages. There is certainly nothing in the law now that was not in the law before to stop them. Of course for a time, while the bill was being debated, there was a great deal of ado about it in the papers. As to the Enforcement Act as it is called, there were never any remarks made upon it scarcely; that was not called the Ku-Klux bill or anything of the kind. They did not seem to know or care what that was. But Mr. Shellabarger's bill, when it came up this year, was a very stringent one and excited the feelings of the conservative classes of the community there very greatly."

"By Conservative you mean Democratic?"

"Yes, sir. They are adherents of the Democratic Party, but since they do not want to be democratic, or even to be called Democratic, they call themselves Conservatives. When the Shellabarger bill—which would have been a very effective law if enacted—came up, they took exceptions to it, and called it the loudest names of anything I ever heard in that section of the country. But after it was cut down to nothing and passed, they no longer seemed to care about it."

"So far, then, as regards the protection of life and property, you think that people in that section are no more secure under the operation of that law than before?"

"If that law had repealed the Enforcement Act, instead of supplementing it, they would be even less secure."

"How would that follow?"

"Because the sixth section of the Enforcement Act makes the banding together and going in disguise upon the public highways et cetera a felony, punishable by fine not exceeding $5,000, and by imprisonment not exceeding ten years, whereas this new Act makes the offense a misdemeanor, and does not affix any very definite penalty to it at all."

"Will not prosecutions under this new Act be more likely to result in convictions in the United States courts, than was formerly the case in the state courts?"

"I do not think that such will be the result, at least in the end. 'You can sue a beggar and catch a louse,' as the old saying is, and that is all you can do under the new Act. The criminal process is not any different as far as I can see; and the civil remedy, enabling the victims to sue the culprits for damages, is nothing at all."

"Is not the new law more effective by virtue of authorizing the judge to administer to the witness an oath as to whether he belongs to any secret organization?"

"These men I should not believe in any case. There is no oath which any human being could take which would make me believe him, if I believed he belonged to this organization."

"Are we to understand you then as saying that you believe a part of the system of this organization is to obstruct the administration of justice against its members?"

"I do most decidedly. I believe it is part of their practice as well as their creed to clear each other from criminal prosecutions."

"By what means?"

"By any means that may be necessary."

"Including perjury?"

"Yes, sir. I do not imagine that any of them hesitate to perjure themselves to clear their companions any more than they hesitate to commit any other crime in the world."

"Have you any knowledge on that subject?"

"I am only satisfied from testimony that comes before me and in the manner in which they do it."

"Is not the organization of such character that it may be quiet or active according to the pleasure of its members?"

"I look for it to pervade all the counties in the coming election for convention."

"On what ground do you found such an opinion?"

"From the antecedents of the organization; from the fact that it has always come up in political campaigns."

"You do not seem to have a very hopeful view of the future or of the power of Congress to deal with this organization. What do you think is the remedy?"

"I think the remedy is to hold counties responsible, as they do in other countries, and as the Shellabarger bill in its original form provided. If the counties are made to pay a fine for permitting such violence to go unprosecuted, it will stop."

"Striking that clause out of the Ku-Klux bill did not meet with your approbation?"

"If you had struck out everything except that, I would have been willing to go bond myself for the peace and security of North Carolina, and every citizen in it."

"I Wanted to Get Out of It"

"My name is John Harrill, and I live in Rutherford County, North Carolina. I was born there, and am going on twenty-three years."

"What political party have you been acting with?"

"I belonged to what they call the Invisible Empire of America."

"Do you belong to the Republican Party or the Democratic Party?"

"The Democratic Party."

"State whatever you may know in regard to the preservation of law and order, the safety of life and property, in the County of Rutherford. Have there been any outbreaks of any sort?"

"Yes, sir. There has been a right smart of outbreaks within the last five or six months."

"Of what character?"

"People being whipped out—breaking down their doors, and taking them out of their houses and whipping them."

"What sort of people mostly—colored or white?"

"Some of both."

"You said you were a member of the Invisible Empire of America. What is the business of this Order? What connection has it with such outrages, if any?"

"That is what we called ourselves—what people call the Ku-Klux."

"How came you to join it?"

"There was a man got at me to join it. He asked me if I liked this and that and the other, and got me to join."

"Who was that man?"

"Richard Martin."

"What did he tell you?"

"He told me there was no harm in it; that it was to see how strong the Conservative Party was, so that they could carry their points. When I got into it, I found there was something else . . ."

"Was he a man of property?"

"His father is about as well-doing a man as any there in that country there."

"Did he tell you where you should go to join?"

"He swore me in himself—one Sunday, at preaching."

"Did you attend a meeting of the camp afterward?"

"Yes, sir. The first meeting was close to the Burnt Chimneys. A man by the name of Jesse DePriest was the chief."

"What was the purport of the obligation administered to you?"

"Well, it denounced the Radical Party, and all such as that."

"Was anything said about the means by which that was to be accomplished?"

"Well, if they could not do it in one way they would do it in another.

If they could not do it by whipping about, they were going to kill some of the leading men."

"Was there an obligation that bound you to secrecy?"

"Yes, sir. If we divulged anything it was death."

"Death how?"

"By the hands of a brother—'death, death, death at the hands of a brother.' That is the last of the oath."

"Was there anything in the obligation about obeying your officers?"

"Yes, sir. We were sworn to obey all orders given by our chiefs in all respects."

"Was there any chief officer for the district?"

"Yes, sir, a man at Charlotte. Jones was his name—Ham Jones, I believe they called him."

"Do you know of any other chiefs in your county?"

"Yes, sir. Madison McBrayer was one. There were Elias Hambrick, John Witherow, William Webster, and Mac Deck. I have heard that Bill Edgington is another."

"Did you have a general chief of the county over the others?"

"Yes, sir—Randolph Shotwell. The *Rutherford Vindicator* was the paper he had some connection with."

"Did you meet in disguise in these dens?"

"Yes, sir. We just disguised ourselves on the head. Some had gowns, but a heap of them did not."

"What did you do with your disguises in the daytime?"

"We kept them hid."

"Did you go armed?"

"Those that had arms took them; they generally had repeaters."

"Were you ever at one of these meetings when it was decided upon to go on a raid?"

"Yes, sir."

"State the particulars of the first case when there was a raid proposed."

"There was a raid proposed—I never was on but two—to go to an old Negro's place and give him a little brushing out."

"Who proposed it?"

"The crowd. I don't know which one of them now—I believe it was George Dogwood, as we called him."

"What did you do?"

"They just took him out; pulled down the door, I believe, and took him out and gave him about twenty-five lashes. They went back on him the Thursday night afterward and gave him about twenty-five more.

They heard of him talking of swearing to some men that were there, so they went back and gave him his orders, and gave him another little brushing out."

"What sort of orders did you give him?"

"Orders never to swear to any men; that if he did they would kill him. And I believe some of them told him that if he went to the election it would be death, or something that way."

"Was there any obligation in your den that you were to help each other or stand by each other?"

"O, yes, sir! We were to swear for them, to help them in distress, and everything that way."

"Do you mean that you were to swear falsely in court for them?"

"Yes, sir."

"To get them clear?"

"Yes, sir."

"Was there anything in the obligation in regard to releasing them from prison when confined there?"

"Yes, sir, that was talked of."

"State any other meetings that you had when there was anything done."

"That was all the meeting I was ever at. I was on one raid afterward. About three weeks after that I went with another den to another darky's house. They sent our den word for some of us to go, to change the thing, so they would not be recognized."

"Did you go of your own accord, or were you sent?"

"We were ordered to go."

"What did they do on that raid?"

"They went to a Negro girl's house, and gave her about fifteen or twenty lashes for fighting with a white man."

"Were you ever on other raids?"

"No, sir. I knew when the town raid was going to be made."

"State how you knew it, and who proposed it."

"I was in town the Friday before, and Shotwell took me in a room and told me all about it. He said they were going to make a raid on the town on Sunday night, and he told me he wanted me to go. He said they were going to take Jim Justice out and kill him, and burst up the office of the *Rutherford Star* and kill old Biggerstaff."

"What were they going to do that for?"

"Well, it was political. The *Star* is a Republican paper."

"Were you in that raid?"

"No, sir. I did not want to go, and I told my daddy about it just about an hour before I was going. He said he would do anything to me before he would have me go into such an arrangement as that. My father belonged to it."

"He told you not to go?"

"Yes, sir, and he tried to persuade Gaith Trout to not go. He was against any raiding that ever was to be done. He got into it, and after he got into it he said that if they ever had any raiding or whipping to do he was done with it!"

"You may state anything that has been told to you since, if you believe it to be true."

"Washington Trout was on it. He just told me the next day that he was on it, and what they had done. He said he was one of those that kept them from killing Jim Justice."

"When a proposition was made in camp to do anything, was it put to a vote?"

"It was not put to a vote. There was a committee appointed and they decided upon it, but whenever orders came from the chief they had to obey."

"It has been stated in evidence that some operation was noticed as going on during court week. Who were active in swearing in men at that time?"

"Some said Plato Durham was. He knew I was in, and I had been told he was. I gave him a sign and he gave it back to me. He said that Beatty Carpenter, George Logan, and them fellows must be killed if they did not stop taking up men that had been sworn to."

"You mean there had been arrests by these United States Commissioners?"

"Yes, sir."

"How many men do you suppose belong to this organization in Rutherford County?"

"I guess about three hundred. I expect there are six or eight hundred in Cleveland."

"Have you any idea how many there are in the whole state?"

"I don't recollect whether they have ever told me or not. I have heard there was about eight million in the United States."

"Are there men of some age and property who belong to this organization and do not go out on raids?"

"Yes, sir, about as wealthy as any in the county."

"Do you know where these men got their arms?"

"They just bought them from the stores, just wherever they could get them. I have heard that Smith Wood's den had sent off to New York for one hundred six-shooters. I heard some say that the South Carolina men had taken some from the Government—had captured some arms out of a depot one night."

"Do the Negroes there seem to be afraid of this organization?"

"Yes, sir, they did, and some white men, too. Some mighty innocent good men got their orders that if they did not keep their mouths shut, and hush talking, they would get their backs slashed. My father's own uncle—a preacher right close to me—got his orders like that."

"To keep his mouth shut about what?"

"About politics, and to stop talking against the Ku-Klux. They would not allow any man to talk about them. If he did he was in danger of getting a whipping or, maybe, being killed."

"Do you know anything about the White Brotherhood?"

"Well, it is all the same thing—Ku-Klux. The name 'Invisible Empire' was so that when they swore in court they could swear that they never belonged to the Ku-Klux; that they never knew a Ku-Klux, or anything that way."

"How many men belonging to this organization have been arrested in your country by United States authority?"

"I expect there are from fifty to one hundred."

"Have any of them confessed?"

"About seventy-five, I guess, have confessed."

"What made you confess?"

"I wanted to get out of it, and I was glad they were confessing."

"What made these other men confess? Was it because the United States Government had sent down troops and begun to arrest? Did they think it would be safer then for them to confess than it was before?"

"Of course they did. If we had confessed before that, we would have been killed. They would have done it in the daytime. I would not have confessed before for anything."

"Then all these confessions were brought about by the protection given by the United States Government down here?"

"Yes, sir, of course."

Kluxers: "I Was Approached by Several Gentlemen"

"My name is Plato Durham, and I am a practicing lawyer in Cleveland County, North Carolina. I am a native of this state."

"State what public positions you have held."

"I was a member of the legislature of North Carolina at the session of 1866–67. I was a member of the constitutional convention which assembled in our State under the Reconstruction Acts of Congress, in January, 1868. I was also elected, in April, 1868, to another term in the legislature."

"The object of this Committee is to ascertain whether the laws of your state are efficiently executed, and whether property and life are safe there."

"I do not think that the existing laws of North Carolina, particularly those of the criminal code, have been enforced as they ought to have been since 1868."

"What is the general tenor of the teaching of the Carpetbaggers and others to the Negroes of your state?"

"The general tenor of their teachings has had a very bad influence upon the Negroes. First and foremost, I think in 1867 and 1868, about the time the Union and Loyal Leagues were being organized, or rather reorganized, the influence of these men was very bad indeed. The Negroes were made to believe that the white people were their enemies—that they were seeking the first opportunity to put the Negroes back into slavery. The Negroes at one time expected the confiscation of the property of the Southern people—there is no doubt about that. I have myself heard several Negroes say that they were told that the lands of the Southern people would be confiscated, and that they were promised land, horses, et cetera—forty acres in real estate for each Negro, I believe, and a horse or a mule."

"The Reconstruction measures and the manner in which the state government was organized caused a great deal of dissatisfaction in your state?"

"Yes, sir."

"Did they look upon it as a violation of the pledges of the United States Government made at the time of the surrender?"

"They did look upon it in just that way; and they believed that the men who came down there professing to love the Negroes so much, and those who suddenly turned over and became such lovers of the colored population, were not in earnest. We told the Negro that they were not in earnest. I am satisfied that the whole difficulty has grown out of this doctrine of universal suffrage for the Negro."

"How do the people of your state look upon the legislation of Congress in regard to the Southern country? Do they consider it to have been dictated by a spirit of hostility?"

"They do. There can be no question about the fact that a large number of the best people of that country—the property owners of the country, the men representing the intelligence of the country—look upon that legislation as hostile in the extreme."

"We have had evidence before us from two or three witnesses who profess to have been members of the Ku-Klux order as it is called, and who stated that there was an order known as the Ku-Klux, or Invisible Empire, and that its object was political—to prevent Negroes from voting, or compel them to vote the Democratic ticket. They stated that they are secret organizations, and oath-bound."

"I know of no such organization."

"I think that some parties had made confession and implicated you, and it was believed you were a leading man of the order—that you were the chief."

"Well, sir, I am not the chief of the Ku-Klux. I am neither the head of it, nor any part of it; nor am I the chief of any other secret organization, or any part of it."

"Do you know of any secret organization in your state?"

"No, sir, not at this time. I know of an organization which did exist in that State."

"What was that organization?"

"It was an organization for mutual protection and defense."

"What was its object and purpose?"

"The people thought that the lessons which the Negroes were being taught in the Union Leagues were leading them on. About that time I was approached by several gentlemen and told of the existence of an organization for self-protection and self-defense. The obligation was to support the Constitution of the United States and the constitution of North Carolina, to protect each other, and to protect the women and children of the country in case of necessity, and to vote for white men for office. So far as regards the idea that the outrages upon Negroes have been committed by that organization, it is in my opinion preposterous."

"Are not the laboring white men of the country far more jealous of the privileges which have been granted to the Negroes than any other class of the people?"

"They are the ones who are jealous, of course. There is no necessity on the part of the higher and more intelligent classes for that jealousy toward the Negroes which exists between the poor white man and the Negro. There is a feeling among the poorer classes of the white men that they and the country would be a great deal better off if the Negroes were entirely out of the country; and they would unanimously vote for colonizing them. The common white people are at times very much enraged against the Negro population. They think that this universal political and civil equality will finally bring about social equality. In fact, it is commencing to do it already; there are already instances in the county of Cleveland in which poor white girls are having Negro children. The white laboring people feel that it is not safe for them to be thus working in close contact with the Negroes."

"Do the colored people behave on the average as well as the whites?"

"No, sir! They have not done so, and they never do anywhere, so far as I know."

"Has there ever been in your county an organization known among its members, or designated by parties who are not members, as the Ku-Klux organization?"

"I do not know that there has ever been such an organization. Of course the Ku-Klux organization is spoken of there as it is all over the South, but I do not know anything about its existence."

"Do you know of any organization known as the White Brotherhood?"

"No, sir."

"Do you know of any known as the Constitutional Union Guard?"

"No, sir."

"Do you know of any commonly designated as the Invisible Empire?"

"Yes, sir. That is the one I spoke about a while ago—at least that is what it was said to be at the time I became a member of it."

"Was it in January, 1869, that you joined it?"

"I think it was somewhere along there, but I am not sure."

"Did that organization extend to any other county?"

"I expect it did. I do not know that it did. I have heard that it did."

"As to the membership, were you bound to secrecy?"

"I believe that was the understanding. I forget now, but I believe it was."

"Did they have signs and pass-words?"

"Yes, sir, they had some signs, but I do not recollect all of them."

"Do you recollect that a person was hailed with these words, 'Who goes there?' and the answer was, 'A friend'?"

"I do not recollect that."

"Then the response was, 'A friend of what?' and the answer was, 'To our country.' "

"No, sir. I do not recollect anything about the hailing part of it."

"Who was the chief officer when you were admitted?"

"I do not think they had any."

"Did you occupy any office in the organization?"

"No, sir, nothing at all."

"Does each one of the klans have a chief?"

"I reckon so."

"Have the members of that organization at any time had disguises which they wore on occasions?"

"I do not know. I never saw any persons whom I knew to be members have disguises."

"Do you know whether a part of the actual operations of this Invisible Empire has been to ride about in disguise?"

"No, sir, I do not know that."

"Have you ever heard that it was so?"

"The Invisible Empire?"

"These klans or councils, whatever they are."

"No, sir, I never heard that it was part of their operations. I have heard that parties ride in disguise, but I do not know that they were parties belonging to this organization."

"Have you not heard that they meet in council and consider and discuss propositions to inflict punishment on persons?"

"I have heard that from the opposite Party and from people whom I do not know whether to credit with truthfulness or not."

"You have never heard anything of that sort from persons who had been members of the Invisible Empire?"

"I may have heard it from some of them, but I do not know whom."

"You think this organization was formed for the purpose of protection?"

"I know it, so far as my knowledge extends—for mutual protection, and for the protection of the country in case of emergency. I will make a statement with regard to these outrages. I firmly believe that if the proceedings of these Union Leagues and their leaders, those organizations being generally composed of Negroes and white men of very disreputable character, had been allowed to go on without some check by the courts or otherwise—if they had been permitted to continue to threaten and to attempt to deter and intimidate the people, I really do not know what would have been the condition of the Southern states today."

"Least Said Is Best Mended"

"My name is Isaac Hawkins. I am about twenty-eight years old, and I live about three miles from Unionville, South Carolina."

"What is your occupation?"

"Well, sir, I have been riding for the sheriff ever since the war. I was crippled in the war, and have been acting as constable."

"Were you here upon the night that the last raid was made upon the jail?"

"I was not."

"Did you know anything of that occurrence, that raid?"

"Not until the next morning, about an hour before day."

"Did you meet Hughes, the keeper of the jail?"

"I did."

"Where did you meet Hughes?"

"At Steen's Hotel."

"Was that the first you learned of the raid?"

"Yes, sir."

"Were you not at the jail between 11 and 12 o'clock?"

"I was not."

"You were in the jail the night before the raid occurred, in your capacity as constable?"

"Yes, sir."

"But you were out on the night the raid did occur?"

"I was."

"Had you any knowledge that there was going to be a raid that night?"

"I did not."

"Are you a member of the Ku-Klux?"

"How? I am not."

"What is the name by which that organization is known in this country?"

"You know as much about it as I do."

"I am asking you the question."

"What is it known by?"

"Yes."

"The Ku-Klux."

"Has it any other name?"

"Not as I know of."

"Have you ever taken an oath in any secret organization since the war?"

[A pause.] "I don't know to what you allude."

"You can answer that question. Have you taken an oath in any secret organization since the war?"

"I have."

"In what association?"

"In a Masonic."

"In any other?"

"No, sir."

"Is there an organization known as the Invisible Circle in this state?"

"Not that I know of."

"Is there any organization, in this place, of the Ku-Klux?"

"Not that I know of."

"Or of any society known by any other name whose object is the same?"

"I know of none."

"Do you know any of the signs of the Ku-Klux organization?"

"No, sir. I know nothing of it."

"Have you ever been in a Ku-Klux meeting here?"

"No, sir. I don't know as they have ever had a meeting."

"Were you in the Rebel army?"

"Yes, sir."

"What are your politics?"

"Well, I am nothing as far as that is concerned. I have never voted in my life, and never expect to."

"Are you not a citizen of the United States?"

"Yes, sir, I am. I have the right to vote, but I am not obliged to use it unless I want to."

"Why do you not vote?"

"That is my business."

"Is it because you do not want to acknowledge allegiance to the United States?"

"Well, 'least said is best mended,' as the old fellow said. That is my right. I can enjoy that right, if it is a poor one."

"For what reason did you go off and leave the jail that night?"

"Because I was worn out with watching."

"Where did you sleep before?"

"In a room in the jail."

"Why did you not sleep there that night?"

"Because I didn't care to sleep there."

"For what reason?"

"For several reasons."

"What were they?"

"I don't know that I am obliged to tell it."

"We will ask you to tell."

"Well, sir, I will tell you my main reason. That will satisfy you, I hope.

It was because I supposed Negroes were coming to take out the prisoners, and would kill me if they found me there."

"When you met Hughes at the hotel the next morning, did he tell you the Ku-Klux had come to the jail and taken out the Negro prisoners and killed them?"

"There was a parcel of men there. I believe he was the first one told me."

"What was your answer to that?"

"I don't remember now."

"Did you not say you were glad of it?"

"I don't know as I did; I don't know as I didn't."

"How was it? Were you glad of it?"

"That is sort of a self-concern, I think."

"We want you to answer."

"Well, I didn't care."

"Your business there, according to your testimony, is to assist in guarding the prisoners, and yet you say when you learned that the Ku-Klux had taken them out and shot them, you were rather glad of it?"

"I did not say so yet; I said I didn't care."

"Answer the question. Were you not glad of it?"

"If they were the guilty party, I was glad of it."

"Did you not believe they were guilty?"

"Yes, sir."

"As an assistant in the jail, you were willing to see them taken out and shot, and you were glad of it?"

"You are not trying me now."

"But you are a witness here."

"Put your questions in a proper shape, and I will answer them."

"As an assistant to the sheriff, whose duty it is to keep the prisoners safely, you say you were glad they were taken out and shot?"

"I say if they were guilty I was glad of it. That is all you will get."

"Without trial?"

"Yes, sir. If they were guilty, without trial."

"You have rather sympathized with these movements of the Ku-Klux in taking prisoners out of jail—rather thought it a good thing?"

"Well, I don't know."

"How did it happen that everybody stayed away from the jail that night?"

"I don't know."

"You did not know what the Ku-Klux might do if they came?"

"No, sir, I did not; but what I did I did as conscientiously as anything I ever did in my life."

"So Help Me God!"

, "My name is John Tomlinson. I was born and raised here in Yorkville, South Carolina. I am a druggist, and am near thirty."

"We desire to examine into the existence in this county, or in any portion of this state, of any secret organization which has committed or encouraged violence. Have you any knowledge of such an organization?"

"I have not."

"Is there any organization in this county which is popularly known as Ku-Klux?"

"Not that I know of."

"Is there any organization known as the 'Invisible Circle'?"

"Not to my knowledge."

"Any organization known as the 'White Brotherhood'?"

"Not to my knowledge."

"Or the 'Invisible Empire'?"

"Not to my knowledge."

"Are you a member of any secret organization?"

"I suppose I did join the Sons of Temperance, but the organization broke up."

"Are you a member of any other secret organization?"

"No, sir, I believe not—only the Masons."

"Do you know anything about the taking of ammunition from the office of the probate judge in this place?"

"I do not."

"Were you not in the office of the probate judge shortly before it took place?"

"I was there with Mr. Bloodworth and Judge Harris. I suppose we were the last men in the office."

"Have you no knowledge of a key being prepared by Bloodworth that evening to enter?"

"I have not."

"Had you any conversation on that subject with a man named Samuel Smith."

"I did not."

"Have you any knowledge of where the ammunition was put that was taken from there?"

"None whatever."

"Have you any knowledge of the time when, and the persons by whom, a man named Anderson Brown was killed in this county?"

"I have heard of him. I heard he was killed. I could not swear it. I suppose the coroner could tell."

"About that time were you in company with a man named William Colcock?"

"You mean that night?"

"Yes."

"In town?"

"Any place."

"Colcock and I room on the same floor, and we might have been together."

"Was John Hunter in your company on that night Anderson Brown was killed?"

"He also rooms on the same floor, and we might have been together."

"Do you recollect of coming into town, you and Hunter and Colcock, on the morning after Anderson Brown was killed just before daylight?"

"Most positively we did not do it; most emphatically we did not do it! I did not. I was not with them."

"Where were you that night?"

"That is a delicate question . . ."

"We want to know."

"For a young man and single, he might be in places where he would not want to tell where he was. It is a little delicate. I was in town. I will tell you that. That is satisfactory."

"Was Mr. Hunter with you that night?"

"I do not know what night it was. I do not want to swear a lie."

"Had this killing of Anderson Brown excited some attention?"

"It did not with me, because we have heard rumors all about of this thing and that thing, in these excitable times here."

"Was that an event that made no impression on the community at all?"

"Really, I can't express the community's feelings; I can only express my own. It did not on mine. I did not know Anderson Brown; I never knew the Negro before. I did not know whether he was a Negro or a white man."

"Did you learn that he was killed by a tree falling on him, or by a gunshot?"

"I never heard. I heard the Ku-Klux killed him."

"Do you belong to any organization whose hailing sign is three taps on the left ear with the left hand?"

"I do not."

"And whose reply is the right hand in the pocket thrust out, with the left foot advanced?"

"That might be a Masonic sign or might not be."

"Do you belong to an organization whose hailing word is 'I s-a-y,' and the reply is 'N-o-t-h-i-n-g'?"

"I do not."

"Do you belong to any organization whose word of distress is 'Avalanche'?"

"I do not."

"Have you ever taken or administered this oath: 'I do solemnly swear that I will support and defend the "Invisible Circle"; that I will defend our families, our wives, our children, and brothers; that I will assist a brother in distress; that I will never reveal the secrets of this order, or anything in regard to it that may come to my knowledge; and if I do may I meet a traitor's doom, which is DEATH, DEATH, DEATH: So help me God, and so punish me, my brethren.' "

"I do not."

"Have you ever taken or administered that oath?"

"Not just as it is there."

"Have you ever taken an oath similar in form or substance to that?"

"That is a question I can't answer."

"Why not?"

"For this reason: The Masonic order I belong to. I have taken the obligation. There may be things almost similar to that."

"I am asking in reference to this organization, without regard to Masonry. When you answered that you did not take an oath exactly like that, did you mean similar in effect?"

"I will say outside of Masonry I did not. I did not say I did in Masonry, but outside of Masonry I did not."

"Have you no knowledge whatever of the existence, either in the persons or objects, of this organization, commonly known as Ku-Klux, let its real name be what it may?"

"I joined an order called Ku-Klux. I do not deny it."

"Who initiated you?"

"So help me God, I could not tell the man!"

"Do you know who he was?"

"I do not know who he was. Here is the point: I took an obligation then, which, of course—"

"We want to know what that obligation was."

"So help me God, I could not tell you! I was sworn to secrecy."

"What was its purport?"

"Its purport was, I know, opposition to the Union League and the Republican Party—to break up all the meetings of the Union League, if possible."

"Just a moment ago, you said you did not know, so help you God, who initiated you?"

"I said I did not know who gave the oath."

"Who was the chief of that Ku-Klux organization?"

"I do not think I can tell that."

"But we require an answer."

"I am sworn to secrecy."

"The Act of Congress which I will read to you, if necessary, does not relieve you from the duty of answering questions that may be necessary."

"Shall I violate an oath? The Order are played out. I do not know what it is called—whether it was Ku-Klux."

"You say you do not know whether it was called Ku-Klux or not?"

"He called it Ku-Klux, although in initiation I do not know what it was called. I could not swear."

"Who else was initiated with you?"

"There is another point where I am sworn to secrecy. I will tell you this much—nobody was initiated."

"How many persons were present?"

"I do not know, because the room was dark."

"What building in this town were you initiated in?"

"It was not in a building—it was in an old field here. I will tell you now it was in a building—I told a lie there. But I do not want to tell where it was. It played out."

"So much the easier to let us know all about it."

"But it is not in existence, and I do not know whether my obligation is stopped or not. Ben Briggs is the man who initiated me—it was in his house."

"Who is Benjamin Briggs?"

"He is our member of the state legislature."

"Was he the man you said a little while ago you did not know?"

"I told you I did not know who administered the oath, and I do not know."

"You say he initiated you?"

"I mean he persuaded me to go there. He came to me and said, 'It is a secret order got up here, and may be of service to you.'

"I said, 'Anything of service to me, I am with it.' He went on and explained, and talked to me and I went there."

"That one person did all the initiation?"

"Yes, sir. Mr. Briggs. He administered the oath."

"Did they tell you that Ku-Klux was the name of the organization?"

"Yes, sir."

"Do you know of any acts of violence committed by the organization?"

"I never heard of any. Major Briggs can tell."

"Is not the Ku-Klux which you were initiated into the same organization which has been riding in disguise and whipping people in this county for the past three years?"

"I do not know them to be."

"Did you see the men who were engaged in breaking into the county treasury that night?"

"I saw them passing on the street."

"Were they masked?"

"Yes, sir, their heads were covered."

"Did you go out on the street?"

"Yes, sir."

"Were you among them yourself at any time?"

"I was not."

"At first you declined to give the names of other persons who were initiated when you were. I return to that point. I want the names of all who were there."

"I don't know them. I never asked."

"You say now, that although initiated into the Ku-Klux three years ago, you have no knowledge of the Ku-Klux of this year in this county?"

"I do not believe it is the same thing."

"To what do you attribute the whippings of Negroes and Republicans?"

"I do not know and do not want to know anything about it. That is the whole truth of the matter."

"Do you deny that the Ku-Klux exists in this town?"

"I do not know anything about it—so help me God, I do not know!"

"No Desire to Hide Anything"

(Nathan Bedford Forrest, who had been a trader of horses, cattle, and slaves before the war, and who had been in command of the Confederate cavalry who carried out the Fort Pillow Massacre of 300 captured blacks, had been elected Imperial Wizard of the Ku-Klux Klan at its Nashville klovokation in the spring of 1867. He was one of the first witnesses to be heard by the Joint Committee, at a hearing held in Washington, D.C., on June 27, 1871. Even as he spoke, the hooded night riders who were sworn to obey his every order were on a bloody rampage all across the South—author.)

"We desire to ascertain the manner in which the laws are executed in the Southern States, and the security there enjoyed for person and property. So far as your observation enables you to speak, will you state what are the facts in this respect?"

"So far as I know, I have seen nothing that prevented the law from being executed. I am president of two railroads, mostly between Memphis, Tennessee, and Selma, Alabama, and have been very busy establishing factories and foundaries. I came out of the war pretty well wrecked. I went into the army worth a million and a half dollars, and came out a beggar. I have given all my time since then, so far as was in my power, to try to recover."

"Do you know anything of any combination of men for the purpose of preventing the execution of the law?"

"I do not."

"I have observed in one of the Western papers an account of an interview purporting to have been had with you in 1868, in which you are reported to have spoken of the organization of what was called the Ku-Klux . . . You recollect the article to which I refer?"

"Yes, sir."

"Upon what information did you make the statement in regard to the organization and constitution of the Ku-Klux?"

"Well, sir, the whole statement is wrong. The reporter did not give anything as it took place . . . It was reported that there was such an organization, but I knew nothing about its operations."

"Is the whole account of this interview a misrepresentation?"

"Not all of it. I was suffering very much with a headache at the time, and told him I could not talk to him. He asked me a few questions."

"Is this statement as reported in that interview correct: 'Can you or are you at liberty to give me the name of the commanding officer of this State?' 'No; it would be impolitic.'?"

"No, sir. I never made that statement."

"I will now ask if, at that time, you had any actual knowledge of the existence of any such order as the Ku-Klux?"

"I had, from information from others."

"Will you state who they were who gave you that information?"

"One of them was a gentleman by the name of Saunders. I heard others say so, but I do not recollect the names of them now."

"Under what name is it your belief it existed at that time?"

"Some called them Pale Faces; some called them Ku-Klux."

"What did you understand to be the purpose of the organization?"

"There were a great many Northern men coming down there, forming Leagues all over the country. The Negroes were holding night meetings; were going about; were becoming very insolent; and the Southern people were very much alarmed. Parties organized themselves so as to be ready in case they were attacked."

"Who were understood to belong to this Ku-Klux organization?"

"Men of the Southern states, citizens."

"Did they deny or admit its existence?"

"They did not do either."

"When they proceeded to carry out the objects of the organization, did they do it in numbers, by riding in bands?"

"I do not know. I never saw the organization together in my life . . . I understand that they patrolled communities, rode over neighborhoods."

"Had you ever seen a constitution of the Order?"

"I saw one, yes, sir."

"Who had it?"

"Well, it was sent to me in a letter."

"Have you that constitution yet?"

"No, sir."

"What has become of it?"

"Well, I burned up the one I had."

"Who sent it to you?"

"That I cannot tell."

"Did it come anonymously?"

"Yes, sir, it came to me anonymously."

"What was the name of the organization given in that constitution?"

"Ku-Klux."

"It was called Ku-Klux?"

"No, sir, it was not called Ku-Klux. I do not think there was any name given to it. As well as I recollect, there were three stars in place of a name."

"Signifying that the name was to be kept secret?"

"You are to place your own construction on that."

"Look at this, and say if it is a copy of the Prescript that you received . . ."

"I cannot say to you whether it is or not."

"Did you act upon that Prescript?"

"No, sir."

"Did you take any steps for organizing under it?"

"I do not think I am compelled to answer any question that would implicate me in anything. I believe the law does not require that I should do anything of the sort."

"Do you place your declination to answer upon that ground?"

"I do not."

"I only wish to know your reasons for declining to answer. I will communicate to you the fact that there is an Act of Congress which provides that such a reason shall not excuse a witness from answering. I will repeat the question: Did you take any steps for organizing an association or society under that Prescript?"

"I did not."

"Did you show it to anyone, read it to anyone, or allow anyone to read it?"

"I am not able to answer that question. I might have shown it and I might not have shown it. I do not recollect."

"Can you tell us any single member of that organization?"

"Well, that is a question I do not want to answer now."

"You decline to answer?"

"I would prefer to have a little time, if you will permit me."

"What is your reason for wanting time?"

"I want to study up and find out who they were, if I have got to answer the question."

"Do you know what any of their signs and passwords were?"

"I did know. You will have to let that pass over a little while, if it is necessary to answer it, for it is a matter that has gone out of my knowledge for eighteen months or two years."

"How did you get to know the sign?"

"It was given to me by one who, I suppose, was one of the members."

"Did he understand you to be one?"

"No, sir, not at that time."

"How came he to give it to you?"

"I asked him to give it to me in order that I might try and check the thing—I was trying to keep it down as much as possible."

"Did you want to suppress that organization?"

"Yes, sir. I did suppress it."

"How?"

"Had it broken up and disbanded. I talked with different people that I believed were connected with it, and urged its disbandment. I wrote a great many letters to people, and counseled them to abstain from all violence, and to be quiet and behave themselves, and let these things take their course."

"Did you get any answers to your letters?"

"To some of them I did."

"What did you do with them?"

"Perhaps I have some of those, but most of the letters I burned up, for I did not want to get them into trouble."

"How came these people to write to you?"

"I do not know—I suppose they thought I was a man who would do to counsel with."

"Against whom did this organization operate?"

"I do not think it operated against any person particularly. I think it was, as I said before, an organization for the protection of Southern people against mobs, and rapes, and things of that sort. I never knew any portion of the organization to commit any deed."

"Did you never understand that they went out and took persons from their homes and whipped them?"

"That was the newspaper rumor."

"During the last year or two has there been any serious trouble among the people, white or black, along your line of railroad?"

"I have heard of but three cases. One is where they took out a man who had been arrested and put in jail for stealing horses. Another was at Greensboro in regard to the probate judge. I understand these men came to his house; in fact, Judge Blackford came to me for protection, and I did protect him for a week."

"How long ago?"

"I suppose five or six months ago."

"What was the pretext for annoying him?"

"He was looked upon as a man who had given a great deal of bad advice to the Negroes, and kept them in confusion, and off the plantations. He was a Southern man, who had been in the Confederate Army, and had gone over to the Radical Party. He had large meetings of the Negroes at his house . . . and it had become very dissatisfactory to the people."

"In the course of your experience have you heard of a man being molested for his political opinions upon one side or the other?"

"This man Blackford I suppose was molested because he was thought to be tampering with the Negroes and preventing them from working."

"Had Blackford advised violence?"

"It was a rumor through the town that he had been talking with the Negroes."

"Had he been advising violence?"

"I heard him once advise violence . . . I do not recollect exactly his words, but it was something about fighting their own way, and if people did not let them have it, make them do it, stand up to them. It was very offensive."

"There has been some intimation in the testimony about your railroad being used to carry men in disguise. Has there been anything of that sort done on your road with your knowledge or consent?"

"I am satisfied there has been nothing of that sort done."

"I have before me a communication published in a paper called the *Southern Argus* at Selma, Alabama, February 3, 1871. I will read it:

The Late Greensboro Affair

Sir, I see from your article in your last issue that you accuse a body of disguised men of going to Greensboro, and releasing a man from the jail of that place who had been confined for horse stealing. We inform you, sir, that your author has told a malicious falsehood. The man who was released on that evening was not confined for horse stealing, but for killing a Negro and the taking of a Yankee's horse, openly, that it might enable him to make his escape from a court (like Blackford's) of injustice; and we say to you, sir, that the party did not visit Greensboro for the purpose of releasing this man Mc-Crary, but for the purpose or catching and giving Mr. Blackford what he lawfully deserves, and will get before the 1st day of March.

We do not communicate to you for the purpose of clearing ourselves of but one thing, and that is the release of a horsethief. Sir, it is not our object to release thieves; but, on the other hand, it is our sworn duty to bring them all to justice; and we in this section of country intend and will see that all thieves shall be punished to the extent of the law; and in cases where the law cannot reach them, the party that released the man in Greensboro will give them all they deserve, and perhaps a little more.

Yours truly,
Knights of the White Camelia

P.S.—The writer is a subscriber to your paper, and would be pleased to see this and an additional article by you in your next issue.—K

"Do you think that the sentiment contained in that article—that killing a Negro is a less offense than stealing a horse—is countenanced by the community?"

"No, sir, there is no man who believes that the offense of killing a Negro is less than killing a white man."

"Did you say that you believed the Ku-Klux was organized only in middle Tennessee?"

"No, sir. I remarked that I thought it originated there. I have no idea what place, or who started it."

"Have you never heard?"

"It has been said I organized it—that I started it."

"Is that so?"

"No, sir, it is not."

"You do not know who did?"

"It was afterward said that it was gotten up at Johnson's Island when there were Rebel prisoners there. But nobody knows, I reckon, where it was started."

"Did not the Ku-Klux admit young boys?"

"I think not. My information was that they admitted no man who was not a gentleman, and a man who could be relied upon to act discreetly; not in the habit of drinking, boisterous men, or men liable to commit error or wrong, or anything of that sort."

"Did you ever hear of the Knights of the White Camelia?"

"Yes, they were reported to be there."

"Were you ever a member of that Order?"

"I was."

"You were a member of the Knights of the White Camelia?"

"No, sir, I never was a member of the Knights of the White Camelia."

"What order was it that you were a member of?"

"An order called the Pale Faces—a different order from that."

"Where and when did you join it?"

"In Memphis. It was in 1867, but that was a different order from this."

"What was that?"

"Something like Odd Fellowship, Masonry, orders of that sort, for the protection of the weak, defenseless, etc."

"Something on the same principles that the Ku-Klux afterward had?"

"Something similar to that, only it was a different order."

"Who invited you to join?"

"Some of the members."

"Who were they?"

"I cannot tell you now."

"Why not?"

"I do not recollect."

"Where did they meet?"

"In a hall or room."

"In Memphis?"

"Yes, sir."

"Where in Memphis?"

"Well, I do not recollect that now."

"Do you remember who were present?"

"I do not remember. I might, if I had time to think the matter over, recollect these things."

"So far as you know, these Pale Faces were the best class of Southern citizen?"

"I do not know whether you might term them the best class or not."

"Let us have your understanding of it—were they men of substance and property?"

"My understanding is that those men were young men mostly; men who had been in the Southern Army, and men who could be relied upon in case of a difficulty."

"Were they men of sufficient substance and means to go about from one place to another?"

"Well, they were in the habit of going almost everywhere and anytime without much assistance."

"You desired time to consider whether you would give us the names of those persons whose names were asked of you. Who are they?"

"One was named Jones. I am trying to think who the other was; I cannot call his name to mind now."

"Are those all the names you wish to give or can give?"

"I might give you more names if I had time to think about the thing. I am disposed to do all I can to try to fetch these troubles to an end. I have no desire to hide anything from you at all."

(Upon emerging from the hearing, Forrest was asked by waiting journalists how it had gone.

"I lied like a gentleman!" he replied with a wink.)

THE SECOND SECESSION

✠

CHAPTER 10

✠

After taking thirteen volumes of such testimony, the joint committee in the spring of 1872 reported to Congress[1] that it had found "revolutionary conditions" as the result of "a Southern conspiracy against Constitutional law and the Negro race."

"The Ku Klux Klan does exist, and it has a political purpose which it seeks to carry out by murders, whippings, intimidation, and violence," the report of the majority concluded, going on to say that "the evidence was decisive that redress cannot be obtained against those who commit crimes in disguise and at night."

While noting that there had been some diminution of Klan activity as a result of the Ku Klux Act, the committee cautioned: "This should not lead to a conclusion that communities would be safe if protective measures were withdrawn. These should be continued until there remains no further doubt of the actual suppression and disarming of this widespread and dangerous conspiracy."

Declaring that suspension of habeas corpus in South Carolina had proven to be "the most and perhaps only effective" means for the Klan's suppression, the committee recommended that the president's emergency powers in this regard be extended by Congress. It further recommended that additional federal judges be temporarily appointed in the Southern states in order to "secure speedy and certain justice" and "leave no hope of impunity to criminals by the law's delay."

Although acknowledging that not even apologists for the Klan had attributed its existence to the continued disfranchisement of some Confederate soldiers, the committee went out of its way to recommend that Congress fully restore their rights to vote and hold office. Not content with this and the willingness of the committee majority to take and report testimony to the effect that the Klan was a necessary means of combatting alleged "bad legislation, official incompetency, and corruption," a Democratic minority on the committee submitted a separate report declaring that the accounts of Klan terrorism had been "grossly and willfully exaggerated."

The minority *Report* was authored in the main by Philadelphia Van Trump, Democratic congressman from Ohio. In it, he characterized the 167 black witnesses as having "the most forbidding personal appearance" and displaying "the very lowest grade of intelligence belonging to human beings." Little would be lost, the Congressman declared, if their testimony were to be thrown out in its entirety.

Nor was Trump any more favorably impressed by the Southern and Northern whites who had been victimized by the Klan. To him they were the "malicious scalawag" and "venal carpetbagger," describing the latter as a "demon of discord and anarchy, his infernal schemes and intrigues with the negroes have thrown a whole people into utter and hopeless despair."[2]

Although 1872 was a presidential election year, no one was inclined to use the *Report* on the "Condition of Affairs" as a campaign piece. There was, as has been noted, a systematic campaign not just to cover up but to physically wipe out the *Report* and its thirteen volumes of testimony.

In the fall of 1871, while the committee was still taking testimony, Sumner had made a last desperate appeal to the Senate, introducing a far-reaching civil rights bill that not only would have covered the political rights of blacks but also would have specifically assured access to jury boxes and places of public accommodation, including churches and cemeteries.[3] In the hope of making black rights more acceptable, Sumner included restoration of all rights of former Confederates. The bill failed by one vote.

In the spring of 1872, after the "Condition of Affairs" report was in, Sumner reintroduced the measure.

"I appeal for the sake of peace, so that at last there shall be an end to slavery, and the rights of citizens shall be everywhere under the equal safeguard of the national law," he said. "Humbly do I pray that the Republic may not lose this great prize, nor postpone its enjoyment."

But while Sumner was thus pleading and praying, the banking and railroad magnate Henry Cooke was writing "friends" in Washington: "You know how I have felt for a long time in regard to . . . the ultra-infidelic radicals like Sumner, Ben Wade, Stevens. They are dragging the Republican Party into all sorts of isms and extremes . . . These reckless demagogues have had their day and the time has come for wiser counsel."[4]

Wiser or not, the Congress chose to postpone equality by voting to restore the political rights of former Confederates but refusing to do anything more in support of political and civil rights for blacks. "You must be just to the colored man before you are generous to former rebels," Sumner said sadly, but to no avail.

By its action the Congress threw the weight of all former Confederates into the scales on the side of white supremacy, and, in a separate move that virtually abolished the Freedmen's Bureau, deprived Southern blacks of that modicum of freedom from economic sanctions that the bureau had afforded. As if all this were not enough, a bipartisan agreement (presaging the Deal of '76) was reached, to the effect that the Enforcement Act against the Klan "could not" be enforced.[5] In such manner the stage for the election of 1872 was set.

By this time Republicans across the nation had gravitated into three camps: conservatives loyal to Grant; those who styled themselves "liberal" or "reform" and followed the lead of such men as Carl Schurz and Rutherford B. Hayes; and the remaining "radicals" who stood beneath the equal rights banner held aloft by Sumner.

A bit of a split in Republican ranks had already emerged in 1870, over a difference of opinion as to tactics to be followed in Missouri. But now in the spring of 1872 the "reform/liberals" decided to stage a convention of their own. Held in Cincinnati, it nominated for the presidency of the United States none other than Horace Greeley—he who had unwittingly achieved immortality by his urging "Go West, young man, go West!" Now he was urging capital to go South, and Northern troops to go back where they came from. Although Greeley played liberal to the extent of urging votes for blacks as well as rebels, he had this advice for blacks, which he addressed to them through the pages of the New York Tribune. "Be realistic. Political equality is far off. Social equality will remain forever out of reach. Don't expect free gifts of land. Segregate yourselves; employ each other. Who are your best friends?—Sound, conservative, knowing white Southerners."⁶

In June the rest of the Republicans convened in Philadelphia, where they acted as though no rump Republican convention had taken place, and proceeded to nominate Grant for a second term. The Democrats met in July—and endorsed Greeley and his platform as their very own! The coalition of racist Republicans and Democrats that Andy Johnson had sought in vain to bring together under his "National Union" banner in 1866 was at last a reality.

On the national level the center had shifted so far to the right that equal rights advocates felt they had no champion. When word got out that Sumner had taken the floor in the Senate to berate Grant for his conservatism, multitudes flocked to witness the phenomenon. As the presidential contest unfolded, supporters of Greeley were to quote Sumner's words as if to prove that no one liked Grant, while Grant supporters used the same castigations to prove how nice and conservative Grant was.

The election of 1872 was ostensibly not a referendum on the question "Shall the United States of America be an apartheid nation?" but in reality it was precisely that. Moreover, on the presidential level there was no way for voters to register a clear-cut "no."

If there was bitter irony in Sumner's feeling obliged to cross swords with the Great Liberator, Ulysses S. Grant, there was still more in the spectacle of men who called themselves "liberal Republicans" flying the flag of states' rights and racial segregation and racist Democrats rushing to join them. The nifty thing about this amalgam for all concerned was that it was somewhat difficult to determine who was capitulating to whom. The label on the candidate and the platform read "Republican," but the contents were purely Democratic. They all called it "national reconciliation," but in reality it was the North being reconciled to the South, not vice versa, nor each to the other. As for America's blacks, North as well as South, this reconciliation between American whites left them no choice but to sweat it out or die. Nobody had even asked them about any reconciliation. They had long since reconciled themselves to Ole Massa's being a congenital fiend; the only trouble was, he refused to be reconciled to their humanity, much less citizenship.

In the South as in the North, the Greeley ticket and platform were not without supporters who defected from Republican ranks. These gentry were of course Pale Faces, in the main men of some substance who before the war had voted as Whigs. A good many had opposed slavery and/or secession and had thus come to be regarded as Unionists. As such, they had gravitated into leadership roles in the Republican Party, where they felt a certain moral obligation to go along with the Reconstruction program of political rights for blacks. Many had felt uncomfortable about the social relations with blacks that this often entailed, and when their brethren in the Democratic Party intensified their appeal for racial solidarity, they responded to the call. In doing so, however, they seldom conceded that their defection was based upon race, attributing it instead to some moral motive, such as disaffection with the fraud alleged to be found in Republican ranks.

What the South had which the North lacked, however, was a mass of black voters who, despite the holocaust unleashed against them, stood steadfast for equal rights and the only presidential candidate who offered any hope for attaining them, Grant. The problem confronting white supremacists, therefore, was, as usual, one of keeping blacks from voting and equal-rights advocates from running or, if elected, from serving. In the hope of accomplishing these things the usual methods were employed, with the usual results.

Congress had long since ceased to be a seat of power to which victims of the terror could address appeals for help with any hope of being answered. In the breach, petitioners had addressed themselves to the national Republican Party, as if it were able and willing to do something. But now, presaging the soft peace (hard on blacks) which was to come in 1876, the national leadership of the party curtsied to the states' rights/ home rule posture of the Greeleyites. Chairman William E. Chandler went so far as to let it be known that the GOP high command was primarily interested in garnering electoral votes for Grant, and did not much care what happened on the local and state levels down South.[7] Southern blacks, and what remained of their white allies, were pretty much on their own.

Even so, some letters were written. One, from a white Republican in Greensboro, North Carolina, offered this analysis and prognostication: "The old aristocracy and slave owners of the South are sore-headed . . . Their hostility to the Republican Party and their hatred of the U.S. Government drove them into the Ku Klux organization. They hoped that by means of that wicked order they would get undisputed control of the South, and with the assistance of Tammany they would walk into the White House in 1873."[8]

The campaign proved to be a replay of past performances staged by the white supremacists. In South Carolina, for example, when Republican Governor Daniel H. Chamberlain addressed a rally in Barnwell County it was broken up by a band of six hundred of Wade Hampton's mounted Red Shirt terrorists, who emitted rebel yells as they charged the crowd, denounced the governor as a "carrion crow," and urged his hanging then and there.[9] In Mississippi, Republican state Senator Charles Caldwell was assassinated by a fusillade so massive that his body was "grotesquely turned completely over by the impact of innumerable shots at close range."[10]

One of the few innovations in disfranchisement to appear during the campaign was the introduction by Georgia of a poll tax as a prerequisite to voting. (This device, eventually adopted Southwide, was destined to be a cornerstone of the white rule of the region and the South's rule of the nation, which was to prevail for three-quarters of a century.)

As seen from the other side of the fence, the *New York Tribune*, backing Greeley, declared: "Had it not been for carpetbag mismanagement, this country [the South] today would be filled with millions of Northern and foreign yeomanry carving out farms, or working in . . . iron, copper, coal and marble."[11]

As the election drew near, the South's white supremacists, elated at having won over a segment of the Republican Party and Northern voters, once again raised the old bugaboo that if they did not get their way they might again resort to civil war. (Latter-day attempts to whitewash the white terror—as exemplified by Dunning disciples J. G. Randall and David Donald[12]—would have us believe that "Ku Klux Klan prosecutions were pushed in the South to discourage Democrats that might put too much pressure on Negroes; and the colored vote was rounded up by the Union Leagues." The truth of course was that the Congress had seen fit to carry out that portion of the recommendations of its joint committee that called for restoring the political rights of ex-Confederates, and voting down those portions that called for an extension of presidential emergency powers and the sending of more federal judges into the region.)

Mockery, not democracy, was the keynote on election day.

"To say that the election was a farce fails to express the truth; it was a mob, controlled by the Democratic bullies, and ended in *crime*," is the way one Georgia Republican described it in a letter to national secretary Chandler.[13]

Another report from Georgia described the scene in similar terms: "Never since the formation of this government was there a more shameful outrage upon free suffrage than the one just perpetrated in Georgia in the name of democracy. The colored men were intimidated and driven away from the polls by the hundred-and-one devices of the Democrats, and where words would not do, bloody deeds soon taught the negroes that to vote against the wishes of their white employers and neighbors was to risk death."[14]

In spite of everything, many Southern blacks went to the polls and voted. A white observer in Tallahassee, Florida, was moved to describe their fortitude in these terms: "The opposition may talk of the 'everlasting nigger', but it is beginning to learn that it has in the black man a foe whose opinions are born of honesty and whose native instincts assisted by six years' education in the exercise of the suffrage, and his naturally Christian heart, make him at this time their most formidable enemy, and the finest and most progressive friend of the Republican Party."[15]

Owing in good measure to the courage of black voters, and a boycott of the election by many Northern Democrats who did not share Greeley's proverbial views, the coalition candidate carried only six states—Texas, Louisiana, Tennessee, Maryland, Kentucky, and Missouri—and died before the electoral votes were counted. But in terms of capturing control of local and state governments in the South, white supremacy scored major victories. In the manner aforesaid, racists regained control of Georgia, ending two years of a Republican majority in the legislature. Texas, Tennessee, Maryland, Kentucky, and Missouri were also taken over by the forces of the neo-Confederacy.

Despite the rising tide of white supremacy that threatened to engulf the entire South, some redoubts of republican government managed to survive the election of 1872. In no less than three states, both camps claimed victory, resulting in the spectacle of two-headed states for a time.

Perhaps the most chaotic of these was Louisiana. Henry Clay Warmouth, though governor of the state by the grace of black votes, was wont to boast that he had not a drop of Northern blood in his veins, and that some of his best friends were big planters. On the occasion of the rump "reform" Republican convention in Cincinnati, Warmouth had arrived with a coterie of 125 delegates. Though somewhat embarrassed by the support of someone with Warmouth's clouded reputation, the reformers were persuaded to bend their principles when Warmouth assured them he could deliver Louisiana's electoral votes.[16]

Back home, Warmouth's black lieutenant governor, onetime slave Oscar Dunn, was acting as governor and warning his constituents that Warmouth was off on a mission "to sell us out to the Democrats, and we must nip it in the bud." About this time a congressional investigating committee turned in a report highly critical of Warmouth's wheeling and dealing. Impeachment was threatened, but upon his return to the state Warmouth succeeded in killing all of Dunn's initiatives, and soon after Dunn himself was dead—some said through foul play.[17]

Louisiana Democrats nominated as their gubernatorial candidate the former Confederate General John McEnery, in whose parish the most devastating of the "Negro hunts" had occurred. After trying in vain to bring about a fusion ticket between Greeley Republicans and the Democrats (to be headed by McEnery), Warmouth went all the way and backed McEnery on the all-out racist Democratic platform. On election day voters had a choice among McEnery, a Greeley Republican slate, a Grant Republican slate, and still another Republican ticket headed by Confederate General P. G. T. Beauregard, campaigning on a platform of "Justice to all races, creeds and political opinions, and full equality in all public places, vehicles and schools."[18]

Though duly flabbergasted by such words coming from such a source, Louisiana blacks opted to stand firm for the Grant Republican ticket, headed by W. P. Kellogg (who had come from outside the state) and his black running mate, C. C. Antoine. Kellogg was elected, and made ready to occupy the statehouse, only to be barred by Warmouth who was reported to be keeping the gubernatorial seat warm for McEnery—by some means of ascension not specified. In December Warmouth was impeached, and for forty-three days Louisiana had a black acting governor, Pinckney Pinchback, who had succeeded the deceased Oscar Dunn. During the Pinchback interregnum antiblack massacres erupted in New Orleans and elsewhere in the state, and when proposals were made to arm blacks for self-defense, shudders of horror were said to engulf not only the white South but the white North as well (presumably the slaughter of innocent and unarmed blacks was less horrifying).[19]

Eventually a canvasing board confirmed Kellogg's victory, and he proceeded to occupy the governor's mansion, only to be forcibly evicted by troopers from General McEnery's private army. President Grant had previously urged Congress to send more U.S. forces into Louisiana to maintain law and order, and, when Congress declined the honor, he sent them in himself. Now these troops were thrown into action, and Kellogg was reinstated.

In his inaugural address of March 4, 1873, Grant exulted that peace prevailed throughout the nation. Even as he spoke, however, Governor Kellogg had again been forcibly evicted and there was fighting in the streets of New Orleans. Again U.S. troops were called into action and

Kellogg was seated for the third time. McEnery, upon being ushered out, declared matter-of-factly: "We shall carry the next election if we have to ride saddle-deep in blood to do it."[20]

Although this time Kellogg managed to hold on, Louisiana was far from being pacified. On Easter Sunday, blacks who had barricaded themselves into the Colfax courthouse for protection were cannonaded out by racist forces. Sixty-one blacks were cut down by artillery fire, and thirty-seven more were captured and executed.[21] When some little effort was made to prosecute those who were responsible for the massacre, the "conservative" press of the state insisted that the blacks had only gotten what was coming to them.

A rather similar chain of events had unfolded in neighboring Alabama. There black votes gave the election victory to the Grant slate, but white supremacists, undaunted, forcibly took possession of the state house, obliging the Republicans to try to run the state from the U.S. courthouse. Congress turned a deaf ear to appeals for help, leaving it to Grant to intervene. Under a compromise worked out under his auspices, a division of power was agreed upon, conceding the gubernatorial victory to the Republicans but surrendering many another state office to champions of white rule.

A third two-headed state for a time was Arkansas, where the fused Democrats and Greeley Republicans mounted an armed challenge to the victorious Grant slate. Although both groups called themselves Republican, the Greeley camp was almost entirely white, and the Grant camp almost entirely black. One group held the statehouse; the other operated from the railroad station. Pitched battles between the rival "Republicans" took place in Little Rock, tearing up the capital's streets. In Helena and Austin, armed blacks fought off attempts by whites to forcibly oust their elected officials. (It was not quite the civil war that had been promised, but it came close. Dual administrations persisted in Arkansas until 1874, when the regular Republican victory was finally confirmed. The "victory" was short-lived, however, for the forces of white rule made a clean sweep in Arkansas's state elections that same year.)

In Texas the terrorists were able to bar enough blacks from the polls to make possible a Democratic victory on paper. The incumbent Republican regime, backed by black militiamen, refused to surrender the statehouse and appealed to Washington for help. In this situation not even Grant was willing to "go behind the returns" and take into account the forcible disfranchisement, and Texas was returned to white rule.

The election of 1872 marked the first participation of recalcitrant Vir-

Black Louisianians gathering their dead and wounded after the Colfax massacre (*Harper's Weekly*, May 10, 1873).

ginia since before the war. Abjuring a candidate of their own, the state's Democrats backed the "reform" Republican gubernatorial candidate Gilbert C. Walker, a former Northern Democrat. Walker won, and Virginia was also returned to white rule.

But while the abandonment and betrayal of republican government resulted in a widespread restoration of white power over much of the South in 1872, some formidable redoubts remained, and black determination to exercise the rights of citizenship continued strong. Besides holding on in Louisiana and Florida, republican government persisted also in South Carolina, where, despite some inroads by the fusionist forces, four of the state's five congressmen following the election were black. In Mississippi—the other state with a major black majority in the population—black leadership and discipline produced black sheriffs, magistrates, and other county officials throughout much of the Black Belt.[22] Thanks to black support, the gubernatorial victory went to the regular Republican Adelbert Ames, despite Democratic support for the "reform" Republican James L. Alcorn. So pervasive was black power in the state by this time that blacks also served on juries in Black Belt counties, moving one white editor to lament: "Nine out of ten who sit on the juries

Blacks hiding in the Louisiana swamps to escape the perpetrators of the Colfax massacre (*Harper's Weekly,* May 10, 1873).

are ignorant, without property, and yet are permitted to judge what is best for the interest of property holders."[23]

By innumerable acts of omission and commission, the United States government had permitted unfree elections in the Southern states, knowing full well that the outcome would be white rule. Having once embarked upon this course, it was really too much to expect Uncle Sam to about-face and set aside the "results" of those unfree elections.

When it was all over, only the South's blacks were still manning the ramparts of equal rights, free elections, and republican government. The Congress, architect of the Reconstruction, which had been dedicated to all these things, had surrendered. The Supreme Court, ordained defender of the Constitution, had deliberately rendered integral portions of it dead letters. The Republican Party, the party of emancipation, had rededicated itself to economic expansion at any cost. And Grant, that hero of Appomattox—without party, Congress, or court to back him—must have wondered what the war had been about.

On the whole, that which took place in 1872 amounted to nothing less than a second secession.

To be sure, there was no firing upon a federal military installation, as at Fort Sumter. Johnny Reb did not quite make good his threat of a resumption of the Civil War, but his massive armed defiance of federal authority enabled him to seize effective control over much of the region—and to get his big foot in the door of the rest.

And while there was no adoption of Articles of Secession by any state legislature, countless declarations of independence served unmistakable notice that the white South did not intend to be bound by anything in the Constitution or laws of the United States so far as black rights were concerned.

Thus, while the first secession had been formal and total, and the second informal and partial, it was the latter and not the former which achieved the basic goal of both: the continued subjugation and exploitation of blacks.

Moreover, while the first had been fleeting, lasting a scant four years, the second was to prove to be long-lasting, enduring for nearly a century. And whereas the first had given rise to the short-lived Confederate States of America having but regional jurisdiction, the second represented an imposition of the white Southern will upon the entire nation. It put Ole Massa back in the saddle, not only in his own stomping ground, but in the halls of Congress and electoral college as well.

It would remain for the Deal of '76 to finalize the Rout of '72, but the racist configuration of America's future could be clearly seen.

Appomattox was well on its way to being reversed.

RETREAT AND PANIC

✠

CHAPTER II

✠

And so Grant, with a new four-year lease on the White House, stayed on.

As he took the oath of office for his second term, an aura of seeming prosperity pervaded the land, and there was much talk of finally pacifying the (white) South and getting on with the business of the expanding and developing nation. But before the year was out, both of these bubbles had burst.

In what would later be referred to as the "Retreat of '73," pacification proceeded to take the form of a general abandonment of the national commitment to free elections, republican government, and equal rights in the South, and a resultant drift toward becoming an integrally racist apartheid nation. Then, hard upon the heels of the Retreat, there came an economic crash, the Panic of '73. In short, Grant's second term was marred at the outset by two national catastrophes, the one moral/political and the other economic/social. Together, the Retreat and Panic of '73 helped pave the way to the Deal of '76.

The Retreat was well under way on all fronts—legislative, executive, judicial—before the Panic burst upon the scene. On the face of things, the election of '72 had chalked up some black gains. The lust for citizenship that enabled so many Southern blacks to cast ballots while look-ing down the barrels of cocked guns sent six new black congressmen to Washington.

Among them was Pinckney Pinchback of Louisiana, bearing impec-cable credentials as having been elected to serve in both the House and Senate simultaneously. Debate over where to seat him raged through three months and a special session of Congress.[1] Some said the contro-versy had to do not so much with credentials as with a reluctance on the part of other senators' wives to entertain Mrs. Pinchback. Be that as it may, the *New York Commercial Advertiser* was moved to observe that Pinchback was "the best-dressed Southern man we have had in Congress since the days when gentlemen were Democrats."[2]

But while the election of 1872 put more black faces into the Forty-third Congress than there had been in its predecessor, it also sent up more ex-Confederates than had been seen on the Hill since the lily-white Johnson restoration immediately after Appomattox. In the new senate, the bipartisan camp favoring "Home [white] Rule" for the South was able to claim a substantial majority, consisting of 88 Democrats and 5 "Reform" Republicans—and no one knew how many of the remaining 49 "Regular" Republicans were leaning in that direction. In the House, 195 Regular Republicans still nominally constituted a majority, but the opposition had swelled to 88 Democrats, plus 4 Reform Republicans.

Business interests—as ever the power behind the throne—were keep-ing a sharp eye on the changes that were taking place and let it be known that they were willing—nay, eager— to do business with anyone in a po-sition to do business, regardless of race, creed, political persuasion, or pre-vious condition of rebelhood.[3] Since the traditional proprietary class had regained title to the natural resources of the South and were fast getting their hands back upon the levers of political power as well, Northern cap-ital had far more to gain by cultivating them than the poor but honest black politicos.

Ole Massa was not only in a position to deliver the goods for such ex-tractive industries as timber and mining; in more and more Southern ju-risdictions it was he who was in a position to grant the necessary fran-chises and other inducements that the public sector had to offer. To such men, therefore, the paramount issue of the times was not whether or not blacks would be able to get at ballot boxes, but whether, for example, Democratic financier August Belmont and his Louisville and Nashville Railroad, through its subsidiary North and South Line, would get the franchise to tap the ore fields around Birmingham—or would the prize go to Republican financier Jay Cooke and his Alabama and Chattanooga Railroad?[4] The only implication such titanic struggles as this had for Southern blacks was "Who would provide the tracks they would be compelled to live on the other side of?"

It would appear to be axiomatic that, throughout human history, political power sooner or later follows economic power, and the postwar South was proving to be no exception. What the Retreat of '73 really meant was that democracy in the South was being systematically destabilized and displaced by the traditional white oligarchy. Needless to say, those who were engaged in the process did not speak of it in those terms; rather, the rape of republican government was carried out under the cloak of moral duty. This is how those latter-day apologists for the rapists, J. G. Randall and David Donald, put it: "Powerful Northern economic interests also turned against the carpetbag regimes. New York businessmen, never enthusiastic about the Radical program, came to view the continuation of the corrupt Republican Administration, together with its Southern supporters, as more dangerous than a return of the Democrats to power."[5]

Then (as now) all that was necessary to get people to kill their fellow man was to mutter a few imprecations such as "corrupt," "radical," and "carpetbagger." What few objective studies have been made have been unanimous in concluding that graft and corruption at the time knew no sectional, racial, or partisan boundaries, and that the blacks in public office were, if anything, less given to corruption than their white detractors. This individual integrity was coupled with a sense of responsibility in carrying out the public trust, which manifested itself in conservative handling of fiscal affairs. It was not really the corruptibility, but the incorruptibility, of the "radical" regimes that bothered the "reformers" and "redeemers," and made their efforts at discrediting and destabilizing so frustrating. The verities of the situation were frankly stated in 1873 in the *Floridian*: "No greater calamity could befall the State of Florida while under the rule of its present officials than to be placed in good financial credit. Our only hope is the State's utter financial bankruptcy, and Heaven grant that may speedily come!"[6]

It is of utmost significance that what little money Congress provided for the prevention of the subversion of free elections in the South by Klan terror was diverted to cope with the threat posed by big-city machines to honest elections in the North.[7] In an America caught up in the throes of "redemption," almost everyone it seemed (except blacks) was agreed that political machines based upon graft had to go and political machines based upon racist terror were quite all right. That is to say, it was all wrong for Northern political bosses to fleece Northern whites but all right for Southern bosses to fleece Southern blacks.

With big business embarked upon a course of "business as usual" with the title holders of the South, and the nation's press assiduously cultivating the public mind to go along, it was becoming progressively easier to sell capitulation under the false label of reconciliation. In keeping with this vogue, all sorts of strange things began to happen. The Klan's Imperial Wizard Forrest, for example, saw fit to issue his proclamation: "The Invisible Empire has accomplished the purpose for which it was organized . . . Therefore the grand Wizard, being vested with power to determine questions of paramount importance, now declares the Invisible Empire and all subdivisions thereof dissolved and disbanded forever."

According to the book *KKK*, by C. Winfield Jones—which bears the imprimatur of the Klan—"some of the klans obeyed this proclamation and some did not." At the time of the purported dissolution, some said that the wizard never intended for that to take place, that he was merely trying to cover his tracks in the event that the Klan leadership was to be prosecuted by the federal authorities. In any event, there was no abatement of the terror, which went on by day and by night, in robe and out.[8]

Although the terms were not in popular usage in this country at that time, *detente* and *rapprochement* between North and South continued apace. Within the South, moreover, some little effort was made, once again, to achieve a reconciliation between whites and blacks. But just as reconciliation within the nation meant the capitulation of North to South, reconciliation within the South would have entailed the capitulation of blacks to whites—and blacks were still far from being reconciled to any such fate. Oldtime Southern Whigs were in the forefront of this proffer of a crown of thorns disguised as an olive branch, which came to be known as the Unification Movement.

Only in New Orleans did this movement strike a genuine note of conciliation. There, Confederate General Beauregard, joined by such men as James L. Day, president of the Sun Mutual Insurance Company; Auguste Bohn, president of the Mechanics and Traders Bank; and Isaac M. Marks, president of the Firemen's Charitable Association, made the remarkable pledge: "That we shall maintain and advocate the right of every citizen of Louisiana . . . to frequent at will all places of public resort, and to travel at will on all vehicles of public conveyance, upon terms of perfect equality."[9]

The Unification Movement foundered in Louisiana upon the shoals of white trepidation that nonsegregation would lead to "social equality," and elsewhere in the South, where it made no such pledge of equal treatment, it ran afoul of black unwillingness to accept anything less.

"Reconciliation" was not the only ploy of all those who had a stake in consummating a peace that would be soft on Southern whites and hard on Southern blacks: they also tried diversion. Something new in "irrepressible conflicts" had emerged on the national scene, and these same people sought to make the most of it. It being bruted about that the North/South conflict had been resolved at Appomattox, the nation was increasingly turning its attention to an East/West conflict of interest. That this served the diversionary purposes of the white South very nicely was evidenced by such editorials as the following from the *Petersburg* (Va.) *Express*: "Between these two great sections there can be no congeniality. On the antagonism to slavery they were able to make a show of harmony. The link is now broken. New issues . . . begin to assert themselves. Finance, taxation, the tariff—all suggest issues to the Western states. There is an irrepressible conflict between the two sections—the bondholder of the East, and the taxpayer in the West."[10]

The currents plunging headlong toward the dead sea of a spurious reconciliation did not stop at the White House doors. The man inside had chosen for his attorney general during his second term of office one Edwards Pierrepont, a New Yorker who had been a Democrat before switching his party allegiance in 1868. Pierrepont's chief claim to fame appears to have been his heading of a two-man commission that had freed hundreds of Northern men Lincoln had jailed for obstructing the war effort. After the war he had been an outspoken critic of Reconstruction. With such a man as the chief law enforcement officer of the land, it was hardly surprising that under him the trend became one of nonenforcement of black rights. The days when federal courts had indicted hundreds and convicted eighty-two Klan terrorists in South Carolina (1871–72) were gone forever.

Grant's appointments to the judiciary were as disastrous to human rights as those in the realm of law enforcement. When he first took office the number of Supreme Court justices had been increased from seven to nine. His appointees included attorneys William Strong of Pennsylvania, Ward Hunt of New York, and Joseph P. Bradley of New Jersey. The latter was said to be "owned" by Tom Scott, promoter of the Texas and Pacific Railroad project.[11] None were calculated to make the Supreme Court a bulwark of constitutional rights.

It was this Court that in 1873 did its bit to make the South safe for white oligarchy by handing down a decision that went a long way toward vindicating the hope which Confederates, even in the ashes of defeat at Appomattox, had placed in it. Although the Court did not go so far, in the tradition of its prewar Dred Scott decision, as to reaffirm a right of white Southerners to "buy and sell niggers," it did send white Southerners a signal that they were free to do just about anything else they pleased with them.

The occasion seized upon for this virtual reversal of Appomattox ostensibly had nothing whatever to do with blacks (thus conveniently shielding the justices from any charge of racism). Known as the Slaughterhouse cases,[12] up from Louisiana, the question posed was whether that state, by creating a closed monopoly in the butchering trade, was infringing upon a constitutional right of would-be butchers to engage in a legitimate occupation.

Written by Justice Samuel F. Miller, and handed down while Salmon P. Chase was chief justice, the Slaughterhouse decision held that certain basic rights "belong to citizens of states as such . . . [and] are left to the state governments for security and protection, and not placed under the special care of the Federal Government." What went unsaid, of course, was the fact that the state governments that were thus being called upon to protect black rights were, or soon would be, lily-white.

To the legalistically astute promulgators of white rule, the Slaughterhouse decision seemed to have possibilities for perversion to their cause. If, as Slaughterhouse affirmed, it was the exclusive prerogative of the states to set the standards for such "basic rights" as to who could and could not be butchers, why then should it not be left up to the states to say who could and could not vote? The reasons why the states could not were obvious enough, the most conspicuous being the constitutional guarantee of a republican form of government throughout the Union, a matter requiring free elections. Then there was the implicit right of the sovereign U.S. to determine who can vote for its elected officials. Specious though their rationale was, they were not letting any straws in the wind pass them by . . .

Slaughterhouse took the nation back beyond the Enforcement Acts, the Fourteenth Amendment, and the "Congressional Understanding" and Civil Rights Act of 1866, all of which were predicated upon a concept of dual federal/state citizenship envisioned as concentric and complementary circles. The outer circle was seen as consisting of certain rights arising out of a citizen's direct relations with the federal government, whereas an inner circle of "ordinary rights" were remanded to the states for protection, albeit with the federal authority as their ultimate guarantor. By forsaking this conception, Slaughterhouse reenthroned the Confederate notion of separate and exclusive federal and state areas of jurisdiction over the rights of citizens.

As historians would later politely put it, Slaughterhouse "divested the Fourteenth Amendment of its Constitutional vitality."[13] By so doing, it was scarcely less than a formal surrender to those who had surrendered "unconditionally" at Appomattox seven years earlier. As if to assure still more decisions in the same mold, when Chief Justice Chase died later in the year Grant replaced him with Morrison R. Waite, an Ohio Republican known to take a dim view of equal rights for blacks.

As for the Panic of '73, it made its debut on September 18, when the New York offices of Jay Cooke and Company closed its doors. Two days later the stock exchange followed suit. The panic and depression that ensued were destined to blight all of Grant's second term and beyond. Already during 1872 there had been business failures with liabilities totaling $120 million. During 1873 another five thousand enterprises, with liabilities of $228 million went under. Agriculture was just as hard-hit. Corn, for example, which had brought seventy cents per bushel before Appomattox, was going for twenty-four cents.[14]

It was a time not only of bankruptcy and foreclosure but also of falling wages, unemployment, lockouts, blacklisting, blackjacking, and union-busting. The ranks of organized labor had grown since Appomattox to some 300,000 members, affiliated in the main with the National Labor Union. William Sylvis, president, was remembered for having said back then: "No man in America rejoiced more than I did at the downfall of Negro slavery. But when the shackles fell from the limbs of those four million blacks, it did not make them free men: it simply transferred them from one condition of slavery to another . . . We are now one family of slaves together."

Even so, eight years after the event, a nation that was worried about where its next meal was coming from was not inclined to be overly concerned about where blacks' next ballot was coming from.

THE SHOTGUN PLAN

❖

CHAPTER 12

❖

When Johnny Reb fired on Fort Sumter, U.S. soldiers inside had fired back. And when the Southern states seceded and formed the Confederate States of America, what was left of the United States of America mobilized its armed forces to teach the South that the nation was indivisible. It had taken four years of bloody fighting, and 622,511 American lives, to drive that lesson home.

Now, however, a little more than a decade later, neo-Confederates employing terrorism and civil disobedience had regained control over most of those states, sworn to reestablish white rule over the entire South, and openly proclaimed their intent to govern it independently from the U.S.A. insofar as federal "guarantees" of free elections, republican government, and civil rights for blacks were concerned.

This time no one shot back, and no one mobilized. Uncle Sam, preoccupied with other matters, chose to ignore Ole Massa's qualified declaration of independence and armed rebellion against federal law and authority. The nation had evidently made up its mind that, so long as the South remained inside the Union and did not go back into the business of buying and selling blacks, it could do what it damned well pleased with them.

"Southern Rebel: 'Come on, boys! Old Grant's bluster about our killing Republicans is only a military scarecrow, after all' " (*Harper's Weekly*, September 26, 1874; courtesy of the Florida State Photo Archive).

No public record reflects that on such-and-such a date any such national decision was ever taken, either in the halls of Congress, or the Supreme Court, or the White House; but it was taken nonetheless and for nearly a century remained in full force and effect as the highest law of the land. It was almost as if Grant had surrendered to Lee at Appomattox, and not the other way around.

The neo-Confederates were quick to realize that at last the ideological and political victory was theirs for the taking. There was nothing any longer standing in the way of their seizure of absolute power except black resistance—and they resolved to make short shrift of that.

This realization/resolution was the incubus that begat the so-called Mississippi Plan, more appropriately referred to as the Shotgun Plan.

Whiteside historians would have us believe that this plan—formulated and advertised throughout the South in 1874, put to the test in the Mississippi election of 1875, and fully operational in the presidential election of 1876 (putting an end to free elections South of the Mason-Dixon line)—called for nothing more than a conspicuous display of weaponry by white voters at the polls and that this show of force proved to be all that was necessary to deter blacks from voting, then and thereafter.[1]

But the blacks in America had been subjected to far too much force to be intimidated by any mere show of it. Nor were token applications—whether in the form of floggings, lynchings, assassinations, or even an occasional massacre—sufficient to prevent them from seeking to exercise the freedom they had tasted and found sweet. Nothing less than a regionwide holocaust would do, and that is just what the Shotgun Plan prepared for and provided.

Mississippi's off-year election of 1875 was seen as an ideal testing ground of the plan for a final takeover of the region in the presidential election of 1876. The realization that there would be no noteworthy federal intervention enabled the Confederate underground to emerge aboveground. The covert armed rebellion was transformed into an open one. The GHQ was transferred from the Klan den to the county Democratic club.

The struggle was transformed from one of section against section to one of Southern whites against Southern blacks, the former armed, the latter not. In some respects, the freedmen were even more defenseless and friendless than they had been as slaves. No longer were there powerful abolitionist societies in the North to urge them on, no John Brown to launch a raid against their masters, no Underground Railway leading to freedom anywhere. They were on their own, but they gave a good account of themselves.

So determined was black resistance, in fact, that the plan was obliged to resort to ever more stringent measures in order to put it down. At the outset in the Mississippi campaign, the private cavalry attached to the county Democratic clubs was content with charging Republican rallies, firing fusillades over their heads, and demanding "equal time" on the platform for Democratic advocates of white rule. When this failed to get the desired results, Republican rallies were "captured" and forced to sit "under the gun" and listen to racist diatribes. When blacks and their few remaining white supporters still failed to get the message, the plan proscribed black gatherings for political purposes altogether. Any who did gather were dispersed by gun and cannon fire, not always aimed over their heads.[2]

From such as this the plan proceeded to adopt techniques whereby *agents provocateurs* were employed to create "disturbances," which in turn served as excuses for the launching of pogroms and massacres known as

"General Grant: 'Who has been mutilating this tree?' Ku-Klux: 'Mr. President, I can not tell a lie—that Nigger done it.' " Cartoon by Bellew (*Harper's Weekly*, October 17, 1874; courtesy of the Florida State Photo Archive).

"Negro hunts." And finally the high command in charge of executing the plan issued an ultimatum affixing a price tag of "One Vote, One Life" on black balloting, gave white Republican officeholders and candidates the choice of coming over to the Democratic Party, getting out of the South, or dying, and left black politicos no choice but abdication or assassination. With a scenario such as this, the bloody events that were to transpire in Mississippi in 1875 and throughout the south in 1876 were altogether predictable.

As the year 1875 dawned, Governor Adelbert Ames was holding the fort of republican government in the state capitol at Jackson. With the forces of white supremacy openly proclaiming their intent to block free elections in the fall and overthrow republican government by force if necessary—and all the while openly mobilizing, arming, and training to carry out these purposes—Governor Ames deemed it expedient in January to ask the Mississippi legislature to empower him to raise a state militia to maintain law and order during the campaign and police the polls on election day. The house barely approved by a vote of forty to thirty-eight, and the measure was killed in the senate by a vote cast along strictly racial lines. Thus, with little or no help to be expected from Washington, the die for a holocaust was cast.

During February, President Grant did ask the Congress to enact legislation authorizing the U.S. government to itself protect the right of U.S. citizens to vote for U.S. officials. In his message Grant made reference to the Colfax massacre of 1873 as a harbinger of atrocities yet to come should Congress fail to act. As reasonable as the Grant proposal might sound to nationals of other republics, the American Congress turned it down. The Speaker of the House confided to a black member of that body that it was the concensus of most Republicans that passage of such a measure would result in the defeat of their party in the coming year—so they voted to defeat the measure instead.

On March 1, however, the Congress did enact the Civil Rights Act of 1875, incorporating certain provisions of the CRA of 1870 and the Ku Klux Act of 1871 that had not yet been stricken by the Supreme Court. The new act stated that "all persons" in the U.S. "shall be entitled to the full and equal enjoyment of the accommodations, advantages, facilities, and privileges of inns, public conveyances on land and water, theaters and other places of amusement; subject only to the conditions and limitations established by law and applicable alike to citizens of every race and color regardless of any previous condition of servitude."[3]

It was not quite the "darling of Sumner's heart" for which he had pled so long and passionately, for it stopped short of assuring desegregated schools and cemeteries; but it came close. Not that it mattered much, for the measure was never enforced during the eight years that transpired before the Supreme Court struck it down, leaving the way clear for an apartheid future. The white South did not wait to declare the measure void, so far as their region was concerned. "Any Negro or gang of Negroes who attempted to act on the bill would do so at their peril," one Louisiana journal warned even before the measure became law, in a statement that was to serve as official policy wherever white rule held sway during the ensuing hundred years.[4]

Drawing the Line

It was abundantly clear from the outset of the Mississippi campaign that the only issue was white rule. Although some conciliatory Whigs managed to slip an "equality" plank into the Democratic/Conservative platform, all but a few of the coalitions' constituents were quick to disavow any such thing. [The] only issue in the election was whether the whites or the blacks should predominate," one color-line Democratic leader said at the time. "There was no other politics that I could see in it. Men that had been Republicans all their lives just laid aside republicanism and said that they had to go into the ranks then."[5]

The choosing-up of sides and candidates on the basis of race was viewed in this fashion by J. S. McNeily, who was among those prominent conservatives who were carried along by the tide: "It was part of the creed of a desperate condition, one easily understood, that any white man, however odious, was preferable . . . to any negro however unobjectionable individually."[6]

Mississippi's press led the flight of conservative and native white Republicans into the Democratic fold. By May of 1875 those original enunciators of the color-line *politique* in 1874—the *Vicksburg Herald, Handsboro Democrat, Vicksburg Monitor, Okolona Southern States, Columbus Index,* and *Yazoo City Banner,* had been joined by the *Hinds County Gazette, Newton Ledger, Brandon Republican, Forest Register, Jackson Clarion,* and *Meridian Gazette.*[7]

By way of rationalizing their adoption of the color-line, these papers asserted that it was the blacks themselves who had drawn the line. In evidence thereof they pointed to the fact that blacks in the legislature had voted as a bloc in opposing white efforts to cut funds for public education, that in the Republican state convention of 1873 they had asked that blacks be nominated for three of the state's seven elective posts, and so forth.

There was general agreement (among whites) that it was unthinkable to allow blacks to take part in the political process, the editor of the *Newton Democrat* adding that he would "as soon try to reason with a shoal of crocodiles or a drove of Kentucky mules."[8]

Econolynch, Once More to the Fore

Colonel McCardle of the *Vicksburg Herald* (who early on in Reconstruction had been arrested and tried by U.S. military authorities for writings calculated to undermine their authority) had this classic bit of Ole Massa plantation psychology to offer the politicos: "The way to treat Sambo is not to argue with him or to reason with him. If you do that, it puffs his vanity and it only makes him insolent. Say to him, 'Here, we are going to *carry* this election; you may vote as you like; but we *are* going to carry it. Then we are going to look after ourselves and our friends; you can look out for yourself,' and he will vote with you."[9]

To reinforce such threats of economic lynching of every black who dared vote Republican, lists were prepared and published of those who were known Republicans, and alongside these were printed lists of blacks who had promised to vote the Democratic ticket. These lists were accompanied by notices that there would be watchers at the polls on election day, that the names of all who voted Republican would be published and retribution swift and sure. Neither they nor their wives could expect to ever find employment thereafter, it was threatened. As if that were not intimidatory enough, some white physicians published notices that they would deny treatment to all members of any family in which the male persisted in voting Republican. In short, the terrorist diktat was: vote for white rule, or not at all.

"Dead Books"

Democratic clubs throughout the state began ostentatiously to compile what they called "dead books," inscribing therein the names of all active Republicans. Republican voters, officeseekers, and officeholders were all given to understand that they must desist or they would be dead men. At first armed Democratic bands made a practice of "invading" Republican rallies and demanding equal time on the platform. But soon they were "capturing" Republican rallies and forcing the audiences at gunpoint to listen for hours to racist harangues. Toward the end of the campaign the terrorists were simply routing any and all black gatherings with musket and cannon fire.

In some instances, native white Republicans—of which there were once some twenty to thirty thousand—were assiduously appealed to, on the basis of their whiteness, to join ranks with their brethren in the Democratic Party. Those who balked at making the transition were socially and economically ostracized by the white community, the *Canton Mail* and other papers going so far as to publish lists of those who "should no longer be recognized on the streets" and whose attentions "must be scorned by every true Southern woman."[10] Given inducements such as these, many white Southern Republicans made the switch. As one of them put it, "the Democrats were making it too damned hot for us to stay out."

Northern white Republicans were another matter. Colonel McCardle was not inclined to deal as leniently with these as he was with "Sambo." In tones highly reminiscent of those employed by Klan Wizard Forrest in his press interview in 1868, McCardle urged that the "deluded" blacks be spared and their white leaders killed.[11] Concurring, the editor of the *Columbus Index* announced, "The White League is resolved to kill hereafter only those white wretches who incite negroes to riot and murder."[12] Rioting and murdering (by whites, of course) were the order of the day up to and including election day, and the victims were far more often black than white. White Republicans were targeted, however, and this knowledge compelled many of those who survived to leave the state altogether.

"Grand Affairs"

Part and parcel of the Mississippi Plan for the disfranchisement of blacks by force and intimidation was the staging of "spectacular" political demonstrations in virtually every city and hamlet in the state. (Insofar as the resources of the time and of the Democratic Party permitted, these events—each of which was billed as "The Grandest Affair of the Campaign"—anticipated the massive rallies that facilitated the rise to power of the Nazi Party in Germany, not to mention some of the flag-waving presidential campaigns and shameless "victory celebrations" staged in our own country later in the century.

Intended as a show of force, these events featured parades by armed rifle companies and red-shirt brigades, as well as the firing of (Confederate) cannon, of which every self-respecting county Democratic committee had at least one. A typical "Grand Affair," paid for with five thousand dollars from the county Democratic club and subscriptions from private citizens and staged at Panola, was described by one of its sponsors: "Our purpose was to overawe the negroes and exhibit to them the ocular proof of our power . . . by magnificent torchlight processions at night and in the day by special trains of cars . . . loaded down with white people with flags flying, drums beating, bands playing, the trains being chartered and free for everybody."[13]

The Vicksburg Formula

Although many white Mississippians were evidently carried away by such displays, many black Mississippians evidently were not. To make the desired impression upon such as these, power would have to be applied after the manner of the Vicksburg massacre of the preceding December, the *Vicksburg Monitor* opined (in the same month the CRA of 1875 was adopted): "The same tactics that saved Vicksburg will save the State, and no other will."[14]

In this spirit of carnage, other editors invoked the memory of the Meridian massacre of 1871 in which a Negro hunt "bagged" at least thirty victims, as a promising pattern for victory at the polls in 1875. "The time has come," the *Jackson Clarion* declared in a virtual ultimatum, "when companies that have been organized for protection and defensive purposes should come to the front . . . Let every citizen hold himself in readiness to join one of these companies. The shameless, heartless, vile, grasping, deceitful, creeping, crawling, wallowing, slimy, slippery, hideous, loathsome political pirates must be wiped out!"[15]

The Big Negro-Hunt of '75

Such calls to arms had their effect, not only in Mississippi but throughout the former Confederate States of America. For the remainder of that election year it was truly open season on blacks in Mississippi. A bare-bones account of the series of "Negro hunts" staged in that state up to and including election day, paraphrased from the work of revisionist Vernon Lane Wharton in 1949, includes the following:

Vicksburg. Blacks staging a Fourth of July celebration mobbed by whites, two killed.

Water Valley. Also during July, this community was disturbed by a rumor that Negroes were going to attack the town. An exploring party found a group of Negroes concealed under a cliff. An unknown number of Negroes were killed.

Louisville. A meeting of black Republicans during August succeeded in raising a disturbance. Result, two negroes wounded, no white men hurt. "Will the negro never learn that he is always sure to be the sufferer in these riots?"

Macon. Same month. A group of whites, including more than a hundred horsemen from Alabama, were out looking for a Negro political meeting. After they had failed to find one, they were told by a rumor that several hundred Negroes had gathered at a church, where they were preparing to carry aid to those of their race in Vicksburg . . . the Alabamians disobeyed the order of the deputy sheriff and fired into the crowd. Twelve or thirteen Negroes were killed."

Yazoo City. A few nights later. A band of white Democrats, "led by their 'rope-bearer' H. M. Dixon," invaded a Republican meeting. In the confusion that followed, a native white Republican was killed, and several Negroes wounded. The white [Republican] sheriff escaped with his life by fleeing to Jackson. White militia [of the Democratic Club] then took charge of the county, and systematically lynched the Negro leaders in each supervisor's district.

Clinton. Three days later. A band of 500 armed white Democrats, traveling by special train, invaded a Republican rally and picnic attended by 1,500 blacks and 500 whites. The Democrats demanded equal time on the platform, and although their request was granted fighting broke out. The audience was stampeded, their food destroyed, and their horses stolen. One white Republican and two white Democrats were killed. "The number of Negroes killed is unknown; estimates varied from ten to thirty. Two thousand Negroes in wild panic rushed to the woods or to Jackson. By nightfall, armed whites, including the Vicksburg 'Medocs,' had control of the entire area. During the next four days they scoured the surrounding country, killing Negro leaders. Estimates of the number killed varied between ten and fifty."

Utica. On the same day as the Clinton massacre, armed white Democrats "captured" a Republican rally and forced the audience to listen to their speakers, only.

Satartia. A few days later. "A minor skirmish in which one Negro was killed."

Coahoma County. Early September. The black sheriff was driven out of the county after an encounter in which five Negroes were killed and five wounded. One white was killed from ambush; another shot himself by accident. (Political affiliation of white victims not stated.)

All of these massacres, lynchings, and assassinations of blacks were widely reported in the white folk's press, with much the same glee as is evidenced in Wharton's recounting three-quarters of a century after the events. "Long before the day of the election, a Democratic victory was assured," Wharton deduced, with good reason.[16]

The mere rumor that Republicans were planning to hold a political rally brought on the mobilization of terrorist bands to break them up. In many a Black Belt county, Republican sheriffs, whether white or black, were forcibly driven out and obliged to seek sanctuary in the state capital. The white militias of the Democratic clubs seized control of the towns and picketted the roads.

Governor Ames was obviously faced with a state of (white) insurrection. From Yazoo City he received one of countless pleas for help: "I beg you most fulley to send the United soldiers here; they have hung six more men since the killing of Mr. Fawn; they won't let the Republican have no ticket . . . ; fighting commense just I were closing, 2 two killed . . . help; send troops and arms pleas . . . Send help, help, troops."[17]

A similarly desperate appeal came from Noxubee County:

> Last Saturday, the 30th, the democrats was in Macon town in high rage, raring around and shooting of their canons all up and down the street, and shooting all their pistols also, and which they have already swored to you for peace; and I don't think they act much in that way last Saturday, for there was Richard Gray shot down walking on the pavements, shot by the democrats, and he was shot five times, four times after he fell, and was said shot because he was nominated for treasurer, and further more, because he made a speech and said he never did expect to vote a democratic ticket, and also advised the colored citizens to do the same.[18]

A like note reached the governor from Warren County advising that there were 108 blacks in a certain precinct who would not register and vote "for we cannot hold a meeting of no description without being molested and broken up; and further our lives are not safe at nor in our cabins, and therefore we deem it unwise to make a target of our body to be shot down like dogs and have no protection."[19]

Finally, there was a succinct plea from Vicksburg, "The rebels turbulent; are aiming themselves here now today to go to Sartartia to murder more poor negroes. Gov., aint the no pertiction?"[20]

Indeed, there was not any, though Ames did his best to mobilize some, on both the state and federal levels. Having been rebuffed in January by the state senate's refusal to allow him to organize a militia, Ames in the midst of the general insurrection that prevailed in September, issued an executive order commanding the private white militias and terrorist bands to disband. The order's only effect was to evoke a scornful response from the *Jackson Clarion* that echoed all over the state: " 'Now, therefore, I, A.A., do hereby command all persons belonging to such organizations to disband.' Ha! ha!! ha!!! 'Command.' 'Disband.' That's good."[21]

Governor Ames, with no military or police force capable of enforcing his government's authority, was in a real sense a palace hostage of private militias. Of course the Constitution of the United States of America has always prohibited the raising of private armed forces—but no one in Jackson or Washington in September 1875 was bold enough to bring the prohibition to bear.

Ames tried. To Attorney General Pierrepont he wrote for troops, adding, "Let the odium, in all its magnitude descend on me. I cannot escape. I am conscious in the discharge of my duty toward a class of American citizens whose only offense consists in their color, and which I am powerless to protect."[22]

While the hero of Appomattox was pondering how to react to this latest round of armed rebellion in the South, he was visited by a delegation of Ohio Republicans. White rule over the state of Mississippi was a fait accompli, they argued; it was too late for federal troops to restore the republic. As a clincher they added that in the forthcoming election Ohio would be lost to the Democrats if he took the unpopular step of sending troops to Mississippi. "The whole public are tired of these annual autumnal outbreaks in the South!" Pierrepont counseled his commander in chief.[23]

Grant informed Ames that the federal government would do nothing until all state resources had been exhausted. With the election only weeks away, Ames set about the forlorn task of trying to mobilize a state militia capable of keeping the way to (and from) the polls open and safe. For this purpose he turned to Brigadier General William F. Fitzgerald, a onetime Confederate who had joined Republican ranks. Ames envisioned a militia composed of an equal number of white and black companies. At first many Democrats, led by J. Z. George (who had effective control of the Democratic 'militias'), favored the idea. But the white rank and file would have none of it, and by October 15 only two companies had been mobilized, one white and one black, and these were stationed around the capitol in Jackson.

The fugitive white Republican sheriff from Yazoo County feared that sending in state militia would result in open war and argued against it. A caucus of black legislators revealed that they were well-nigh unanimous in fearing that any attempt by state militia to assert authority over the election would do more harm than good. Blacks did not want a confrontation because it was all too apparent that the white supremacists had been allowed to establish a monopoly over firepower. Even so, the white-rulers did not want a confrontation either, because they feared that might reintroduce federal arms into the area in behalf of the blacks.

Terrorists as Poll Watchers

Out of this mutual desire to avoid an armed conflict between the races came a conference between Governor Ames and the commandant of the terrorist militias, J. Z. George. With a seemingly uncaring Uncle Sam asleep in the background, Governor Ames felt that he had no choice but to surrender the police powers of the state to the terrorists. In what amounted to a formal treaty, the governor agreed to cancel plans for arms distribution and to disband the two companies of state militia in return for which the terrorist chieftain pledged that the armed bands under his command would guarantee a "fair and peaceful election."[24]

As must have been expected, the election proved to be more peaceful than it was fair, which was not saying much. Such peace as prevailed was of that variety that comes about when one man has a gun pressed against the temple of another who has no weapon.

The mayhem did not wait for election day to dawn but broke out in Columbus on election eve. There, where blacks were in the majority, they staged a parade. The white strategy for precipitating a "riot"—as massacres of blacks were invariably called—was to have some white lads charge the parade with knives and cut the heads out of the drums. Then, someone set fire to a couple of sheds, and word was passed that the blacks were trying to burn down the town.

"The Columbus Riflemen and a large number of visiting Alabamians immediately took charge, and Negroes began to flee for safety" is the way

Wharton describes what ensued. "Those who refused to halt were fired upon; four men were killed, and several men and one woman were wounded."[25]

When the polls opened the next morning, Columbus's black majority was still hiding in the swamps, with good reason. There, the election went off "as quietly as a funeral," the Democratic mayor gloated.

"It was a very quiet day in Jackson—fearfully quiet," said an observer in the state's capital.

"Hardly anybody spoke aloud," was the word from Yazoo City.

As someone said at the time, blacks dared not raise any ruckus—and the whites didn't need to. The funereal aspect that characterized the election in many places was not inappropriate, for on that day, free elections, democracy, republican government, and black rights were all being buried, and would remain interred for a long time to come.

All was not entirely quiet on the Mississippi front though. Despite the terror, very many blacks went to the polls and voted Republican—so many went, in fact, that the white supremacists had to throw out their ballots or not count them in order to carry the day.

The role actually played by the white Democratic Party militias on election day was not unexpected (these militias, like the KKK, were prototypes of the latter-day Death Squads bent upon repressing democracy in Latin America, as Jim Crow was to apartheid in South Africa).

In pledging to Governor Ames that they would see to it that it was a fair election, what the militias had in mind was that it would be fair enough if Democrats and no one else were allowed to vote; and they enforced this to the best of their ability. As for that portion of their pledge having to do with keeping the election peaceable, this they did to their own satisfaction by pacifying would-be black voters by opening fire on them.

In Scott County, for example, as reported by Wharton, "Negroes who were carrying Republican tickets for distribution at the polls were fired on 'by accident' by Democratic squirrel hunters. They fled, abandoning both the tickets and their mules. At Forest, the county seat, it was arranged for boys with whips to rush suddenly into the crowd of Negroes. The voters, already frightened and nervous, feared that this was the beginning of an outbreak, and left in a panic."[26]

Wharton's sardonic account of how "Home Rule" was restored that day goes on to say: "At Okolona, the Negroes, with women and children, gathered at a church in the edge of town, intending to go from there to the polls in groups. The Democratic army marched up and formed near the church. When guns went off by accident, the Negroes stampeded, paying no attention to Democratic invitations for them to come back and vote."[27]

At Aberdeen, in an effort to keep blacks penned up in an area where no polling places had been established, a drawbridge was opened and armed pickets posted along the banks of the Tombigbee River. Nevertheless, many blacks were at the polls when they opened. According to Wharton: "E. O. Sykes, in charge of the Democratic war department, posted the cavalry he had imported from Alabama, surrounded the Negroes with infantry, loaded a cannon with chains and slugs, and then sent a strongarm squad into the crowd to beat the Negroes over the head. They broke and ran, many of them swimming the river in search of safety. The Republican sheriff, an ex-Confederate, locked himself in his own jail."

At Grenada, when a white man started beating a black man over the head with an ax handle, the "Democratic captain" sent for his cannon, and his men went scurrying for their weapons, which they had stashed in a nearby store. "General E. C. Walthall quieted the crowd, but the Negroes had stampeded, and would not return," Wharton reports with mock wonderment and chagrin.

In Meridian "the White League seized the polls, while the Negroes, 'sullen and morose,' gathered in a mass across the street. Any Negro who approached without a white Democrat at his side was immediately crowded away from the ballot box . . . At Holly Springs, about 250 Negroes voted with the Democrats, offering their open ballots as proof."

As a result of the terrorists' tactics, the shutout of black Republican voters was total in some localities, and nearly so in others. Not one was allowed to vote in Auburn; in the predominantly black county of Hinds only two voted in Utica; there were four in Kemper, twelve in Tishomingo, and just seven in Yazoo City (where in 1873 a total of 2,427 Republican votes had been cast).

That the Democratic Party itself served as GHQ for the virtual state of martial law—whose order of the day was that blacks vote Democratic or not at all—was frankly brought out in an accounting published subsequently in the *Aberdeen Examiner:*

the firmest word was "victory"—to be achieved by arms if necessary. When the central power made treaties in Jackson involving the laying down or stacking of arms, the people in this state burnished their arms and bought more cartridges, and each county conducted the campaign upon its own plan . . . each looking to winning its own home fight in its own home way, and each ready and willing to support its neighbors physically and morally whenever the emergency demanded aid, as was not unfrequently the case . . . here and elsewhere in the dark counties we guaranteed peace by thoroughly organizing for war; and . . . at the call of the [Democratic] County Executive Committee it was easy—as demonstrated on several occasions—to put seventeen hundred well-mounted horsemen into line, that could be transposed into a brigade of cavalry at a moment's notice, to say nothing of a thoroughly organized artillery company and a company of Infantry armed with needle guns, purchased by our citizens, for home service. In addition to this, our eight hundred square miles of territory was so thoroughly connected by courier lines and posts, that we could communicate with every voter within its borders within a few hours.

Considering the intensity of the terror, the very substantial number of Republican votes cast on that day in Mississippi stands as a monument to the courage of all those who cast them. In some places the blacks, armed with clubs and sticks, old swords and pieces of scythe blades, marched to the polls "after the manner of soldiers."

In the only administrative state office at stake, that of treasurer, the Democratic candidate W. L. Hemingway "won" with 96,596 votes to the 66,155 mustered by his Republican opponent, George M. Buchanan, a former Confederate.

The state senate which emerged from the election consisted of twenty-six Democratic advocates of white rule and only ten Republicans (of these, only five were blacks, and they were holdovers from previous elections). In the legislature, white-rulers occupied a total of ninety-five seats, leaving twenty for Republicans, sixteen of whom were black. Sixty-two of the state's seventy-four counties were brought under white control. Democrats captured four of the state's six congressional seats, and a fifth was won by a Democratic sympathizer in Republican clothing. At the time, there were sixty thousand more blacks in Mississippi than there were whites.

Congress went so far as to investigate. Its investigators reported that the newly elected legislature was not a legally constituted body and that the state of Mississippi had "fallen under the control of armed men whose common purpose is to deprive the Negro of the free exercise of the right of suffrage and to establish and maintain the supremacy of the white-line Democracy."

But, having found as much, the Congress of the United States elected to do nothing about it. Thenceforth, it was clear to all concerned that the Fourteenth and Fifteenth Amendments to the Constitution, and the Federal Civil Rights Acts designed to enforce those amendments, were dead letters so far as the South was concerned.

The white rulers of Mississippi interpreted this acquiescence on the part of Congress, the president, and the attorney general as a license to liquidate what few Republicans still clung to public office in that state. (Some had been active ever since the constitutional convention of 1867.) One Republican member of the legislature was hanged by the White League. Another was shot down in the streets of Clinton, a third in the full light of day, a fourth in the courthouse at Yazoo City. And the body of a fifth was pulled from a waterhole. The terrorists then laid seige to the homes of others, and those who managed to escape from the state with their lives were deemed fortunate.

The Mississippi Plan had accomplished what it set out to do—return the state to white rule. Now in its alter ego the Shotgun Plan was cocked and loaded to extend the victory over the entire South in the presidential campaign of 1876.

ON THE CENTENNIAL OF THE REPUBLIC

CHAPTER 13

It was just Uncle Sam's luck to have to decide on the centennial of the republic—when all the world was watching—whether to hold on high the standard of popular sovereignty raised by the founding fathers and refurbished by Lincoln or trudge on down the road toward a bicentennial with the shameful pennants "White Man's Government" and "Apartheid" attached.

When in 1776 the assertion was made on the North American continent that governments derive their just powers from the consent of the governed, very few people anywhere on the planet had ever heard of any such thing. It had been a revolutionary notion then, causing many a throne to quiver, and now, one hundred years later, it was revolutionary still.

When first the tocsin was sounded, no one had felt it necessary to make mention that women and slaves were not to be included, and so the United States of America had rocked along some ninety years as a republic of white males. Not until then did it dawn upon the nation that there was something unseemly about a republic—particularly one professing the "all men are brothers" doctrine of Christianity—sanctioning and practicing the buying and selling and flogging and execution of human beings as slaves.

So the Civil War was fought to change all that. (Women would have to wait.) Following that bloodletting, the "just powers" of the American republic no longer had to rest upon the dubious formula, "consent of the governed, except slaves." For a brief decade after Appomattox, the black freedmen who had been slaves shared in the democracy. And yet all that turbulent while, their former owner-masters were conspiring to render them political eunuchs once more. The "Except Slaves" flag surrendered by the Confederacy at Appomattox was soon flying again, this time reading "Except Blacks."

Whether or not Uncle Sam would go along with this editing job was the basic question that the impending presidential election of 1876 was destined to decide.

And so it was that, while all manner of preparations were being made for a gala centennial celebration, the former slaveholders were making all manner of preparations to carry the election in such manner as to assure that in their section of the country at least, government would be of, by, and for white people and that Southern society would be as apartheid as they could make it.

In all but three of the former slaves states, white rule had already been reestablished and was vigorously carrying out its program of liquidating all vestiges of black participation in politics, establishing a one-party (all white) political system, and reinforcing apartheid by a barbed-wire maze of law and regulation. In these states which had already been "redeemed" from republicanism and restored to white rule, the election of 1876 presented somewhat less of a problem to anti-Republicans than it did in the three states where republican governments were still nominally "in power." Even so, as was demonstrated in Mississippi the preceding year, it was one thing for republicans to control the state house and quite another for them to control the countryside. The inability of these governments to recruit whites they could depend upon for militia duty left them no alternative but an all-black militia, which in turn posed the risk of race war and black annihilation.

The bitter choice thereby presented to Republican incumbents was either to leave their regimes and themselves unprotected and face the prospects of forcible overthrow and personal assassination with what grace they could muster, or to put up a fight that in all probability would lead to the mass extermination of their constituents. Although it would be difficult to say which path was the more valorous, the former was chosen.

State of the Union

The fact that the Panic of '73 was still going strong in 1876 was to have a pronounced effect upon the election. The nation's white farmers and workers, plagued by rock-bottom prices for farm produce and by unemployment, were on the whole too preoccupied with their own plight to give much thought to that of Southern blacks.

The South's prewar role as king of the world cotton market was no more; India, Latin America, and the Middle East had garnered much of it. Cotton was down to 9.7 cents per pound, as compared to 16.5 cents in 1869. Wheat was bringing but 77 cents per bushel, in contrast with the $1.57 it had fetched in 1869; and the prices for tobacco, sugar, and other commodities were down proportionately. All this was reflected in a rash of farm mortgage foreclosures and tax sales, and business bankruptcies too were to total nine thousand for the year.[1]

One thing had not changed since before the war: the South's economy was still a colonial one, dependent for the most part upon "foreign" (Northern) capital for the wherewithal to launch and conduct such extractive industries as timber, minerals, and coal. The North's financial and railroad interests were feverishly interested in "opening up" the South. In the course of the years that had transpired after Appomattox these interests had been made increasingly aware that the South's antebellum proprietary class had regained title to the region's natural resources and moreover were once more firmly ensconced in the halls of government. Thus it was they who were in a position both to enter into contracts and to grant franchises. If it wanted to do business down South, the North was obliged to do it with such former Confederate politicos as Jefferson Davis and Alexander Stevens, and such former Confederate generals as Joseph E. Johnston, P. G. T. Beauregard, John B. Gordon, Nathan Bedford Forrest, and Wade Hampton. But business was business, then as now, and the financiers were fully prepared to sign on the dotted line with anyone who could deliver the goods, regardless of political persuasion.

Already the financial establishment was playing a role as something of a shadow government, and the influence of the railroads and the banking houses of the Morgans, Drexels, Cookes, and Sage upon the selection of candidates, conduct of the campaign, and concoction of the Deal of '76 was to be very considerable. These gentry, needless to say, were far more interested in building their respective financial and industrial empires than they were in building democracy or economic and social

justice in the South or anywhere else on earth. The three surviving re-
publican/Republican state governments in the South—concerned as
they had to be with such basics as survival against armed attack, defense
of black rights, and land reform—had come to be regarded as anachro-
nisms, even within the national Republican Party that had given them
birth. It was small wonder, therefore, that these beleaguered regimes
were treated like redheaded stepchildren, and abandoned as such when
the time came to strike the Deal.

WASP Country

Although the "WASP" label had not yet been invented in 1876, the
White-Anglo-Saxon-Protestant majority was giving a hard time to many
a minority that did not fit into that "mainstream" category. Along with
the economic gloom that hung over the nation there was a miasma of
racism and bigotry that manifested itself in various forms from coast to
coast. It was almost as though the centenarian republic was deliberately
trying to shed its mantle as something of a liberator, which it had but recently acquired as a result of its civil war against slavery and Lincoln's
rededication at Gettysburg. For example, Democratic senators attached
to a Senate committee appointed to investigate the terror in the unfree
Mississippi election of 1875, turned in a minority report in 1876 attach-
ing the Fifteenth Amendment itself. "The relations of the African to the
white race in the United States do not stand alone for consideration,"
these Senators warned. "On our Pacific coast the dark shadow of an Asian
horde hangs lowering over the white population, and has aroused their
gravest apprehensions."

The Fifteenth Amendment, as they saw it, opened "to the teeming
oriental populations unobstructed opportunity by their mere number, to
control our elections, and our Governments, State and Federal." It was
not the rights of blacks or Asians that should concern the nation, they
suggested, but those of America's own Southern whites: "no people had
ever been so mercilessly robbed and plundered," they averred, "so wan-
tonly and causelessly humiliated and degraded, so recklessly exposed to
the rapacity and lust of the ignorant and vicious portion of their own
community and other States, as the people of the South have been."[2]

In voicing such sentiments the senators were not out of step with the
American public. From the Atlantic to the Pacific, the United States were
indeed united—in their hatred of one ethnic group or another. The
white South was almost solidly united in its antipathy to blacks. In New
England, descendants of the founding fathers were looking askance at

newcomers from central and southern Europe, and at the Irish Catholics as well. The midwest was venting its spleen upon the "pesky Redskins," and Pacific Coast settlers were banding together to stem the "yellow tide" of "bandy-legged simians" from across the sea.

The mobsters who had begun lynching Chinese on the West Coast in 1870 were of course blood brothers of the Ku Klux Klansmen whose favorite sport was the lynching of blacks down South, and they were in no less need of being reconstructed.

Today there may be some who argue that racism was a virtual necessity for the expanding young republic, as it was for Britain and European colonial powers at the time. Necessary or not, the rationale originally applied by the Puritans in New England that the land rightfully belonged to whoever made the "best" use of it was proving to be a great consolation to the settlers of the West as they went about the business of exterminating the indigenous Indian inhabitants. "Nits make lice," is the way Colonel John M. Chivington put it, in ordering the Colorado militia to put Indian women and children to death too.[3]

It was not merely coincidence, but a national and human tragedy, that even as the Philadelphia Exposition celebrating the centennial was opening its doors to visitors of every hue from the four corners of the earth, Chief Crazy Horse, flanked by paleface cannoneers, was leading his people out of their ancestral home in the Black Hills westward into bondage and oblivion.

Such being the spirit of the times, it was not surprising that both of the nation's political parties were displaying a willingness for blacks to be put back beyond the pale.

Candidates and Issues

This, then, was the climate in which the two parties met to nominate their candidates for ushering the republic into its second century.

The Republicans convened in Cincinnati and, after seven votes, chose a local lawyer, Rutherford B. Hayes. During the war Hayes had risen to the rank of major general and had served Ohio as both congressman and governor. He had a record of supporting Reconstruction legislation, hard currency, and the resumption of specie payments—the redemption of Union war bonds in dollars worth what they were at the time of the purchase, as was so fervently desired by the Eastern establishment.

The Democrats, meeting in St. Louis, put forth as their candidate Governor Samuel J. Tilden of New York. Tilden had for some years been rather closely associated with the political machine of "Boss Tweed," but

when a movement to overthrow the machine developed he took a leading role in it. This had led to his election as governor in 1874, and in that
office too he had earned a reputation as an opponent of corruption. The
Democratic platform devised for him to stand on read more like a criminal indictment of Republicanism than it did a political credo. With this
emphasis upon reform went an advocacy of soft money, which had a decided appeal to Western voters.

As for matters racial, Tilden went so far as to embrace the notion aired
by the Democratic senators in their minority report on the Mississippi
"election," that the Fifteenth Amendment asserting that the right to vote
could not be denied on grounds of race was a menace to American society and ought to be repealed. If elected president, he pledged to work
to that end. Hayes, for his part, catered to the nativist Know-Nothing
movement of the North and West by sounding alarms at the incoming
waves of Catholic immigrant laborers from Ireland and southern and central Europe.

For some ninety days following the nomination of Hayes, Southern
Whigs toyed with the idea of resurrecting the "reform coalition" that had
fallen into place behind Horace Greeley's candidacy in 1872 by throw-
ing their support to Hayes. The idea as conceived by them was to purge
the national Republican Party of any last vestiges of "radicialism," abandon the remaining Republican regimes and black voters in the South to
their fate, and rebuild the party in that region upon a conservative white
constituency. In return for this support, Hayes would be asked to name
a Southern Whig to his cabinet. The *Washington Nation* liked the whole
idea so much that it offered to serve as the official organ of such a coalition.[4]

The manner in which the tar brush of corruption was used to smear
the Reconstruction governments in an effort to discredit, destabilize, and
overthrow them has been dealt with in earlier chapters. A bit more needs
to be said, however, on the role that the smear was to play in the final
rollback of republican government that took place in 1876.

Nothing new was added: the smear was simply dusted off for the occasion. Not that the white South required any rationale; it was opposed
to black participation in politics, period, and was frank to admit as much
as a matter of "principle." Nor were bigots elsewhere in the country any
less frank about their purely racist and/or sectarian prejudices against political rights for Asian, Catholic, and other recent immigrants. But the
charge of corruption looked good in the press and sounded good from
the rostrums of the time (and would stand historians in good stead in

making future generations of Americans feel comfortable about what was taking place).

As has been previously noted, the Reconstruction governments were if anything less prone to graft than their counterparts elsewhere in the country, and in comparison with the big city political machines were relatively immaculate. The prayer of a white supremacist that the Reconstruction government in his state be so profligate as to bring on bankruptcy and thus hasten its own demise has been previously cited. Now, in 1876, South Carolina's black Congressman Alonzo Ransier restated the truth of this matter, as follows: " I am no apologist for thieves . . . Nor am I lukewarm on the subject of better government for South Carolina . . . [but] such is the determined opposition to the Republican Party . . . that no administration of our affairs, however honest, just, and economical, would satisfy any considerable portion of the champions of white rule."[5]

It will bear repeating (the smear having been so oft repeated) that it was not black corruption but black integrity that angered the whites who were trying to drive them from public office. Benjamin Cardozo of South Carolina and Oscar Dunn of Louisiana, for example, were regarded as archfiends precisely because they could not be bought.

This is not to suggest that there was no black corruption whatever, they being "only" human. But in matters of principle, such as Black Codes and legislation to enforce apartheid, black votes were not for sale. On the other hand, such things as franchises, then as now, were up for sale to the highest bidder, and black lawmakers sometimes joined the receiving lines. One such realist was moved to remark: "I've been sold eleven times in my life—but this is the first time *I* got the money!"[6]

Democracy Disarmed

Without waiting for any political decision at the polls or backroom deals by the nation's power brokers, the Supreme Court of the United States handed down a number of decisions that had the effect of insuring that none of the branches of the federal government—executive, legislative, or judicial—could or would interfere with the impending white-power-grab down South.

While these decisions on the occasion of the centennial did not quite vindicate the hope of the Confederates at Appomattox that the High Court would yet let them preserve slavery, they came close—close enough to make them feel that the long years they had spent upon the battlefield and in subsequent night riding had not been in vain.

What the Court did was to emasculate the enforcement acts that Congress had enacted to implement the Fourteenth and Fifteenth Amendments, thereby rendering these amendments virtual dead letters. Southern whites took this to mean that the Supreme Court had declared open season on blacks, so any prospect for a free election was off, and a Southwide Negro hunt was on. Although the Court did not precisely reverse the verdict of Appomattox, it effectively tied the hands of the federal courts and law enforcement agencies so far as black political rights were concerned, thus leaving the way open for those who were intent upon reversing the verdict by intimidation, force, and violence.

As one of three coequal partners in the American system of government by checks and balances, the Court is responsible for seeing to it that this is a government of laws, not men. In this instance, it failed miserably to do so. By its actions, it set the stage for the unfree election and Deal of '76, which made America safe for apartheid and something less than democracy.

One of the spikes that the Court drove into the coffin of republican government, free elections, and black rights in 1876 was its decision in *U.S.* v. *Cruikshank*, up on appeal from Louisiana. This case, it will be recalled, had to do with the indictment of some one hundred white terrorists (under Section 6 of the Enforcement Act of 1870) for conspiring to deprive blacks of their rights to vote, assemble, and bear arms, and to equal protection of life, liberty, and property, as affirmed by the Fourteenth and Fifteenth Amendments. This deprivation, it will further be recalled, had to do with the Colfax, Louisiana, massacre of 1873, when terrorists had broken up a black political rally, cannonading sixty-one to death, and executing thirty-seven more.

The indictments had already been thrown out in 1874 by Justice Joseph P. Bradley, then sitting on the U.S. Circuit Court in Louisiana, on the grounds that the Fourteenth and Fifteenth Amendments were directed only against acts of deprivation by *states* and did not cover such acts by the *private sector* (such as the KKK and other terrorist bands). The framers of the Enforcement Act had failed to make this distinction clear, Bradley said, and the federal prosecutors who drafted the indictment of the Colfax terrorists had likewise neglected to make a case for the killings having been *racially motivated,* or that the state had made itself responsible by not prosecuting. Pursuant to this line of reasoning, the killers had been set free.

Now, two years later, the case was before the Supreme Court on appeal. By this time Bradley was himself a member of the Court. The decision, as authored by Chief Justice Morrison R. Waite, not only embraced Bradley's earlier verdict but went still farther in emasculating the amendments and the Enforcement Acts. The rights that the Colfax blacks claimed had been violated were not attributes of U.S. citizenship but were bestowed by and were the responsibility of the state, the Court held. "That duty was originally assumed by the state; and it still remains there" is the way the decision put it.

As for the Fourteenth Amendment guarantee of due process, to uphold the Colfax indictments would imply that blacks were entitled to special treatment, which was not the intent of the amendment, the Court went on to rule. Finally, with reference to the earlier Civil Rights Act of 1866 and its guarantee of equal protection of the laws, the Court said the Colfax indictments were flawed because they neglected to aver that the violations had been racially motivated and condoned by the state—both conditions being essential if the federal courts were to assume jurisdiction.

Not content with having thus knocked the props out from under the amendments, the Court went on to strike yet another blow at black rights in this crucial election year. In *U.S.* v. *Reese* it threw out the indictment of a Kentucky official who had refused to count a black's vote.[7] The Fifteenth Amendment did not bestow upon U.S. citizens any right to vote for U.S. officials but merely prohibited the states from restricting that privilege on racial grounds, the Court expressly held. Even though in this case an official of the state was the culprit, the Court held the indictment to be invalid because the CRA of 1870 was itself invalid, having failed to limit itself *expressly* to state action that was racially motivated. Once again, Southern blacks stood defenseless before their former masters.

Whatever reasons the republic as a whole may have had to celebrate its centennial that year, these two decisions by the highest court in the land occasioned a vast amount of celebration in the semiautonomous region of the country that had dedicated itself to white rule and apartheid.

The hard-won Fourteenth and Fifteenth Amendments to the Bill of Rights were still *in* the U.S. Constitution, but the statutes designed to enforce them had been largely wiped *out*. Black rights as dead letters were something the South's white supremacists could live with.

Exporting the Counterrevolution

With what was left of democracy in the South thus disarmed, the stage was all set for the election campaign of 1876. The overthrow of the antebellum slavocracy and its replacement by democracy had represented a veritable revolution, and now the forces of counterrevolution were fully primed and determined to seize absolute power and restore the white plutocracy.

The Shotgun Plan, which had served this purpose in Mississippi the preceding year, was ready for export to smash the three remaining republican state governments and consolidate the counterrevolution in all the other states where white supremacists had already gained the upper hand.

The election of 1876 was rightly regarded by all parties as the final showdown. White supremacists all over the South had made the pledge of Louisiana's General McEnery (upon being evicted by federal troops from the state house where his terrorist band had installed him) "to carry the next election if we have to ride saddle-deep in blood to do it." Black blood had not flowed quite that deeply in the Negro hunts that swept Mississippi in 1875, but it was deep enough to accomplish the white folks' purpose. Now it was to be South Carolina's, Louisiana's and Florida's turn.

As had been the case in Mississippi, the new democracy had put down deep roots in South Carolina that would not be easily extirpated. Despite all the strenuous efforts of the KKK and Red Shirt terrorists, this republican form of government had survived ever since its inception in 1868. From 1872 until 1874 the state had been governed by Franklin J. Moses, Jr. (whom latter-day whiteside historians were wont to dub "a notorious and corrupt scalawag"). Moses was followed in office by D. H. Chamberlain, a "reform Republican" who sometimes collaborated with the white supremacists. This was not good enough for white South Carolinians in 1876, however, who were resolved to field a candidate dedicated to unadulterated white rule.

Such a candidate was forthcoming in the person of the old familiar Confederate General Wade Hampton, who in August decided to leave his Mississippi plantation and return to his native South Carolina to run for governor. "The white population was for the first time in eight years united in a definite, fixed purpose," one historian has said of Hampton's homecoming.[8] That purpose, needless to say, was to elect Hampton and return the state to lily-white rule.

Hampton had never relinquished either of his two hats as grand dragon of the Carolina Klan and Red Shirt commander. During his sojourn in Mississippi he had had an opportunity to observe firsthand the efficacy of the Shotgun Plan (and no doubt play a part in it). As transplanted by him onto Carolina soil, the plan called for terrorists to ride as Red Shirt cavalrymen by day and robed Klansmen by night.

These "last word" cohorts were preceded by what might be called an emphasis upon "one-on-one" terrorism. In an effort to avoid if possible the mass bloodlettings of the Mississippi Negro hunts (and the risk of federal intervention that went with them), Candidate Hampton promulgated a policy of "force without violence," to be enforced by violence only when necessary.

"Every Democrat must feel honor-bound to control the vote of at least one Negro, by intimidation, purchase, keeping away, or as each individual may determine how he may best accomplish it," the general publicly urged. "Never threaten a man individually. If he deserves to be threatened, the necessities of the times require that he should die."[9]

While Hampton's call for one-on-one terrorism was to prove highly effective, it did not in the least cramp the style of the Ku Klux or Red Shirts, who interpreted their leader's policy of "force without violence" to mean that they first fire above Republican heads before firing at them.

"The Red Shirts rode like the cavalry of Hampton's old brigades, paraded in towns, and attended meetings of both parties in impressive numbers," is the way Manly W. Wellman describes the action in his *Giant in Grey*. "Radical speakers, including [Governor Daniel H.] Chamberlain, found themselves repeatedly challenged before large audiences as 'liars, thieves, and rascals.' "[10]

The Red Shirts did not confine themselves to firing verbal insults at Republican speakers but were in the habit of galloping up in a cloud of dust and firing cannon over their heads. Hearing the commotion, nearby residents thought the Civil War had broken out all over again. One Red Shirt company in Columbia boasted twelve four-pounder cannon in its arsenal. When President Grant ordered all such armed bands to disband, this one cheerily made a public announcement that it had changed its name to the "Hampton & Tilden Musical Club, with twelve four-pounder flutes."[11] None disbanded, and as the campaign progressed arms were shipped in from neighboring neo-Confederate states, packed in "drygoods" crates and barrels.[12]

In Louisiana and Florida the Shotgun Plan was applied without much variation on its original theme. Louisiana in particular had a long record of prior experience in Negro-hunting, as for example in the New Orleans slaughter of participants in the constitutional convention of 1866, the Colfax massacre of 1873, the Cousahatta massacre of August 1874, and the massive New Orleans Negro hunt that took place in September of that same year.

In conformity with the Mississippi pattern of 1875, the county Democratic Party clubs assumed responsibility for applying the terror in

Louisiana in 1876. President Grant sent orders to General Sheridan, who was still nominally in charge of the Louisiana/Texas military district, to enforce the peace; but there was no peace. "Organized clubs of masked men, formed as recommended by the central Democratic Committee, rode through the country at night, marking their course by the whipping, shooting, wounding, maiming, mutilation and murder of women, children and defenceless men whose houses were forcibly entered" is the way Ohio Congressman John Sherman described the Louisiana scene at the time.[13]

And in Florida, the third state where counterrevolution (more politely referred to by the counterrevolutionaries as "redemption") was the order of the day, the election campaign was scarcely less bloody. Indeed, Republican candidates and black voters were under heavy fire all across the South, as the counterrevolution pressed forward its mopping-up activities.

As election day drew near, the Congress—which earlier in the year had turned a cold shoulder to Grant's request for a new law that would give the U.S. government power to monitor U.S. elections—grew panicky as anarchy spread over the South. But instead of adopting the law he had asked for, the lawmakers merely adopted a resolution calling upon the president to do something to stop the violence "at all costs."[14]

Time had almost run out, but the old warrior did what he could. It was to be his final effort to tame his perennial rebel adversaries. Law or no law, he appointed 11,501 deputy U.S. marshals and 4,813 polling supervisors, stationing them not only across the South but also in Northern wards where big-city political machines had also made a mockery of the election process. In addition, he sent still more troops into South Carolina, appealing the while to practitioners of force and violence in other states not to make further military intervention necessary.[15]

These last-ditch measures were helpful in enabling some blacks to vote, but overall it was a matter of too little too late. The logistics of intervention meant that the terrorists could have a free hand on election eve and election day, and it would be all over before any troops could get there. In some instances, when U.S. marshals sent in by Grant sought to give blacks safe conduct to the polls, the blacks were shot and the marshals along with them.[16]

There was little to distinguish that election day of 1876 from those that had preceded it down South without benefit of federal policing except that, pursuant to the Shotgun Plan, virtually the entire white electorate was up in arms to see to it that there would be little or no black electorate. In all other respects, it was a repeat and climactic performance.

In many localities whites had managed to gain control of the election machinery, and from this vantage point they came up with a device that was to stand white supremacy in good stead for generations: hide-and-seek polling places. Last-minute, unannounced changes in the location of polling places caused many would-be black voters to "get lost." To make doubly sure, armed white pickets were posted to intercept any who might find the way. Lerone Bennett, Jr., described the way the hide-and-seek ballot box worked: "Polling places were located in bayous and on islands, in barns and fodder houses . . . In one Louisiana parish . . . the whites gathered at the white church and were told, in whispers, how to reach the polls. In another county, the polls opened in the dark of the morning and whites voted by the light of candles. When the Negro voters showed up, the polls were closed for the day. In Mississippi, white men from Alabama and Louisiana streamed across the state lines and voted early and often."[17]

Burning the Midnight Oil

Around midnight that November 7, Hayes went to bed saying, "I am of the opinion that the Democrats have carried the country."[18] But there were others in the Republican camp who were not prepared to accept that verdict. In their view, the neo-Confederates had, by rendering the Republicans' Southern black constituency hors de combat, had stolen a victory that rightfully belonged to the Republicans— and they were determined to get it back if at all possible.

To this end the editor of the Republican New York Times, Whitelaw Reid, kept the midnight oil burning, conferring with his staff on what headline to run in the morning's first edition.The returns indicated that Samuel J. Tilden had 184 undisputed electoral votes and Hayes 165. To win, a candidate had to have 185 electoral votes. Someone at that press meeting took note of the fact that if Hayes were to carry the three Southern states still under Republican administrations—Louisiana with its eight electoral votes, South Carolina with seven, and Florida with four— he would have the necessary 185 votes and be the winner by a margin of one.

On the strength of this "discovery" they woke the sleeping Republican chairman Zachariah Chandler and persuaded him to "issue" the statement: "Hayes has 185 electoral votes and is elected."[19] Then, on the strength of Chairman Chandler's announcement, New York Times editor

Reid and that other Republican bigwig William E. Chandler persuaded General Daniel Sickles to send telegrams to the (Republican) state officials in Louisiana, South Carolina, and Florida (with a copy to Oregon) as follows: "With your state sure for Hayes, he is elected. Hold your state."[20] They signed it Zachariah Chandler, chairman of the Republican Party. A bit later, having some misgivings about the wording, Reid and Chandler dispatched a second version which read: "Hayes is elected if we carry South Carolina, Florida, and Louisiana. Can you hold your state?"[21] (Subsequently, both Chandler and Sickles claimed "credit" for sending telegrams.) At 3:00 A.M. South Carolina responded in the affirmative and by 6:00 A.M. Oregon had done likewise.

As for the *New York Times* headline that morning, the first edition declared that the outcome of the election was in doubt and the second suggested that Hayes had won. Democrats across the country set up a howl that the Republicans were trying to steal the election and threatened an armed march on Washington. Grant took the threat seriously enough to deploy troops in and around the Capital and to send troops into the three contested states to protect the incumbents from attack.

(The situation in those states in 1876 was somewhat akin to latter-day close elections, when absentee ballots, coming in belatedly by mail, have upset apparent victories. Untold number of would-be black voters were "absent" on that election day—not from the precincts where they were registered but from the polls as a result of having been told they would be dead men if they went there. It might well be argued that they were as entitled to cast "absentee ballots" as those we have nowadays entitled to do while away on business, vacation, or military service.)

In 1876 the canvassing boards in the disputed states faced the hard fact that the white vote was in and the black vote was not. Short of holding another election made free by federal bayonets, there was no way to set matters aright but to take and count affidavits from blacks who had been prevented from voting Republican, and to throw out such fraudulent white votes as could be identified as such.

In South Carolina the canvassing board seemed inclined to concede that the Democrats had carried the state while claiming that the presidential vote had gone for Hayes. The incumbent legislature took exception to this view and declared that the Republican candidates for the governorship and legislature had also won. Both Hampton and Chamberlain promptly got themselves sworn in as governor, and both slates of contending legislators likewise took the oath of office. Had it not been for the presence of federal troops, a shoot-out between Hampton's Red

Shirts and Chamberlain's (largely black) militia would doubtless have ensued.[22]

In Florida, the Democratic strategy was to set up a howl for a "fair count" of the returns. But needless to say, a "fair count" of returns from an unfair election can only produce an unfair result. After a great deal of affidavit-taking as to whites who had voted more than once and blacks who had not been allowed to vote at all, the state's canvassing board declared that in equity the victory belonged to the Republicans.

In Louisiana, where a so-called "fair count" of returns from the unfair election indicated that from six to nine thousand more Democratic votes had been cast than Republican, the canvassing board finally announced in favor of the latter, declaring that the White League had "by force . . . and intimidation, halting at no enormity of crime . . . [substituted] the rule of violence . . . [for] the will of the majority."[23]

With Hayes's claim to the twenty electoral votes of these three disputed states thus buttressed, the focus of national attention shifted back to Washington, as talk of "Tilden or blood!" and a march on the capital increased.[24]

✠

CHAPTER 14

✠

When they drafted the U.S. Constitution, the founding fathers tried to anticipate every eventuality, but they never anticipated the one that cropped up one hundred years later.

In all of the nation's preceding presidential elections, the Congress in joint session simply recorded the votes and passed them on to the electoral college. When Jefferson and Burr tied in 1800, the House of Representatives decided between them, as provided by the Constitution. The problem in 1876, however, was not a tie but contested returns from several states. It was the constitutional duty of the president of the Senate (a Republican) to "count" the votes—but which set of votes should he, would he, count?

With the Constitution requiring that the new president be sworn into office on March 4, there was no time to lose.

Although both candidates expressed the belief that the Congress itself should resolve the dilemma, a joint committee of that body on January 12 recommended that the buck be passed to a special commission created for the purpose. As approved by Congress, this commission was to consist of fifteen men: each house to name five, with one in each of these delegations to be chosen by lot, and with five members to be drawn from the Supreme Court.

No one was surprised when the House, dominated by Democrats, came up with three Tilden supporters among its delegation of five, and the Senate, dominated by Republicans, produced three Hayes supporters among the five from its ranks. Moreover, the four justices selected from the Supreme Court were equally divided between Tilden and Hayes. These four were to choose a fifth justice—who in the circumstances would hold the presidency of the United States in his hands.

All of the remaining justices on the bench, from among whom the choice had to be made, were nominally Republicans. The one agreed to by Democrats was Joseph P. Bradley of New Jersey. A Grant appointee, Bradley had as previously noted endeared himself to white supremacists by authoring that Magna Carta of private-sector terrorism, his circuit court decision freeing the perpetrators of the Colfax massacre, subsequently embraced by the Supreme Court as the law of the land. Farther back in his judicial career, Bradley had rendered a decision that had enabled Thomas Scott of the Pennsylvania Railroad to acquire the Texas and Pacific scheme to link the South to the West. So some said that the commission consisted of seven representatives of the Democratic Party, seven for the Republican Party, and one representing the Pennsylvania Railroad.[1]

The commission met for the first time on January 31. Tilden's attorneys wanted the commission to "go beyond the returns" from the three disputed states to hear evidence that the Republican canvassing boards in those states had juggled the figures. Lawyers representing Hayes contended, ironically, that to do so would be an invasion of states' rights, inasmuch as the returns in question were the only ones that had been duly signed by the respective state governors. (There was no one there to argue in favor of "going behind the returns" far enough to show that black citizens, en masse, had been kept from voting by terror and intimidation.) The commission took the matter under advisement.

On the following day, February 1, Congress met in joint session to go through the motions of tallying the returns. The galleries were packed with members of the diplomatic corps and foreign journalists, intent upon witnessing and reporting this unscheduled feature of the centennial. The proceedings went forward with outward dignity, set against a backdrop of recurrent rumors that, if the decision were to go to Tilden, President Grant was prepared to stage a military coup, whereas on the other hand if it went to "Rutherfraud" Hayes, neo-Copperhead rifle clubs would form in the North to join forces with neo-Confederate rifle clubs in the South to unseat him.

As the roll call of states got under way alphabetically, no one paid much attention until Florida was called. "The Chair hands the tellers a certificate from the State of Florida, received by messenger, and the corresponding one by mail," Senate President T. W. Ferry intoned. After examining the first set of returns, which had been signed by the governor of Florida, the teller announced that the state's electoral votes belonged to Hayes. But then the second set was examined, and the teller proclaimed that Florida had voted for Tilden.

"Are there any objections to these certificates from the State of Florida?" the senate president asked impartially. There was a brief silence, after which the session exploded with a roar. After heated objections had been heard from both sides, the controversy, as planned, was referred to the commission.

The commission was scheduled to meet on February 8 to decide whether or not to "go behind" the official Florida returns. The night before, Democratic national chairman Abram S. Hewitt invited some of his party's top leaders to dinner in his home. After dinner, Hewitt dispatched a personal friend of Bradley's, a man named Stevens, to go to Bradley's home and sound him out as to his intentions for the morrow. Stevens went, and in a few hours was back, triumphantly reporting that Bradley had read to him a draft of his opinion that the commission should go behind the Florida returns.[2] Taking this to mean that Bradley's decisive vote was going for Tilden, the Democratic leaders toasted their victory in champagne and retired for the evening.

Before that evening was over, however, Bradley received some other visitors. Between midnight and dawn a virtual cavalcade of seventeen carriages carrying Republican dignitaries arrived at the Bradley mansion. Heading the delegation were Senator F. T. Frelinghuysen (himself a member of the commission) and Secretary of the Navy George M. Robeson, both of whom were fellow New Jerseyans and close friends of Bradley's. Also said to be among those present was Thomas Scott of the Pennsylvania Railroad. According to some reports, before the night was over the flag had been waved, Mrs. Bradley had wept, and $200,000 had changed hands—all in behalf of Hayes.[3]

Be all that as it may (and there are those who dispute it), come dawn and the commission session, Bradley was ready with his decision—not the pro-Tilden one he had read to Stevens early in the evening but a pro-Hayes one. And so the commission vote was eight to seven not to go behind the official Florida pro-Hayes returns.

When infuriated Democrats publicly took Bradley to task for a last-minute switch, he reportedly admitted having had two opposing recommendations in hand, both written by him, and had finally opted for the pro-Hayes one. It was common judicial practice, he asserted, for judges to prepare opposing decisions and then to choose between them.

Two days later, on February 10, the commission met en camera and emerged with a recommendation that the Congress count Florida's electoral votes for Hayes. For all practical purposes, Bradley had picked the president of the United States.

Democrats were very far from accepting the verdict. Once again the cry of "Tilden or blood!" was heard in the land. Editor Henry Watterson of the *Louisville Courier-Journal* proclaimed that 100,000 Kentuckians stood ready to march to see justice done for Tilden.[4] Many an editor bemoaned the "Mexicanization" of the American electoral process, and some voiced the fear that a two-headed government, akin to those which over the years had cropped up in many a Southern state, would ensconce "theyself" in the nation's capitol. Grant was sufficiently concerned to deploy more troops around and about on February 16, the day the commission gave a repeat performance by recommending that Louisiana's votes also go to Hayes.

Still undaunted, Democrats launched a filibuster designed to halt the counting of votes until the inaugural date had passed, hoping thereby to throw the decision into the House, where they had a majority. With and without such a hope, they made the most of the time gained to negotiate the best possible deal for the (white) South. Republican Congressmen and railroad lobbyists alike sought to persuade Democratic Representatives that it was their "patriotic" duty to go along with the Hayes decision. But the Southerners especially had many an ax to grind and were not to be bought off for any song. Their patriotism, such as it was, was still sectional, not national.

Even so, there were those whose votes could be had for a price. Some researchers have reported that the railroad lobbyists, fearful of Tilden and reform, swarmed through the halls of the Capitol like maggots through a cheese, openly bidding for Southern votes for Hayes.

Under the joint resolution establishing the commission, only a majority vote of both houses could set aside the commission's decisions. On February 19, following a stormy joint session, the commission's decision that Louisiana's electoral votes should go to Hayes was approved. Five days later, on the 24th, the Democratic Speaker of the House, Samuel J. Randall, let it be known that he was in favor of conceding Hayes the White House.

There was not much time left to finalize who was to get what under

the Deal that was taking shape. On the 26th, key Republican and De-
mocratic leaders met behind closed doors in committee rooms at the
Capitol, and then, the following day, reconvened in Wormsley's Hotel.
There, the Deal was struck.

According to the Associated Press, the Democrats agreed to swap the
Republicans the White House in exchange for the governor's mansion
in Louisiana (and South Carolina and Florida). The incongruity of such
a resolution of the contested election returns did not seem to bother anyone, except Republican James A. Garfield, who was so dumbfounded he
left the room. Not until Democrats had intimated that they might let him
become speaker of the House did he return. All that remained to be done
was to explain to the nation and world how it was that these states had
voted for a Republican for president and Democrats for everything else.

When the commission voted February 28 to award South Carolina's
votes to Hayes, the question of who was to be president appeared to have
been resolved. Still unresolved, however, was the problem of how to nail
down all that the white South was supposed to receive under the bargain. After all, the Treaty of Wormsley's Hotel (as I would dub it) was
not the sort of thing one could bring up on the floors of Congress for debate and ratification. "Hayes' friends can profess his promises" is the way
Louisiana's Democratic Congressman E. John Lewis expressed these apprehensions. "*He* has promised nothing."[5]

All that remained in the hands of the Democrats by way of leverage
was their ongoing filibuster, stalling the roll call of votes and threatening
to throw the decision, come March 4, into the House. The impasse was
seemingly broken when Tilden elected to send a telegram to Democratic leaders, asking them to "let the roll call proceed." Everyone assumed
that was the end of that, but when on February 28 the joint session got
to Vermont, a traditionally Republican state that everyone knew had
voted for Hayes, out of somewhere in the chamber came a voice asking:
"Are there any other returns from Vermont?" Democratic Party Chairman Abram S. Hewitt sprang to his feet, waving a packet. "I hold in my
hand a package which purports to contain electoral votes from the State
of Vermont," he pronounced. "This package was delivered to me by express about the middle of December last."

The packet held by the Democratic party chairman was a duplicate of
originals said to have been sent to the president of the Senate at the same
time. That worthy now said he had never received any such returns. It
turned out that this rival set of returns—so mysteriously produced at the
last minute but laying claim to a certain antiquity—took advantage of the

fact that one of Vermont's three Republican electors had been disqualified, by virtue of already being an officeholder (postmaster). Now his
Democratic runner-up was asserting that he was entitled to replace him—
and cast a vote for Tilden, which was all Tilden needed for victory.

Did this latest sleight of hand mean that the Deal was off? Amidst great
turmoil, the joint session adjourned to consider the matter.

When they reconvened on the morrow, March 1, one observer remarked that the law-makers were "outnumbered by their masters, the
lobbyists."[6]

When the senate president announced that the rival returns from Vermont had been "mislaid" overnight, tempers flared to new heights. The
debate raged on into the night, and by midnight pistols as well as bottles
of whiskey were being openly displayed atop lawmakers' desks.

It was almost dawn when a Louisiana congressman named Levy took
the floor, claiming to have direct word from Hayes that he would carry
out his end of the deal as made. "I have solemn, earnest and, I believe,
truthful assurances . . . of a policy of conciliation toward the Southern
states . . . in the event of Hayes' election to the Presidency," Congressman Levy informed the assemblage.[7]

Not only had Hayes personally endorsed the commitments made in
his behalf at the Wormsley Hotel, particularly with regard to the prompt
withdrawal of federal troops from the South, but President Grant had
given his endorsement as well. (He who had received Lee's sword at Appomattox was now in effect tendering his own.)

There were still a few formalities to be observed, and the two houses
separated to deliberate among themselves. To the House Tilden sent a
telegram asking that the roll call be allowed to proceed; it was his way of
conceding the presidency to Hayes.

The joint session reconvened at 4:00 A.M., and by 4:10 the roll call had
been completed. Hayes had won by a single electoral vote. Speaking to
the silent congressmen, Senate President Ferry intoned: "Wherefore, I
do declare: that Rutherford B. Hayes, of Ohio, having received a majority of the whole number of electoral votes, is duly elected President
of the United States for four years, commencing on the fourth day of
March, 1877."

The following day, March 3, the still rebellious House, by a vote of
137 to 88, adopted a resolution "declaring" Tilden to have been elected
president. But few took the gesture seriously, it being said that the House
was owned by the railroads, who were afraid of Tilden's countercorrup-
tion proclivities.

Die-hard Democratic Chairman Hewitt tried to persuade Tilden to present himself at the White House for inauguration, adding that armed men in fifteen states were ready to march in his support. None other than General George B. McClellan—he who had perched on the safe side of the Potomac for countless months at the outbreak of the war—volunteered to lead such a march on Washington. But, considering the time frame and his record of "having the slows," no one took him seriously either.[8] Tilden's only response to the proposition was to fire Hewitt. Tempers were, however, running high, and someone cautioned Grant not to leave the White House unoccupied over the weekend.[9]

A Washington journalist who suggested in print that the American people deserved to be enslaved if they permitted Hayes to proceed unscathed from the inaugural to the White House was thrown into jail on a charge of sedition.[10]

Having gotten the small end of the bargain, the Republicans were taking no chances of losing even that. Since March 2 Hayes had been secretly installed in the Washington home of Senator Sherman, playing a game of wait-and-see. Since the constitutionally designated inaugural date, March 4, fell upon a Sunday, Grant invited Hayes to the White House for dinner on the evening of March 3. Upon arrival Hayes discovered that he was not the only one who had come to dinner: Chief Justice Salmon P.Chase was also there, and, as soon as dinner was over, the gentlemen adjourned to a private room, where Hayes was privately sworn in by Chase, "just in case."[11]

But inaugural Monday passed without mishap, though Hayes was seen to wince a bit when, as he passed down a Pennsylvania Avenue lined with soldiers, someone touched off a string of firecrackers.

The basic demand of the neo-Confederacy—that federal troops be pulled out of the South and the entire region left free to return to "Home (white) Rule"—was first on everyone's agenda. Hayes had not even waited to take office before taking some initial steps to scuttle the surviving Republican regimes in the South. In late February he had suggested to Louisiana Governor Packard that it was his patriotic duty to resign but to no avail.[12] In Florida, white supremacists had not waited for any initiative from Hayes but had proceeded on their own, the moment the joint session "ratified" the Treaty of Wormsley's Hotel on March 2, to purge Republicans from public office.[13] Louisiana and South Carolina were different matters, however, and Hayes wanted the sacrifice in those states to be a bloodless one if at all possible, and in any case to be cloaked with some semblance of legality, however transparent. The fact that he owed his presidency to the bravery of black voters in these three states was not enough to deter him from selling these supporters back down the river into bondage to Ole Massa.

South Carolina was first on the Hayes hit list for the very good reason that, unlike Louisiana, it did not have two legislatures and two judicial systems in place to make matters difficult.

And so it was that, on the Sunday preceding his official inaugural, Hayes had his confidant Stanley Matthews write a personal note to South Carolina Governor Chamberlain, strongly hinting that he ought to renounce his claim to having been reelected, for the sake of the new administration and the northern wing of the party. For added impact, William M. Evarts, who had been Andy Johnson's attorney general, was asked to add a postscript. Then, as if to add insult to injury, a relative of the Democratic claimant, Wade Hampton, was asked to hand-deliver the communication.[14]

On that same preinaugural Sunday, Hayes also conferred with a Louisiana Democrat on ways and means of putting to death the Republican government in that state. On March 7 Governor Chamberlain penned his reply. Public duty and personal honor alike dictated that he remain in office, he said; and he vowed to do so unless compelled to surrender by "a power which it would be idle to resist." Intent upon bringing just such power to bear, Democratic claimant Hampton simultaneously demanded that Hayes get his troops out of there.

Meanwhile, Hayes had enlisted the aid of Ohio's Republican Senator John Sherman, who in turn enlisted the aid of some New Orleans bankers, in the task of persuading Packard to step down in Louisiana.[15] But Packard, like Chamberlain, stood firm.

Having given the destabilization process these prods, Hayes did not immediately press the issue but busied himself the while making good on some of the other promissory notes that had come due. He had to look to the Hill for approval of his cabinet appointees, and he thought it best to get that done before alienating any of his supporters by surrendering the rest of the South to the Democrats. He thought it would be timely, indeed, to let Congress go home before he let the ax fall.

The cabinet that Hayes proceeded to gather around him was altogether indicative of what was in store for the South and the nation. Making good his promise to appoint at least one Southerner, Hayes chose as his postmaster general the Tennessean and former Confederate David M. Key. This post, considered to be the prize plum because of the vast patronage it carried with it, was quite enough to mark this obligation "Paid in Full." But Hayes did not stop there. As his secretary of state he named William M. Evarts, a "conservative" who had severed Andy Johnson as attorney general during that earlier postwar restoration of white supremacy and had defended Johnson at this impeachment trial. Evarts had, moreover, been an outspoken critic of Grant's use of troops to put down the power grab of the White League in Louisiana following the election of 1874, and latterly served as chief counsel of the railroad empire builders.

With the notable exception of John Sherman as secretary of the treasury, the entire cabinet of seven was composed of men who had, if anything, negative feelings about the goals of Reconstruction. While the white South and Democrats generally were delighted with it, "staunch" Republicans were dismayed.

"What party do I belong to now?" Republican mentor Robert G. Ingersoll asked in despair.[16]

"Greeley adopted the Democratic Party four years ago . . . that he might be made President," observed Wisconsin Senator Timothy O. Howe. "Hayes *is* President, and yet I guess he means to adopt the Democratic Party."[17]

When some Republican senators threatened to vote against the appointments, some members of the Democratic "opposition" threatened to vote for them. In the same breath, these latter urged the president to get on with troop withdrawal.

After so long a struggle, the South's white supremacists were in no mood to postpone their final seizure of power. A Republican was in the White House, and they could see no reason that they should have to wait to install Democrats in the governor's mansions of Louisiana and South Carolina. In the former state they resolved to proceed with the takeover, troops or no troops.

To this end, the Democratic "legislature" placed under arrest black state militiamen attached to the Republican administration. Governor Packard wired Hayes on March 19, pleading for immediate recognition. On the following day the Democratic claimant, Confederate General Francis T. Nicholls (who had lost both an arm and a leg in the conflict) sought to put the blame for the confrontation on Packard, who he said was provoking violence in a bid for federal intervention.

Hayes did not have to decide all by himself. His new cabinet met on March 20 and 21, and the majority gave their endorsement to his contention that he "did not think the wise policy is to decide contested elections in the States by the use of the National Army."[18] It was decided to send in a presidential commission to seek a solution, with the army being called upon to "maintain order" the while.

This decision created considerable panic among the Southern parties to the Deal, who jumped to the conclusion that Hayes had bowed to pressure and was seeking a way to weasel has way out. Louisiana whites in particular, having seen many a congressional committee probe and resolve in favor of Republican state administrations, were taken aback by the prospect of yet another probe. "Our people have been nearly 'commissioned' to death," bewailed one poor white supremacist. So perturbed was Mississippi's Senator Lucius Q. C. Lamar that he rose from his sick bed to write Hayes: "*Do* as you said you would do!"[19]

As it turned out, all the furor was unwarranted. On a frantic telegram of inquiry sent him by Congressman Charles Foster, Hayes noted: "No change of policy contemplated."

The press too took a hand in seeking to persuade the South's "Home Rulers" to "hold their horses." Even the Washington *National Republican,* long a champion of military intervention, now declared that "any settlement is better than an open controversy" and went on to suggest that the contested elections in the three Southern states be "decided according to the Darwinian theory, 'survival of the fittest.' " In the Southern context, the outcome would of course have nothing whatever to do with fitness but only with the fact that an armed white populace was intent upon subjugating an unarmed black population.

The presidential commission as announced in early April was ostensibly balanced as to party and sectional representation but had been carefully handpicked by Hayes. Although told that they had a free hand, the commissioners were also told that, no matter what, troops would soon be pulled out. Almost everyone concluded that the commission's unwritten mandate was "Get Packard out." The Democratic St. Louis *Republican* openly opined that the commission was merely Hayes's way of "looking about to see how the thing can be done without seeming to do it."[20]

It was also a bid for time, during which Hayes hoped to resolve the South Carolina question in such manner as to set a precedent for Louisiana. The fact that South Carolina did not have rival judicial systems in place seemed to hold forth the possibility of a summary resolution of the question as to which party (race) would hold power.

Earlier, through intermediaries, Hayes had invited both Chamberlain and Hamptom to come to Washington and talk things over with him, separately. Hampton, feeling secure, said he would come only if invited personally by the president. On March 22 the cabinet approved withdrawal of troops from the South Carolina capital, and Hayes made his invitation a personal one. In the circumstances, Chamberlain was fully aware that the Washington visitations were intended to provide nothing more than the semblance of an impartial hearing. His family arrived in the capital with all their belongings, ahead of him. He felt it prudent to make the trip alone and incognito.[21]

Confederate General Hampton, in marked contrast, advanced upon the nation's capital like some conquering hero and was greeted as such at whistle-stops all along the way by large crowds (of whites) who cheered and threw flowers at his feet. Bands played, and cannon salutes and firecrackers created an air of a latter-day Roman triumph. In speech after speech Hampton proclaimed that he would accept no commission and no compromise and demanded that the U.S. troops in South Carolina be confined to their barracks and the state government be left in the hands of men "strong enough to sustain it." The "good ole Rebel" actually sounded like he might be going to stage a coup in Washington.

Chamberlain told the president that he would not abdicate voluntarily but admitted he could not hold office without the backing of federal troops. To this end, he asked that a commission be sent in, as in Louisiana. Hampton on the other hand assured Hayes that if troops were withdrawn and he took over, peace would be preserved and "the rights of all respected."[22] (Southern whites were very adept, then and in later generations, at making such declarations, inasmuch as they had in mind full rights for whites and highly delimited rights for blacks.)

This (without the foregoing translation) was of course just what the president wanted to hear, and he promised Hampton that the troops would be removed very shortly. On April 3 he issued the order, and on April 10 they broke camp. On April 11 Chamberlain instructed an assistant to hand over the keys, and Hampton and his men took over the capitol (The Republicans at the time still had a substantial number of representatives in the state legislature, and a majority of one in the state senate; but this situation was promptly "corrected" through the process of impeachment, and special elections held in July, which gave the Democrats a clean sweep.)

In Louisiana, the desired result was achieved somewhat differently. With republican government wiped out and replaced by white rule in South Carolina, it was a foregone conclusion that the same was in the cards for Louisiana. There the commission had been doing its work well the while. When these presidential emissaries arrived in New Orleans on

April 5, such pre-Deal options as new elections or leaving the decision in the hands of the legislature(s) or the state supreme court(s) had gone by the board. It was soon evident, moreover, that the white supremacists had no intention of sharing power with blacks or any other shade of Republicans in any sort of coalition government. There was, in short, and in these circumstances, no other prospect than the pulling out of troops and allowing white rule to take complete control.

The commission did its spadework as gravediggers of democracy well. To make certain that nothing went awry, Hayes during this period removed the feisty General Sheridan from his Louisiana/Texas command, replacing him with the more apolitical General Winfield Scott Hancock. The press did its part in softening up Northern public opinion with contentions (as in the *Boston Herald* of April 11) that the removal of troops did not mean abandonment of Reconstruction but on the contrary would "facilitate its realization through state autonomy."[23] And because white Americans wanted to believe such things, they did.

The strategy devised by the presidential commission, with enthusiastic assistance from the cohorts of white rule, was to bribe enough members of the Republican legislature to defect to the Democratic legislature to give that body a quorum. Once established, that quorum would proceed to "legitimatize" the unofficial election returns purporting to show that white supremacists had won the governorship and other state offices and at the same time endorse the white folk's version of a state supreme court. To raise the necessary bribe money, appeals were directed to New Orleans businessmen, and public lotteries were held.[24]

The day after Congress went home the commission wired the president that the legislature put together by the Democrats was on the verge of having a quorum and that troops could therefore be withdrawn from around the statehouse where Packard's Republican regime was ensconced. On the very next day, word was sent that the quorum had been formed. On the day after that, acting on the recommendation of both the commission and the cabinet, the president ordered the U.S. troops out. When the cathedral clock struck noon on April 24, a military band also struck up, and the United States forces marched to a wharf on the Mississippi River to embark. As they did so, (white) crowds cheered, church bells tolled, and cannon fired parting shots into the sky.

Similar scenes enacted all across the South served to ease somewhat the bitterness that Appomattox had engendered in the hearts of Southern whites. The departing U.S. troops did not lay down their arms as the Confederates had been required to do at Appomattox, and Grant was not there to give Lee back his sword; but the final victory was nonetheless sweet.

No one bothered to asked Southern blacks how it tasted to them. Nor could anyone ask the Union dead.

There was no lack of comprehension at the time of the import of all that had taken place. On April 27, three days after the embarkation, the *St. Louis Globe-Democrat* proclaimed as official Southern policy that extrapolation from the Dred Scott decision and Klan oath: "The Southern negro now has no rights except such as the white people of the South chose to allow him."

The North was scarcely less unfeeling. "Concede the very worst, that blacks are about to descend into political servitude," a New Yorker named Thomas Beecher wrote James G. Blaine. "What of it?"[25]

Even before the embarkation, the *Nation* (on April 5) had foreseen just such a future. "The negro will disappear from the field of national politics," it predicted. "Henceforth the nation, as a nation, will have nothing more to do with him."

This was to prove true as regards any effective national concern for black rights; on the other hand, however, the nation, as a nation—with the concurrence of all three branches of the federal government—went on to embrace warmly the neo-Confederacy's ideology of white supremacy, ape its system of apartheid, and practice gross racial discrimination in employment in both the public and private sectors and in its armed forces. Uncle Sam, in short, did forget the American black as human and citizen but remained keenly aware of his utility as cheap laborer in time of peace and buck private in time of war.

Even as Appomattox was only symbolic of decisive events that had gone before, so too was the embarking of U.S. troops from New Orleans. Nevertheless, that would seem to be as good a place as any to conclude our brief accounting of "How the South Won the War."

Some may yet say that it was the peace that the white South won, not the war. But no matter; it all depends upon one's definition of what constitutes warfare. By the fruit we know full well who the final victors were.

✠

AFTERMATH

✠

That which came to pass following the withdrawal of federal troops from the South was of course altogether predictable, the wishful thinking of the president not withstanding.

By and large the Southern society that reemerged under white rule was not all that different from the status quo antebellum. The dress rehearsal that had been conducted under the aegis of President Johnson had provided a faithful preview of that which was to come. In parting, however, lest any reader be left in any doubt, it might be well to relate just a few of the things that came in the wake of withdrawal.

The Treaty of Wormsley's Hotel was truly a case of winner-takes-(almost)-all, and the neo-Confederacy collected on just about everything it had been promised.

All three branches of the federal government—executive, legislative, judicial—honored the unwritten covenant not to try to enforce in any meaningful way the constitutional rights of blacks in the South.

The vestigial remnant of the Freedmen's Bureau was quietly put to death.

As for any pledge to procure public backing for the Texas and Pacific

Railroad project, this ran afoul of retrenchment forces in Congress. William Lloyd Garrison wrote, while the North was willing to "trust the negro to the South," it was not about to "open its purse strings."[1] Even so, however, public funds were forthcoming for another railroad that was to link the South with the West by 1880; and during the decade that followed the South was to receive more developmental assistance than it had in all its previous years. No one spoke of it as war reparations (by the victor!) but much of it did go to such projects as the repair of war-wrecked levees on the Mississippi River.

Although, so far as is known, the treaty did not include any stipulation that U.S. marshals as well as U.S. troops would be pulled out of the South, the neo-Confederacy chose to put this interpretation upon the generalized understanding that the white South would be permitted to practice "home rule." What good was home rule, they asked themselves, if there were going to be U.S. marshals all over the place?

In an effort to compel the U.S. to accede to this tacked-on peace term, white Southerners in Congress tacked onto the 1877 general appropriations bill just such a mandate. But Hayes balked at this as not having been a part of the Deal. Deprived of funds, many government activities ground to a halt, and a special session of Congress had to be called to get things going again. In the interim, many worked without pay, including U.S. soldiers who were busily engaged in killing Indians and breaking a railway strike.

Whereas Lincoln's claim to fame rested upon his mantle as the "Great Emancipator," Hayes envisioned himself as the "Great Pacificator." The question of course was "Who was to be pacified, and upon whose terms?"

With a view to enhancing this image—and with an eye on the coming fall elections and the reconvening of Congress—Hayes set out upon a speaking tour that took him to New England in June and August, Ohio in September, and the South during late September and October. On the New England leg of this junket he took along his former Confederate Postmaster David M. Key, whom he introduced as a man who "has been greatly wrong in the past, but is greatly right now." Accompanying him into the South was none other than Confederate General/Klan Dragon/Red Shirt commander/South Carolina Governor Wade Hampton.

Carried away by the cordiality of his reception in Atlanta, the president of the United States told his audience: "It is no discredit to you and no special credit to us that the war turned out as it did."[2]

As for his Southern policy, there was nothing experimental about it, he said; rather, it was fixed, irreversible fact. "There has been no other six months since the war when there have been so few outrages committed upon the colored people," he exulted.

But of course things had been rather peaceful *before* the war too, under slavery. In reality, black subjugation was being palmed off as white pacification.

William E. Chandler was moved to observe that Hayes's remarks in Atlanta had "blotted out all distinctions between loyalty and treason, between Union and rebel soldiers, between the torturers of Andersonville and the veterans of the North."[3]

A few old guard abolitionists were also heard from, including William Lloyd Garrison, who berated Hayes for his "policy of compromise, of credulity, of weakness, of subserviency, of surrender," which upheld "might against right . . . the rich and powerful against the poor and unprotected."[4]

"The whole soil of the South is hidden by successive layers of broken promises," added Wendell Phillips. "To trust a Southern promise would be fair evidence of insanity."[5]

Forsooth, Ole Massa lost no time in reestablishing his hegemony over both the South and the nation.

A movement calling itself the "Readjusters" sprang up in many parts of the South, addressing itself to hamstringing or repealing much of the direly needed social legislation that had been enacted during Reconstruction. The fledgling public schools systems were a prime target, and appropriations and bond issues intended for them were either voided or diverted.

"Free schools are not a necessity," declared the governor of Virginia (at a time when 20 percent of the South's whites and 70 percent of blacks were illiterate). "Our fathers did not need free schools to make them what they were . . . [Schools] are luxury . . . to be paid for, like any other luxury, by the people who wish their benefits."[6]

In those days the average term of public schools in the South was three months, and the region was spending one-third as much per pupil as was the North. "The typical free school is kept in a log house, with dirt or puncheon floor, without desks or blackborads," one observer of the Southern educational scene reported.[7]

Along with the repeal of much of the Reconstruction legislatures' social programs—which followed hard upon the heels of the assassination of Republican officeholders, causing the remainder to flee for their lives—a systematic campaign was waged to destroy all *records* attesting what good had been done during the days when free elections and republican government held sway. Presumably the usurpers did not want to leave extant any documents that might at some future date be invoked in support of a Second Reconstruction—or refute their scurrilous version of what had taken place during the first.

After repealing the Reconstruction legislation providing for free schools, orphanages, old folks' homes, and such, the new lily-white legislatures busied themselves with the refinement of the Black Codes, which before the war had governed the conduct of "free persons of color." A first order of business was the enactment of laws and regulations designed to impose an apartheid system of racial segregation in every aspect of Southern life.

As for that long-festering postwar question of whether blacks should be permitted to serve on juries, it was now speedily resolved—in favor of their exclusion. And for all practical purposes, blacks were likewise precluded from testifying against whites.

Despite all such evidence as to what the white South had in mind when it promised "fair treatment" for blacks, Hayes toyed with the notion of appointing a conservative Virginian to serve as his attorney general. Garfield was sufficiently moved to complain that Hayes had "nolled suits" and "discontinued prosecutions" at a time when Southern whites were "whetting their knives for any Republican they could find."[8]

When Congress convened in October, Democrats, who said they had not been privy to much less party to their brethren's implied promise as part of the Deal to let Republican James A. Garfield become speaker of the House and appoint its committees, unceremoniously brushed that "understanding" aside. Far from letting the Republicans have the House as well as the White House as their short end of the deal, the Democrats launched a determined campaign to strengthen their grip via the congressional elections that were held in fifteen states in 1877.

Upset by this double cross, the *Springfield Republican* (with reference to Hayes's Southern junket) had this to say: "Southern Democrats at least should have held the pacification of the South worth something more than a tender of old bourbon and of effusive speeches at railroad receptions."[9]

When the election returns were in, they clearly showed that the Republican Party had been demolished in the South and gravely diminished elsewhere in the country. Even Ohio, Hayes's home state, went Democratic for the first time in twenty-four years. In these fifteen states, the

Democrats polled a net gain of 109,000 votes. Taking note, Hayes in his second annual message to Congress lamented lamely that some Southern blacks were still not being allowed to vote.

When a deputation of Republican congressmen called upon the president to voice their concern over the trend revealed by the election, Hayes sent them away even more dismayed by his cheery assurance that his Southern policy would delivery eight Southern states into Republican ranks in the presidential election of 1880. To everyone except Hayes, apparently, his vision of rebuilding the party in the South under white leadership and upon a white base was clearly a pipe dream. Southern whites were not about to switch their allegiance to a party that, rightly or wrongly, they felt had driven them to a bloody war, robbed them of their slaves, compelled them to rejoin the Union, and tried to force black equality upon them. Intent upon perpetuating white supremacy, they knew full well that the Democratic Party was by far the surest guarantor of it.

With an eye to the upcoming congressional elections of 1878, there were some few Republicans who sought to stir their president into the sort of heroic action that would obviously be required if the Democratic tide were to be turned and free elections restored in the South.

"There is no such thing as good faith among the . . . leaders of the Southern Democrats," James Atkins wrote to Garfield in February of 1878. "One will make a promise with the distinct understanding that his associates are to break it, and allow him to outwardly condemn them for so doing, without any loss of standing among them as associates."[10] Based upon this assessment, Atkins concluded: "No conciliation is possible; it must be *conquer or be conquered.*"[11] It was the latter that came to pass.

When the congressional election of 1878 was over, the Democrats had not only tightened their grip upon the House but also captured the Senate. Of the 294 Southern counties where blacks were in the majority, only 62 were reported as going Republican (as compared to 126 in 1876). In many a predominantly black county, not one had dared to vote.

Declaring that his Southern policy had been based upon "an earnest desire to conciliate the Southern leaders . . . and to soften the asperities of political strife," the would-be Pacificator went on to confess: "I am reluctantly forced to admit that the experiment was a failure. The first election of importance held since it was attempted has proved that fair elections with free suffrage . . . in the South are an impossibility."[12]

A few voices were to be heard in favor of some new enforcement acts and of refusing to seat representatives from districts where blacks had not been allowed to vote; but it was much too late for all such as this. White rule of the South, and South rule of the Congress, were both accomplished facts. With the disfranchised blacks now being counted as whole persons, rather than three-fifths of one as they had been as slaves, Southern whites purporting to represent them garnered that many more seats in the House.

In the Congress that sat in 1879-80, fully 90 percent of the Southern contingent had once served in the Confederate army or government. Among them were no fewer than eighteen Confederate generals. A Confederate newspaper editor served as secretary of the senate, and the former commander of a Confederate prison camp was chairman of the senate committee on military pensions. What the Democrats had was a "shotgun, rifle, and red-shirt majority," wrote Horace Redfield in the *Cincinnati Commercial*.[13] To this Republican Senator Joseph R. Hawley added that the Democratic Party was a "motley compound of all the don'ts, won'ts, shant's, hates, prejudices . . . of the times."[14]

Not only were no new civil rights measures forthcoming; five times during 1879 neo-Confederates in Congress attached riders to general appropriations bills providing for repeal of what little of the existing laws the Supreme Court had left alive. Each time Hayes vetoed, and, as time went by and it became evident that the federal government was not going to make any serious attempt to enforce the remaining laws, the white South became reconciled to living with them as dead letters.

Believers in equal rights were hard put to find any consolation. One black man named Erastus B. Williamson did summon up the faith to write George P. Hoard in 1890: "I thank God for the 15th Amendment. It cannot be annulled *always*. The power is vested and will sooner or later be exercised."[15] (As it turned out, it would be rather later—three-quarters of a century later.)

Whereas Appomattox had failed to achieve a lasting peace, the Deal did. Shots were to be heard for generations to come, but these were no longer a sign of intersectional strife between white Americans. They were merely the sound effects of white Southerners blowing away any black Southerners who took exception to being subjugated.

The Invisible Empire of white supremacy had at long last come to terms with the Invisible Empire of finance capital, and, amidst a semblance of tranquility, the two settled down to the business of turning the nation's natural and human resources to a profit.

✠

ALARUM AND EXCURSION

✠

Some may say that what I have touched upon in this volume is ancient history, and so it is, in point of time; but it is also modern history, in that it was the unfinished business of the First Reconstruction that made necessary that veritable Second Reconstruction, the civil rights struggle of the mid-twentieth century. It is futurism, even, in that we are still far from fulfillment of America's pledge of liberty and justice for all.

If we are so bold as to hold up a mirror to the "progress made" during the long century stretching from Appomattox to the Overcoming, what do we see?

Where once we had segregated racism, we now have desegregated racism.

We may no longer be Jim Crowed, but we are just about as black ghettoed as we ever were.

The Token Negro has been replaced by a token black middle class, but the black masses in the inner cities are as skill-less, jobless, and hopeless as ever.

Crime, seemingly the only career open to many, and inspired by megabuck white-collar banditry in government, banking, and business, has packed penitentiaries with disadvantaged Afro and Hispanic youth.

Most portentous of all, much as the facetious formula "separate but equal" provided a cloak of constitutional sanction for apartheid in America for a century, the equally devious promotion of the "neighborhood school" as guarantor of "parental involvement" (and "only alternative" to the calculated busing of both white and black students for unconscionable distances and hours) in the given context of on-going residential segregation now threatens to bring about the resegregation of education for untold generations to come.

To be sure, the shaking off of apartheid, enforced as it was by both legalistic and extra-legal means, was a major accomplishment, second only to the abolition of chattel slavery; and there have been many appreciable gains besides.

But something has happened in human affairs the while that does have a bearing upon our pursuit of black rights in America and human rights everywhere. It is globalization, and the threats to the globe itself.

As some philosopher once observed, "the forms of exploitation change from time to time." In recent centuries vast segments of mankind have been locked in titanic struggles to throw off such yokes as slavery, colonialism, feudalism, inquisitions, monarchy, autocracy, oligarchy, plutocracy, apartheid, caste, sexism, fascism, and the respective horrors thus far displayed by communism and capitalism.

As the present bloodiest-of-centuries draws to a close, fratricidal strife based upon race, nationality, ethnicity, and religion—ever the curse of our species—appears to be increasing rather than decreasing.

World War I "To Make the World Safe for Democracy" came and went, only to see a wave of totalitarianism engulf much of the planet.

World War II to assure the Four Freedoms for all has left only a few who can name them (freedom of speech and religion, freedom from want and fear).

The ideological battle-of-the-century between the two isms and the accompanying ruinous arms race has bankrupted not just one but both of the longtime superpowers. The big difference may yet turn out to be that we had a national credit card and have not yet had the courage to foreclose on ourselves.

We have been so caught up in celebrating the demise of the former USSR as to lose sight of the many trends that are entirely capable of reducing us to the former USA. A scant threescore years ago our vaunted Western way likewise fell flat on its face, leaving the West quite as destitute as the Soviets are today. Fact is, we are standing in the need of perestroika as much as anybody.

Instead of taking advantage of the changed situation by converting from the endless stockpiling of weapons of war to meeting human needs and balancing our budget, we keep casting about for some new enemy to justify keeping the munitions flowing. This is sheer folly, and no way to compete with the Japanese and Germans. We would do better, actually, to emulate the ancient Egyptians, who squandered their substance by building pyramids in a forlorn bid for immortality.

It is being said that the twenty-first century may be characterized by "ethnic cleansing" as the twentieth was by hot and cold wars. This assumes, of course, that AIDS does not depopulate the plant first.

Should we survive the one and the other, it may well be that we shall live to see what may come to be referred to as the "Global Sweatshop." Such a system would obviate any need for reenslaving peoples from certain continents and putting them to work in others. Rather, it would operate on the principle of "leave 'em and work 'em where they're at."

The trend toward the Global Sweatshop as format of the future is already well under way and rapidly gathering momentum. The flight of capital from industrialized/unionized lands to underdeveloped non-unionized ones—where labor is dirt cheap, taxes are low, and pollution is okay—is spawning human degradation and natural despoliation in a manner not seen since the industrial revolution made its debut.

As for the American workers whose generations of labor and struggle created the capital in question, they are being abandoned to wither on the vine, without so much as a backward glance or fare-thee-well, and they have little to show for their pains besides unpaid mortgages, rusting factories, gutted mines, and tree stumps.

For some centuries the developed world was wont to look upon the teeming millions of the underdeveloped world as surplus people; but now the emergent Global Sweatshop threatens to turn the tables and make it the other way around. And where is the "representative" American government in the face of this calamitous prospect? Far from doing battle with the Evil Empire, which the Global Sweatshop, so rapidly being forged by Runaway Capital, represents, "our" government raises the spurious standard of "Free Trade" and plays the role of Great Facilitator in the betrayal. This is a far cry from the days when Uncle Sam hastened to adopt and enforce the Runaway Slave Act. Time now for a Runaway Capital Act, or we may all soon be wage slaves together, regardless of race, creed, or color.

The history of the industrial revolution has been nothing but conflict between capital's desire to maximize profits and labor's struggle for the right to collective bargaining as its only means of securing decent wages and working conditions. Heretofore the battle has been between individual plants and industries against their workers, with shutdown and lockout the ultimate weapons of the former, and the strike the final recourse of the latter. What capital flight represents is nothing less than permanent shutdown and lockout on an industrywide and nationwide basis, and the biggest union bust in history. Nor is it too much to say that America itself is threatened by shutdown, for where labor goes, up or down, so must go the middle class, whose salaries begin wherever the wages won by labor leave off.

All this has a distinct bearing, to say the least, upon the ongoing struggle of Afro-Americans for equal rights. What shall it profit a person, for example, to gain equal access to jobs, if there are none? No group is more threatened by the *in situ* neoslavery represented by the Global Sweatshop than the descendants of African slaves in America.

This is not to suggest that the struggle for black rights, or those of any other color, be put on a back burner in deference to transcendant global issues threatening us all. The principle involved was well put by A. Philip Randolph during World War II, when as leader of the March on Washington Movement he proclaimed, "Winning Democracy for the Negro is Winning the War for Democracy."

Nowadays freedom fighters the world over need to keep in mind the fact that their struggles are all linked, and that there must be no such thing as the uplift of one people by the put down of another. Moreover, there must be recognition of the fact that equity is indivisible, and that we cannot hope to build such things as cultural equity upon foundations of economic, social, and political inequity.

Ethnic cleansing, crime, and war are all cut from the same cloth of greed, and unless we proscribe them by law and enforce those laws they may singly or in combination provide the "ultimate solution" for us all.

Nor is the ordering of relationships among ourselves the only problem of transcendental importance. Side by side with ethnic cleansing and Global Sweatshop stalk such spectres as the Penis Rampant, AIDS, and the poisoning of the elements. As oceanographer Jacques Cousteau came up from under water recently to ask, "Why should I be down there trying to save one more whale, when there are forces up here bent upon the destruction of all life on earth?"

Unless we forthwith put a stop to all the global efforts now being made to put Mother Earth to death, all causes will be lost ones. Equality in death would be a poor reward for all the freedom fighting mankind has gone through. All the world is indeed a stage, and without one the play could not go on.

In that dire event, the long search of the human race for freedom, security, happiness, and justice would be over, not to mention the infinitely more important miracle of life itself.

Nikita Khrushev, while presiding over the communist world, confidently assured the capitalist world, "We will bury you!"

But it didn't work out that way. At this writing, we are all—West, East, North, South—digging our own graves.

The doomsayers may not know the half of it.

✠

NOTES

✠

Chapter 1: Our Big Lie

1. Joint Committee to Enquire into the Condition of Affairs in the Late Insurrectionary States (hereafter referred to as "KKK Hearings"), *Testimony*, House Report 22, 13 vols., 43d Cong. 2d Sess., 1872. (Extant sets in LC and Schomburg Center for Research in Black Culture NYPL.)

2. *Cincinnati Commercial*, September 1, 1868; reprinted in "KKK Hearings," vol. 13, pp. 132–34.

3. W. T. Couch, "Publisher's Preface," in *What the Negro Wants* (Chapel Hill: University of North Carolina Press, 1944). For detailed verbatim exposition of the Couch "majority rule" rationale for racial segregation, see Stetson Kennedy, *Southern Exposure* (New York: Doubleday, 1946), 334–40.

4. William Blanchard, *Racial Nationalist Program* (Miami: White Front, 1941).

5. Arthur de Gobineau, *Essay on the Inequality of Man* (Paris, 1853).

6. Kenneth L. Stampp, *The Era of Reconstruction, 1865–1877* (New York: Knopf, 1965).

7. Stampp and Litwack, *Reconstruction*, 5.

8. Houston Chamberlain, *Foundations of the Nineteenth Century* (New York: J. Lane, 1910).

9. Stampp and Litwack, *Reconstruction*, 5–7.

10. Thomas Dixon, Jr. *The Clansman* (New York: Doubleday, Page, 1905).

11. Wyn Craig Wade, *The Fiery Cross: The Ku Klux Klan in America* (New York: Simon and Schuster, 1987), 130–39.

12. Ibid., 140–48; Kennedy, *Southern Exposure*, 29.

13. U.S. Congress, *The Ku Klux Klan Hearings*. 67th Cong., 1st Sess., House Committee on Rules (1921), 114–26. An authentic copy of *The Kloran*, procured from the Nathan Bedford Forrest Klavern No. 1, Atlanta, in 1946, is among the

Stetson Kennedy Papers, Schomburg Center for Research in Black Culture, NYPL.

14. Lothrop Stoddard, *The Rising Tide of Color Against White World Supremacy* (New York: Scribners, 1920).

15. Madison Grant, *Conquest of a Continent* (New York: Scribners, 1933).

16. Adolph Hitler, *Mein Kampf* (Boston, 1943).

17. Claude Bowers, *The Tragic Era* (Cambridge, Mass., 1929).

18. Stampp and Litwack, *Reconstruction*, 6.

19. W. E. B. Du Bois, *The Souls of Black Folk* (New York, 1903).

20. W. E. B. Du Bois, *Black Reconstruction* (Cleveland, 1964).

21. Stampp and Litwack, *Reconstruction*, 21.

22. Wade, *Fiery Cross*, 106.

Chapter 2: The Cause Pauses

1. Carl Sandburg, *Lincoln: The Wars Years* (New York: Harcourt, Brace, 1939).

2. Stetson Kennedy, *Palmetto Country* (New York: Duell, Sloan and Pearce, 1942), 88.

3. J. G. Randall and David Donald, *The Civil War and Reconstruction* (Boston: Heath, 1961), 529–32.

4. Kennedy, *Palmetto Country*, 107.

5. Georgia Governor Joseph E. Brown, telegram to President Andrew Johnson, May 7, 1865; Joseph E. Brown Letterbook, Hargrett Collection, UGa.

6. Andrew Johnson Papers, Library of Congress; Whitelaw Reid, *After the War: A Southern Tour* (Cincinnati, 1866).

7. Benjamin P. Thomas and Harold M. Hyman, *Stanton: The Life and Times of Lincoln's Secretary of War* (New York, 1962).

8. Vernon Wharton, *Negro in Mississippi* (Chapel Hill: University of North Carolina Press, 1947), 136–37.

9. George Tindall II, *South Carolina Negroes 1877–1900* (Columbia, S.C., 1952), 160, 161.

10. Report of B. C. Truman, transmitted to the Senate, May 7, 1866. Sen. Ex. Doc. No. 43, 39th Cong., 1st Sess., 5–6.

11. Randall and Donald, *Civil War and Reconstruction*, 337.

12. Ibid.

13. *Columbia* (S.C.) *Phoenix*, 1865.

14. *Charleston News and Courier*.

15. Thomas L. Livermore, *Numbers and Losses in the Civil War* (1901), 39.

16. Charles Willis Thompson, *The Fiery Epoch, 1830–1871* (Indianapolis, 1931), 317.

17. Charles Sumner Papers, Houghton Library, Harvard University.

18. Thompson, *Fiery Epoch*, 348.

19. B. A. Botkin, *Treasury of Southern Folklore*, (New York: Crown, 1949).

20. George P. Rawick, ed., *The American Slave*, vol. 17, *The Florida Narratives* (1941; reprint, Westport, Conn.: Greenwood, 1972); Kennedy, *Palmetto Country*, 89. Transcript of original interviews by WPA Federal Writers Project, ca. 1935, in Library of Congress.

21. Stampp and Litwack, *Reconstruction,* 194.

22. Ibid., 217.

23. Ibid., 197.

24. Ibid., 211–212. See also *New York Times,* March 30, 1865; *New York Tribune,* April 4, 1865; Joel Williamson, *After Slavery: The Negro in South Carolina During Reconstruction, 1861–1877* (Chapel Hill: University of North Carolina Press, 1965), 47–48.

25. Stampp and Litwack, *Reconstruction,* 193.

26. Ibid., 200.

27. Ibid., 201.

28. Susan Bradford Eppes, *The Negro of the Old South* (Chicago, 1925), 121, 122.

29. Stampp and Litwack, *Reconstruction,* 206.

30. Ibid., 213.

31. Booker T. Washington, *Up from Slavery* (New York, 1902), 26–32.

32. William C. Harris, *The Day of the Carpetbagger: Republican Reconstruction in Mississippi* (Baton Rouge: Louisiana State University Press, 1979), 219–37.

33. Randall and Donald, *Civil War and Reconstruction,* 371.

34. K. P. Williams, *Lincoln Finds a General* (New York: Macmillan, 1949).

35. Randall and Donald, *Civil War and Reconstruction,* 371.

36. John Richard Dennett, *The South As It Is, 1865–66* (New York: Viking, 1965).

37. 19 Howard's Reports (60 U.S.), 405–8, 427, 430, 400; F. H. Holder. "Some Phases of the Dred Scott Case," *Mississippi Valley Historical Review* 16 pp. 3–22.

Chapter 3: New Chains for Old

1. Senate Executive Document 6, 39th Cong., 2nd Sess., 192–95, 218–19; Theodore B. Wilson, *The Black Codes of the South* (Auburn: University of Alabama Press, 1965), 96–100; Eric Foner, *Reconstruction: America's Unfinished Revolution,* (New York, Harper and Row, 1988), 199.

2. Wilson, *Black Codes,* 70–75: Foner, *Reconstruction,* 209; Donald C. Nieman, *To Set the Law in Motion: The Freedmen's Bureau and the Legal Rights of Blacks, 1865–1968* (Millwood, N.Y., 1979), 73–96.

3. Michael Perman, *Reunion Without Compromise* (New York, 1973), 62–69.

4. Ibid., 67.

5. Stetson Kennedy, *Jim Crow Guide to the USA* (Paris: Jean-Paul Sartre/Julliard, 1955: London: Lawrence and Wishart, 1956; reprinted as *Jim Crow Guide: The Way It Was* [Gainesville: University Press of Florida, 1990], 58–71).

6. Kennedy, *Palmetto Country,* 95.

7. House Report 22, "KKK Hearings," 1872.

8. *Cong. Globe,* 37th Cong., 1st Sess., 415; Randall and Donald, *Civil War and Reconstruction,* 284–85.

9. Howard K. Beale, *The Critical Year: A Study of Andrew Johnson and Reconstruction* (New York, 1930, new ed. 1958); Foner, *Reconstruction,* 183; Andrew Johnson Papers, Library of Congress.

10. William T. Sherman, *Memoirs of General William T. Sherman, Written by Himself* (New York, 1891), 2:245–52; Robert C. Morris, *Reading, 'Riting, and Reconstruction: The Education of Freedmen in the South, 1861–1870* (Chicago, 1981), 124;

"Colloquy with Colored Ministers," *Journal of Negro History* 16 (January 1931): 88–94; Vincent Harding, *There Is a River: The Black Struggle for Freedom in America* (New York, 1981), 261–65.

11. Janet S. Hermann, *The Pursuit of a Dream* (New York, 1981), 35–87, 121, 183–84, 196–97; James T. Currie, *Enclave: Vicksburg and Her Plantations, 1863–1870* (Jackson, Miss., 1980), 92–144; Steven J. Ross, "Freed Soil, Freed Labor, Freed Men: John Eaton and the Davis Bend Experiment," *Journal of Southern History* 44 (May 1978): 218–30.

12. *Cong. Globe*, 40th Cong., 1st Sess., 203; Foner, *Reconstruction*, 5–7; Eric Foner, *Politics and Ideology in the Age of the Civil War* (New York, 1975), 128–49.

13. *The Nation*, June 27, July 18, 1867.

14. Frederick Douglass, *The Life and Times of Frederick Douglass* (London: Collier-Macmillan, Ltd., 1962); Philip S. Foner, ed. *The Life and Writings of Frederick Douglass* (New York, 1950–1955), 3: 189.

15. Leon F. Litwack, *Been in the Storm So Long*, (New York: Random, 1979) 238.

16. Kennedy, *Jim Crow Guide*, 133–34.

17. O. M. Crosby, *Florida Facts*, 1869.

18. Ledyard Bill, *A Winter in Florida* (New York: Wood and Holbrook, 1869).

19. Foner, *Reconstruction*, 189; Thomas Wagstaff, "Call Your Old Master— 'Master': Southern Political Leaders and Negro Labor During Presidential Reconstruction," *Labor History* 10 (Summer 1969): 323–24.

20. Stetson Kennedy, *Forced Labor in the United States*, transcript of testimony before United Nations Ad Hoc Committee on Forced Labor, Geneva, October 24, 1952. In Stetson Kennedy Papers, Archive of Southern Labor History, GSU, Atlanta; also Schomburg Center for Research in Black Culture, NYPL.

Chapter 4: The Johnson Restoration

1. Martin E. Mantell, *Johnson, Grant and the Politics of Reconstruction* (New York: Columbia University Press, 1973), 12.

2. Bowers, *Tragic Era*, 6, 11.

3. Foner, *Reconstruction*, 44.

4. *Harper's Magazine*, 1865.

5. *Nashville Daily Press and Times*.

6. *Houston Telegraph*, 1865.

7. *New Orleans Times*, 1865.

8. Thompson, *Fiery Epoch*, 324.

9. *New York Tribune*, 1866.

10. Thompson, *Fiery Epoch*, 325.

11. Rose S. Chamberlain, *Old Days at Chapel Hill* (London, 1926), 94–99.

12. Benjamin B. Kendrick, *The Journal of the Fifteen on Reconstruction* (New York, 1914), 264–67.

13. Eric L. McKitrick, *Andrew Johnson and Reconstruction* (Chicago, 1960), 292–93.

14. Edward Wells, *Hampton and Reconstruction* (Columbia, 1907), 340–54.

15. Foner, *Reconstruction*, 240, 241.

16. *Augusta* (Ga.) *Chronicle.*

17. Henrietta Buckmaster, *Freedom Bound* (New York, 1965), 60, 61.

18. Sarah W. Wiggins, *The Scalawag in Alabama Politics 1865–1881* (Tuscaloosa: University of Alabama Press, 1977), 50–53.

19. *Raleigh* (N.C.) *Progress,* August 26, 1866.

20. Edward McPherson, *The Political History of the United States of America during the Period of Reconstruction* (Washington, D.C., 1875), 573–78.

21. *New Orleans Times,* 1866.

22. Gideon Welles, *Diary* (Boston, 1911), vol. 2, p. 385.

23. *New York World,* November 24, 1866.

Chapter 5: Congressional Reconstruction

1. *Cong. Globe,* 39th Cong., 1st Sess., app. 1–5; *Proceedings,* Mass. Hist. Soc., 19, (Nov. 1905): 395–405.

2. Ibid.

3. *Sen. Ex. Doc., No. 2,* 39th Cong. 1st Sess., pp. 5, 13.

4. *Cong. Globe,* 39th Cong., 1st Sess., 107 (Dec. 13, 1866).

5. Edward McPherson, *Political History,* 573–78; La Wanda and John H. Cox, *Politics, Principle and Prejudice, 1865–66* (Glencoe, Ill., 1963).

6. *New York Times,* Feb. 9, 1866; *Christian Recorder,* Feb. 17, 1866; Douglass, *Life and Times,* 382–85.

7. Thomas Frederick Woodley, *Thaddeus Stevens* (Pennsylvania, 1932), 473.

8. James G. Blaine, *Twenty Years of Congress* (Norwich, Conn, 1884), 2:408.

9. *Cong. Globe,* 39th Cong., 1st Sess., 3838–39.

10. Ibid., 319, 474, 1266.

11. James D. Richardson, ed., *A Compilation of the Messages and Papers of the Presidents, 1789–1897* (Washington, D.C., 1896–99) vol. 6, pp. 410–11.

12. Joseph B. James, *The Framing of the Fourteenth Amendment* (Urbana, Ill., 1956), 69, 70.

13. Dee Brown, *Bury My Heart at Wounded Knee* (New York, 1970), 274–300.

14. William A. Dunning, *Reconstruction—Political and Economic, 1865–1871* (New York, 1907), 57, 58.

15. Beale, *Critical Year,* 349–50.

16. *Chicago Tribune,* 1866.

17. Douglass, *Life and Times,* 388–89.

18. Woodley, *Thaddeus Stevens,* 512.

19. *Ex parte* Milligan, 71 U.S. 2; 4 Wallace 2 (1866) 277, 333 (1867).

20. Woodley, *Thaddeus Stevens,* 567.

Chapter 6: The South Reoccupied

1. *Cong. Globe,* 39th Cong., 2d Sess., 252, Jan. 3, 1867; 1317, Feb. 18, 1867; R. N. Current, *Old Thad Stevens* (Madison: University of Wisconsin Press, 1942), 216.

2. *Cong. Globe,* 39th Cong., 2d Sess., 1733, 1976; Randall and Donald, *Civil War and Reconstruction,* 595.

3. Randall and Donald, *Civil War and Reconstruction,* 598.

4. Ibid., 598; Bowers, *Tragic Era*, 161.

5. George C. Gorham, *Life and Public Services of Edwin M. Stanton* (Boston, 1872).

6. James, *Framing of the Fourteenth Amendment*, 69, 70.

7. Ibid., 167.

8. John S. Reynolds, *Reconstruction in South Carolina* (Columbia, 1905), 136.

9. Kennedy, *Palmetto Country*, 96.

10. Georgia Governors Papers, University of Georgia.

11. Lillian A. Kibler, *Benjamin F. Perry: South Carolina Unionist* (Durham, 1946), 449–60; Columbia *Daily Phoenix*, May 30, 1867; Charleston *Daily Courier*, August 29, 1867.

12. Wade, *Fiery Cross*, 37.

13. Ibid., 40–41; Randall and Donald, *Civil War and Reconstruction*, 394.

14. C. Winfield Jones, *KKK* (New York: Tocsin, 1940); Kennedy, *Southern Exposure*, 30, 183–84; Wade, *Fiery Cross*, 51.

15. Thompson, *Fiery Epoch*, 348.

16. *Cong. Globe*, 40th Cong., 2d Sess., July 20, 1868, 4236.

17. Ann. Cyc., 1867; Walter L. Fleming, *Sequel of Appomattox* (New Haven: Yale University Press, 1919).

18. Randall and Donald, *Civil War and Reconstruction*, 630; Wharton, *Negro in Mississippi*.

19. D. M. DeWitt, *Impeachment of Johnson* (New York: Macmillan, 1903).

20. Richard L. Hume, "The 'Black and Tan' Constitutional Conventions of 1867–1869 in Ten Former Confederate States: A Study of Their Membership" (unpub. diss., University of Washington, 1969); see also Hume's "Negro Delegates to the State Constitutional Conventions of 1867–1869," in Howard Rabinowitz, ed., *Southern Black Leaders of the Reconstruction Era* (Urbana, Ill., 1982), 129–53.

21. Johnson Papers, L.C.

Chapter 7: Election Year

1. U.S. Supreme Court decision, February 10, 1868.

2. Foner, *Reconstruction*, 344; Woodley, *Thaddeus Stevens*, 596.

3. I. W. Avery, *History of Georgia* (New York, 1881), 371.

4. Thomas S. Staples, *Reconstruction in Arkansas* (New York, 1923), 129, 135, 141, 143.

5. Cardoza to Rev. George Whipple, October 21, 1865.

6. Joel Williamson, *The Negro in South Carolina after Reconstruction 1861–1877* (Chapel Hill, 1963), 26–30.

7. Kennedy, *Palmetto Country*, 97.

8. Report of the Secretary of War, 1868, pp. xix–xxii, xxiv, 15, 20.

9. Ibid., xxvi–xxxii, 125–28, 308–9.

10. Hume, "Negro Delegates," 129–30; Foner, *Reconstruction*, 354n15.

11. Mantell, *Politics of Reconstruction*, 130.

12. Edwin S. Redkey, ed., *Respect Black: The Writings and Speeches of Henry McNeal Turner* (New York, 1971); Robert P. Sharkey, *Money, Class and Party: An Economic Study of the Civil War and Reconstruction* (Baltimore, 1959), 82, 102–4, 182–83.

13. *New York World,* January 1868, cited in C. H. Coleman, *The Election of 1868* (New York: Columbia University Press, 1933), 87.

14. Blair-Lee Papers, Princeton University; Forrest G. Wood, *Black Scare: The Racist Response to Emancipation and Reconstruction* (Berkeley, 1968), 126–31.

15. William Y. Thompson, *Robert Toombs of Georgia* (Baton Rouge: Louisiana State University Press, 1966).

16. Hesseltine, *Ulysses S. Grant* (New York, 1935), 102.

17. J. G. Hamilton, ed., *The Correspondence of Jonathan Worth* (Raleigh, 1909), 336.

18. Mantell, *Johnson, Grant, and the Politics,* 134.

19. Ibid., 132.

20. Haywood J. Pearse, *Benjamin H. Hill, Secession and Reconstruction* (Chicago, 1928), 308–19.

21. Mantell, *Johnson, Grant, and the Politics,* 148, 149; Litwack, *Been in the Storm,* 297.

22. William E. Chandler to Benjamin F. Butler, August 10, 1869, Butler Papers.

23. Allen W. Trelease, *White Terror* (New York: Harper and Row, 1971), 194.

24. Ibid., 205, 209–10.

25. Ibid., 338–40.

26. Stampp and Litwack, *Reconstruction,* 419.

27. Ibid., 419; Joseph E. Brown Letterbook, Hargrett Collection, UGa.

28. *Augusta Loyal Georgian.*

29. *New York Herald,* February 8, 1870.

30. *Cong. Globe,* March 5, 1870.

31. W. J. Clark to Governor Holden, June 18, 1870, Holden Papers.

32. "KKK Hearings (Georgia), 37.

33. Melinda M. Hennesey, "Race and Violence in Reconstruction New Orleans: the 1868 Riot," *Louisiana Historical Quarterly* 20 (Winter 1979): 77–91; Trelease, *White Terror,* 117–19, 127–32.

34. Carolyn E. DeLatte, "The St. Landry Riot: A Forgotten Incident of Reconstruction Violence," *Louisiana Historical Quarterly* 17 (Winter 1976): 41–49.

35. DeLatte, "St. Landry Riot," 41–49.

36. Wade, *Fiery Cross,* 59.

37. Randall and Donald, *Civil War and Reconstruction,* 124.

38. Theodore C. Peace and J. G. Randall, eds., *The Diary of Orville Hickman Browning* (Ill. Hist. Colls., vol. 20, 1927; vol. 22, 1933).

Chapter 8: The Hero of Appomattox Tries Again

1. *Columbus* (Miss.) *Index,* December 10, 1869.

2. Foner, *Reconstruction,* 342.

3. *Columbus* (Miss.) *Democrat,* December 8, 1869.

4. *Fairfield* (S.C.) *Herald,* October 16, 1871.

5. *Columbus* (Miss.) *Democrat.* December 8, 1869.

6. Ray Granada, "Violence: An Instrument of Policy in Reconstruction Alabama," *Alabama Historical Quarterly* 30 (Fall-Winter 1968): 182–83; Ryland Randolph to Walter Fleming, October 15, 1901, Fleming Papers, NYPL.

7. William S. McFeely, "Amos T. Akerman: The Lawyer and Racial Justice," in J. Morgan Kausser and James M. McPherson, eds., *Region, Race and Reconstruction* (New York, 1982), 396–404.

8. Herman Belz, *Emancipation and Equal Rights* (New York, 1948), 131.

9. William Gillette, *Retreat from Reconstruction 1869–79* (Baton Rouge, 1979), 103, 166–68.

10. Belz, *Emancipation,* 127–28; Harold M. Hyman, *A More Perfect Union* (New York: Knopf), 530, 182.

Chapter 9: Testimonials

1. *Cong. Globe,* 42d Cong., 1st Sess., 394–95, Appendix 299.

2. "KKK Hearings."

3. Ibid.

Chapter 10: The Second Secession

1. Robert Kaczorowski, *The Politics of Judicial Interpretation: The Federal Courts, Department of Justice, and Civil Rights 1866–76* (New York, 1985), 79.

2. David Donald, *Charles Sumner and the Rights of Man* (New York, 1970), 529–34.

3. Edward L. Pierce, *Memoir and Letters of Charles Sumner* (Boston, 1877).

4. Michael L. Benedict, *A Compromise of Principle: Congressional Republicans and Reconstruction 1863–1869* (New York, 1973).

5. Steven Skowronet, *Building a New America* (New York, 1982), 42.

6. George W. Julian, *Journal,* May 9, 1872, Julian Papers; William B. Hesseltine, *Ulysses S. Grant, Politician* (New York, 1935), 277.

7. William E. Chandler to Hayes, November 9, 1876, Hayes Papers.

8. *"KKK Hearings"* (South Carolina), 15, 46th Cong., 2d Sess., Senate Report 693, pt. 2:357, 373, 409, 433.

9. Randall and Donald, *Civil War and Reconstruction,* 690.

10. Albert D. Thompson to Blance K. Bruce, December 8, 1875, Bruce Papers; Foner, *Reconstruction,* 561.

11. *New York Tribune,* May 18, 1872.

12. David Donald, *The Politics of Reconstruction 1863–1867* (Baton Rouge, 1965), 278.

13. Leon B. Richardson, *William E. Chandler, Republican* (New York, 1940).

14. *New Orleans Tribune,* November 18, 1872.

15. Joe M. Richardson, *The Negro in the Reconstruction of Florida, 1865–1877* (Tallahassee, 1965), 205–11.

16. Joe G. Taylor, *Louisiana Reconstructed* (Baton Rouge, 1974), 228–36.

17. Charles Vincent, *Black Legislators in Louisiana During Reconstruction* (Baton Rouge, 1976), 71–83, 201–4.

18. T. Harry Williams, *P. G. T. Beauregard: Napoleon in Grey* Baton Rouge: Louisiana State University Press, 1955, 45.

19. Henry L. Suggs, ed., *The Black Press in the South, 1865–1979* (Westport, Conn., 1985).

20. Taylor, *Louisiana Reconstructed*, 241–55.

21. Kaczorowski, *Politics*, 205–16.

22. Michael Perman, *Reunion without Compromise* (New York, 1973), 145–48.

23. *New Orleans Louisianian*, November 23, 1872.

Chapter 11: Retreat and Panic

1. James Haskins, *Pinckney Benton Stewart Pinchback* (New York, 1973), 105–6.

2. *New York Commercial Advertiser*, October 15, 1873.

3. Arnold H. Taylor, *Travail and Triumph: Black Life and Culture in the South Since the Civil War* (Westport, Conn., 1976), 185–90.

4. Mark W. Summers, *Railroads, Reconstruction and the Gospel of Prosperity: Aid Under the Radical Republicans* (Princeton, 1984), 32–46.

5. Randall and Donald, *Civil War and Reconstruction*.

6. *Tallahassee Floridian*, August 18, 1873.

7. Morton Keller, *Affairs of State: Public Life in Late Nineteenth Century America* (Cambridge, Mass., 1977), 112–40.

8. Taylor, *Louisiana Reconstructed*, 241–55.

9. T. Harry Williams, "The Louisiana Unification Movement of 1873," *Journal of Southern History"* 11 (August 1945): 349–60.

10. *Petersburg (Va.) Express*, November 7, 1873.

11. Willard L. King, *Lincoln's Manager: David Davis* (Cambridge, Mass., 1960), 290–93.

12. James D. Richardson, ed., *A Compilation of the Messages and Papers of the Presidents, 1789–1897* (Washington, D.C., 1896–99), 7:221.

13. Peggy Lamson, *The Glorious Failure: Robert Brown Elliott and the Reconstruction of South Carolina* (New York, 1973), 171.

14. William W. Rogers, *The One-Gallused Rebellion: Agrarianism in Alabama, 1865–1896* (Baton Rouge: Louisiana State University Press, 1970), 76.

Chapter 12: The Shotgun Plan

1. Francis B. Simkins and Robert H. Woody, *South Carolina During Reconstruction* (Chapel Hill, 1932), 460–62.

2. 44th Cong., 2d Sess., Senate Report 704, 605; J. B. Work to James A. Garfield, December 16, 1876, Garfield Papers, LC.

3. Bertram Wyatt Brown, "The Civil Rights Act of 1875," *Western Political Quarterly* 18 (December 1965): 772–73.

4. A. T. Morgan, *Yazoo, Or on the Picket Line of Freedom in the South* (Washington, D.C., 1884), 468–74.

5. "Three Hundred Voters" to Adelbert Ames, September 14, 1875; William Cavely to Ames, October 9, 1875, Mississippi Governors Papers.

6. E. B. B. to Adelbert Ames, June, 1875; James W. Lee to Ames, November 2, 1875, Mississippi Governors Papers.

7. Gillette, *Retreat from Reconstruction*, 159–60.

8. *Newton Democrat*, October 19, 1874.

9. *Vicksburg Herald*, November 23, 1875.

10. *Canton Mail*, March 20, 1875.

11. *Ex parte* McCardle, 7 Wallace, 506.

12. *Columbus Index*, February 25, 1875.

13. Blanche B. Ames, *Chronicles from the Nineteenth Century: Family Letters of Blanche Butler and Adelbert Ames* (Clinton, Mass., 1957), vol. 2, pp. 259, 205–10.

14. *Vicksburg Monitor*, March 19, 1875.

15. *Jackson Clarion*, February 11, 1875.

16. Wharton, *Negro in Mississippi*, 170, 172, 179.

17. Morgan, *Yazoo*, 416–54.

18. 44th Cong., 1st Sess., Senate Report 527, 32–33, 90–96, 863–65, Documentary Evidence 20, 23, 29.

19. John Brown to Adelbert Ames, October 8, 1875, Mississippi Governors Papers.

20. E. Stafford to George S. Boutwell, June 5, 1876, Select Committee to Investigate Elections in Mississippi Papers, NYPL.

21. *Jackson Clarion*, June 9, 1875; Pierrepont Papers, Yale University.

22. Adelbert Ames to Edwards Pierrepont, September 11, 1875, Mississippi Governors Papers.

23. James W. Garner, *Reconstruction in Mississippi* (New York, 1901), 382–87.

24. Ames, *Chronicles*, 2:216.

25. *Columbus Index*, November 9, 1875.

26. Wharton, *Negro in Mississippi*, 174–76.

27. Ibid., 172–77.

Chapter 13: On the Centennial of the Republic

1. Mildred Thorne, "The Grange in Iowa, 1868–1875," *Iowa Journal of History* 47 (October 1949): 291.

2. Senate Report No. 611, Part 2, pp. 17, 20, 28, 29, 387, 389.

3. Kennedy, *Jim Crow Guide*, 12.

4. *Washington D.C. Nation*, October 5, 1875.

5. Alfred H. Kelly, "The Congressional Controversy over School Segregation, 1867–1875," *American Historical Review* 64 (April 1959): 552.

6. Stampp and Litwack, *Reconstruction*, 526.

7. *U.S.* v. *Reece*, USSC.

8. Randall and Donald, *Civil War and Reconstruction*, 689.

9. Manly W. Wellman, *Giant in Grey: Wade Hampton* (New York: Scribners, 1949).

10. Ibid., 265.

11. Ibid., 265.

12. Ibid., 265.

13. Jarrell, *Wade Hampton*, 70.

14. Stampp and Litwack, *Reconstruction*, 489–50.

15. Hesseltine, *Grant*, 409.

16. Harry Barnard, *Rutherford B. Hayes* (Indianapolis: Bobbs-Merrill, 1954), 316–17.

17. Lerone Bennett, Jr., *Black Power USA: The Human Side of Reconstruction* (Chicago, 1967), 378.

18. *New York Times,* November 9, 1876.

19. Chandler to Hayes, November 9, 1876, Hayes Papers.

20. Jerome L. Sternstein, ed., "The Sickness Memorandum: Another Look at the Hayes-Tilden Election Night Conspiracy," *Journal of Southern History* 32 (August 1966): 342–57.

21. Chandler to Hayes, November 9, 1876, Hayes Papers.

22. Bennett, *Black Power,* 376.

23. *New York Tribune,* November 9, 1876.

24. Foner, *Reconstruction,* 582–83.

Chapter 14: The Treaty of Wormsley's Hotel

1. C. Vann Woodward, *Reunion and Reaction: The Compromise of 1877 and the End of Reconstruction* (Garden City, N.Y., 1956), 161, 162.

2. Allan Nevins, *Abram S. Hewitt, with Some Account of Peter Cooper* (New York, 1935), 371, 372.

3. Woodward, *Reunion and Reaction,* 195.

4. Barnard, *Hayes,* 247.

5. Woodward, *Reunion and Reaction,* 196.

6. Henrietta Buckmaster, *Freedom Bound* (New York: Macmillan, 1965), 173.

7. Barnard, *Hayes,* 414–17.

8. Randall and Donald, *Civil War and Reconstruction,* 699.

9. Buckmaster, *Freedom Bound,* 171, 172.

10. Barnard, *Hayes,* 237–38.

11. Ibid., 225.

12. Foner, *Reconstruction,* 582.

13. Jerrell H. Shofner, *Nor Is It Over Yet: Florida in the Era of Reconstruction* (Gainesville: University Press of Florida, 1974), 587.

14. Randall and Donald, *Civil War and Reconstruction,* 700.

15. Foner, *Reconstruction,* 583, 609.

16. Ibid., 567.

17. Timothy O. Howe Papers, State Historical Society of Wisconsin.

18. Randall and Donald, *Civil War and Reconstruction,* 700; Buckmaster, *Freedom Bound,* 172.

19. Lucius Q. C. Lamar to Rutherford B. Hayes, January 19, 1877, Hayes Papers.

20. St. Louis, *Republican,* April 7, 1877.

21. Woodward, *Reunion and Reaction,* 139.

22. Barnard, *Hayes,* 414.

23. *Boston Herald,* April 11, 1877.

24. Foner, *Reconstruction,* 307–8.

25. Stampp and Litwack, *Reconstruction,* 530.

Aftermath

1. Stampp and Litwack, *Reconstruction*, 317.
2. Barnard, *Hayes*, 177.
3. Hayes, *MSS*, February 14, 1877. In Hayes Memorial Library.
4. Thompson, *Fiery Epoch*, 120.
5. Gail Hamilton, *Biography of James G. Blaine* (Norwich, Conn., 1895).
6. Charles H. Wesley, *The Quest for Equality: From the Civil War to Civil Rights* (New York: Publisher's Co., 1968), 28.
7. Ibid., 42.
8. Barnard, p. 520.
9. *Springfield Republican*, 1876.
10. Barnard, *Hayes*, 343.
11. Ibid., 344.
12. Ibid., 357.
13. *Cincinnati Commercial*, 1876.
14. Walter F. Fleming, *Documentary History of Reconstruction* (Cleveland, 1906), 781.
15. Wesley, "Negro Suffrage in the Period of Constitution Making, 1787–1865," *Journal of Negro History* 32 (April 1947).

✠

BIBLIOGRAPHY

✠

Books and Articles

Allen, James S. *Reconstruction: A Study in Democracy.* New York: International Publishers, 1937.

Aptheker, Herbert. *The Negro in the Civil War.* New York: International Publishers, 1938.

Ball, W. W. *A Boy's Recollections of the Red Shirt Campaign of 1876 in South Carolina.* Columbia, S.C., 1911.

Barnard, Harry. *Rutherford B. Hayes and His America.* Indianapolis: Bobbs-Merrill, 1954.

Belz, Herman. *Emancipation and Equal Rights.* New York: Norton, 1978.

Bentley, George R. *A History of the Freedmen's Bureau.* Philadelphia, 1955.

Bond, Horace Mann. "Social and Economic Forces in Alabama Reconstruction," *Journal of Negro History* 23 (July 1938): 290–348.

Brodie, Fawn, N. *Thaddeus Stevens, Scourge to the South.* New York: Norton, 1959.

Bruce, Robert V. *1877, Year of Violence.* Indianapolis, 1959.

Buckmaster, Henrietta. *Freedom Bound.* New York: Macmillan, 1965.

Cell, John W. *The Highest Stage of White Supremacy: The Origins of Segregation in South Africa and the American South.* New York, 1982.

Coben, Stanley. "Northeastern Business and Radical Reconstruction: A Reexamination," *Mississippi Valley Historical Review* 44 (June 1959): 68.

Coulter, E. Merton. *William G. Brownlow, Fighting Parson of the Southern Highlands.* Chapel Hill: University of North Carolina Press, 1937.

Cruden, Robert. *The Negro in Reconstruction.* Englewood Cliffs, N.J.: Prentice-Hall, 1969.

Donald, David. *The Politics of Reconstruction, 1863–1867.* Baton Rouge: Louisiana State University Press, 1965.

————. *Charles Sumner and the Rights of Man*. New York, 1970.

Douglass, Frederick. *Life and Times of Frederick Douglass*. Hartford, 1882. Reprint, New York: Crowell-Collier, 1962.

Du Bois, W. E. B. *Black Reconstruction*. New York: Harcourt, Brace, 1935.

Flynn, Charles L. "The Ancient Pedigree of Violent Repression: Georgia's Klan as a Folk Movement," in Walter J. Fraser, Jr., and Winfred B. Moore, Jr., eds., *The Southern Enigma: Essays on Race, Class, and Folk Culture*. Westport, Conn., 1983.

Foner, Eric. *Reconstruction: America's Unfinished Revolution*. New York: Harper and Row, 1988.

Foner, Philip S., ed. *The Life and Writings of Frederick Douglass*. 4 vols. New York, 1950–55.

————. *Nothing but Freedom, Emancipation and Its Legacy*. Baton Rouge: University of Louisiana Press, 1983.

————, and George E. Walker, eds., *Proceedings of the Black National and State Conventions, 1865–1900*. Philadelphia, 1986.

Franklin, John Hope. *Reconstruction after the Civil War*. Chicago: University of Chicago Press, 1961.

Gibson, Albert M. *A Political Crime: The History of the Great Fraud*. New York, 1885.

Gillette, William. *Retreat from Reconstruction, 1869–1879*. Baton Rouge: Louisiana State University Press, 1979.

Granada, Ray. "Violence: An Instrument of Policy in Reconstruction Alabama. *Alabama Historical Quarterly* 30 (Fall-Winter 1968).

Guthrie, James M. *Camp Fires of the Afro-American*, Cincinnati, 1899.

Haskins, James. *Pinckney Benton Stewart Pinchback*. New York, 1973.

Haworth, P. L. *The Hayes-Tilden Disputed Election of 1876*. Cleveland: Burroughs, 1906.

Hennessey, Melinda M. "Political Terrorism in the Black Belt: the Eutaw Riot," *Alabama Review* 33 (January 1980): 112–25.

Hepworth, George H. *The Whip, Hoe, and Sword; or, The Gulf Department in '63*.

Hesseltine, William B. "Economic Factors in the Abandonment of Reconstruction," 22 (September 1935): 204.

Higginson, Thomas Wentworth. *Army Life in a Black Regiment*. Boston, 1870.

Jones, Jacqueline. *Soldiers of Light and Love: Northern Teachers and Georgia Blacks, 1865–1873*. Chapel Hill: University of North Carolina Press, 1980.

Kendrick, Benjamin B. *The Journal of the Joint Committee of Fifteen on Reconstruction*. New York, 1914.

Kennedy, Stetson. *Palmetto Country*. New York: Duell, Sloan and Pearce, 1946. Reprint, Tallahassee: Florida A & M University Press, 1989.

McKitrick, Eric L. *Andrew Johnson and Reconstruction*. Chicago, 1960.

Klingman, Peter D. *Josiah Walls*. Gainesville: University of Florida Press, 1976.

Lebsock, Suzanne. "Radical Reconstruction and the Property Rights of Southern Women," *Journal of Southern History* 43 (May 1977): 195–216.

Lester, C. Edwards. *Life and Public Services of Charles Sumner*. New York: United States Publishing Company, 1874.

Litwack, Leon F. *Been in the Storm So Long.* New York: Random, 1979.

Lynch, John R. *The Facts of Reconstruction,* New York, 1913.

————. "Some Historical Errors of James Ford Rhodes." *Journal of Negro History* 2 (October 1917).

————. "More About the Historical Errors of James Ford Rhodes." *Journal of Negro History* 3 (April 1918).

————. "The Tragic Era." *Journal of Negro History* 16 (January 1931).

Magdol, Edward. *A Right to the Land: Essays on the Freedmen's Community.* Westport, Conn., 1977.

Mantell, Martin E. *Johnson, Grant, and the Politics of Reconstruction.* New York: Columbia University Press, 1973.

Murray, Pauli. *Proud Shoes: The Story of an American Family.* New York: Harper, 1956.

Nathans, Elizabeth S. *Losing the Peace: Georgia Republicans and Reconstruction, 1865–1871.* Baton Rouge: Louisiana State University Press, 1968.

Nugent, Walter T. K. *Money and American Society, 1865–1880.* New York, 1968.

Olsen, Otto H. "Reconsidering the Scalawags." *Civil War History* 12 (December 1966).

————. *Carpetbagger's Crusade: The Life of Albion Winegar Tourgee.* Baltimore, 1965.

Oubre, Claude F. *Forty Acres and a Mule: The Freedmen's Bureau and Black Ownership.* Baton Rouge: Louisiana State University Press, 1978.

Peek, Ralph L. "Lawlessness in Florida, 1868–1871." *Florida Historical Quarterly* 40 (October 1961).

Perman, Michael. *The Road to Redemption: Southern Politics, 1869–1879.* Chapel Hill: University of North Carolina Press, 1984.

Pierce, E. L. *Memoirs and Letters of Charles Sumner.* Boston: Roberts, 1893.

Rabinowitz, Howard N., ed. *Southern Black Leaders of the Reconstruction Era.* Urbana, 1982.

Rable, George C. *But There Was No Peace: The Role of Violence in the Politics of Reconstruction.* Athens: University of Georgia Press, 1984.

Rachleff, Peter J. *Black Labor in the South: Richmond, Virginia, 1865–1900.* Philadelphia, 1984.

Reid, Whitelaw. *After the War: A Southern Tour.* Cincinnati, 1866.

Richardson, Joe M. *The Negro in the Reconstruction of Florida, 1865–1877.* Tallahassee, Florida A & M University Press, 1965.

Rogers, William W. *The One-Gallused Rebellion: Agrarianism in Alabama, 1865–1896.* Baton Rouge: Louisiana State University Press, 1970.

Roussève, Charles B. *The Negro in Louisiana.* New Orleans: Xavier University Press, 1968.

Schurz, Carl. *Reminiscences.* New York: McClure, 1907.

Scroggs, Jack B. "Southern Reconstruction: A Radical View," *Journal of Southern History* 24 (March 1966).

Sellin, Thorsten. *Slavery and the Penal System.* New York, 1976.

Shapiro, Herbert. "The Ku Klux Klan During Reconstruction: The South Carolina Episode." *Journal of Negro History* 49 (January 1964).

Sharkey, Robert P. *Class and Party: An Economic Study of Civil War and Reconstruction.* Baltimore, 1967 ed.

Sherman, John. *Recollections of Forty Years in the House.* Chicago: Werner, 1895.

Shofner, Jerrell H. *Nor Is It Over Yet: Florida in the Era of Reconstruction.* Gainesville: University of Florida Press, 1974.

Simkins, Francis B. "New Viewpoints of Southern Reconstruction," *Journal of Southern History* (February 1939): 49–61.

————, and Robert H. Woody. *South Carolina During Reconstruction.* Chapel Hill: University of North Carolina Press, 1932.

Singletary, Otis A. *Negro Militia and Reconstruction.* Austin: University of Texas Press, 1957.

Sloan, John K. "The Ku Klux Klan and the Alabama Election of 1872," *Alabama Review* 18 (April 1965).

Somers, Dale A. "James P. Newcomb: The Making of a Radical," *Southwestern Historical Quarterly* 72 (April 1969): 449–69.

Skaggs, W. H. *Southern Oligarchy.* New York: Devin-Adair, 1924.

Stampp, Kenneth M., and Leon F. Litwack, eds. *Reconstruction: An Anthology of Revisionist Writings.* Baton Rouge: Louisiana State University Press, 1969.

Sterling, Dorothy, ed. *The Trouble They Seen.* Garden City, N.Y.: Doubleday, 1976.

Sternstein, Jerome L., ed., "The Sickles Memorandum: Another Look at the Hayes-Tilden Election Night Conspiracy." *Journal of Southern History* 32 (May 1966): 116–20.

Stewart, James B. *Wendell Phillips: Liberty's Hero.* Baton Rouge: Louisiana State University Press, 1986.

Sumner, Charles. *The Works of Charles Sumner.* 15 vols. Boston, 1870–83.

Trelease, Allen W. *White Terror: The Ku Klux Klan Conspiracy and Southern Reconstruction.* New York, Harper & Row, 1971.

Vaughn, William P. *Schools for All: The Blacks and Public Education in the South, 1865–1877.* Lexington, Ky., 1974.

Walker, Clarence E. *A Rock in a Weary Land: The African Methodist Episcopal Church During the Civil War and Reconstruction.* Baton Rouge: Louisiana State University Press, 1982.

Walker, Jonathan. *Trial and Imprisonment of Jonathan Walker, at Pensacola, Florida.* Boston: Anti-Slavery Office, 1845. Reprint, Gainesville: University Presses of Florida, 1976.

Warmouth, Henry C. *War, Politics, and Reconstruction: Stormy Days in Louisiana.* New York, 1930.

Welles, Gideon. *Diary of Gideon Welles, Secretary of the Navy under Lincoln and Johnson,* edited by John T. Morse, Jr., 3 vols. 1911.

Wharton, Vernon L. *The Negro in Mississippi, 1865–1890.* Chapel Hill: University of North Carolina Press, 1947.

Wiley, B. I. *Southern Negroes, 1861–1865.* New Haven: Yale University Press, 1938.

Wilson, Theodore B. *The Black Codes of the South.* Tuscaloosa: University of Alabama Press, 1965.

Wood, Forrest G. *Black Scare: The Racist Response to Emancipation and Reconstruction*. Berkeley, 1968.

Woodward, C. Vann. *Reunion and Reaction*. New York: Doubleday, 1956.

————. *Origins of the New South, 1877–1913*. Baton Rouge: Louisiana State University Press, 1951.

————. *The Burden of Southern History*. Baton Rouge: Louisiana State University Press, 1968.

————. "On Revising Reconstruction History: Negro Suffrage, White Disfranchisement, and Common Sense." *Journal of Negro History* 51 (April 1966).

Congressional Documents

Preliminary Report Touching the Condition and Management of Emancipated Refugees, Made to the Secretary of War by the American Freedmen's Inquiry Commission. Senate Executive Document 53, 38th Cong., 1st Sess., 1864.

Report of Carl Schurz on the States of South Carolina, Georgia, Alabama, Mississippi, and Louisiana. Senate Executive Document 2, 39th Cong., 1st Sess., 1865, Cong. serv. no. 1237.

Reports of the Assistant Commissioners of the Freedmen's Bureau Made since December 1, 1965, and up until March 1, 1966. Senate Executive Document 27, 39th Cong., 1st Sess., 1866.

Report by the Commissioner of the Freedmen's Bureau, of all orders issued by him or any assistant commissioner. House Executive Document 70, 39th Cong., 1st Sess., 1866.

Memphis Riots and Massacres. House Report 101, 39th Cong., 1st Sess, 1866.

Report of the Joint Committee on Reconstruction. House Report 30, 39th Cong., 1st Sess., 1866.

Freedmen's Affairs. Senate Executive Document 6, 39th Cong., 2d Sess., 1867.

Reports of the Assistant Commissioners of Freedmen. Senate Executive Document 6, 39th Cong., 2d Sess, 1867.

New Orleans Riots. House Report 16, 39th Cong., 2d Sess., 1866.

Impeachment Investigation. House Report 7, 40th Cong., 1st Sess., Cong. serv. no. 1314.

Condition of Affairs in Georgia. House Miscellaneous Document 55, 40th Cong., 1st Sess.

Report of the Commissioner of the Bureau of Refugees, Freedmen, and Abandoned Lands, November 1, 1867. House Executive Document 1, 40th Cong., 2d Sess., 1867.

Alabama Election. House Executive Document 238, 40th Cong., 2d Sess., Cong. serv. no. 1341.

Votes Cast for the New Constitution. House Executive Document 284, 40th Cong. 2d Sess. (Cong. serv. no. 1343).

Elections in Southern States. House Executive Document 291, 40th Cong., 2d Sess., Cong. serv. no. 1343.

Correspondence Relative to Reconstruction. Senate Executive Document 300, 40th Cong., 2d Sess., Cong. serv. no. 1345.

Election in Georgia, North and South Carolina. House Executive Document 300, 40th Cong., 2d Sess., Cong. serv. no. 1345.

General Orders—Reconstruction. House Executive Document 342, 40th Cong., 2d Sess., Cong. serv. no. 1346.

Condition of Affairs in Mississippi, House Miscellaneous Document 53. 40th Cong., 3d Sess., Cong. serv. no. 1385.

Testimony Taken by the Joint Committee to Enquire into the Condition of Affairs in the Late Insurrectionary States ("KKK Hearings"). House Report 22, 13 vols., 42nd Cong., 2 Sess., 1872. (Extant sets at LC and Schomburg Center, NYPL.)

Condition of Affairs in Louisiana. House Report 261, 43rd Cong., 2d Sess.

Condition of Affairs in Alabama. House Report 262, 43rd Cong., 2d Sess.

Vicksburg Troubles. House Report 265, 43rd Cong., 2d Sess.

Mississippi in 1875. Senate Report 527, 44th Cong., 1st Sess.

Recent Elections in South Carolina. House Miscellaneous Document 31, 44th Cong., 2d Sess.

Report of Republican Minority on Election in Louisiana. House Report 156, 44th Cong., 2d Sess.

Mississippi Election of 1876. Senate Miscellaneous Document 45, 44th Cong., 2d Sess.

South Carolina Election of 1876. Senate Miscellaneous Document 48, 44th Cong., 2d Sess.

Testimony and Documentary Evidence on the Election in Florida (1876). Senate Report 611, 44th Cong., 2d Sess.

Testimony Taken Before Special Committee on Investigation of Election in Florida (1876). House Miscellaneous Document 35, 44th Cong., 2d Sess.

Testimony Taken by the Select Committee on Alleged Frauds in the Presidential Election of 1876. House Miscellaneous Document 31, 45th Cong., 3d Sess.

✠

INDEX

✠

Columbus (Miss.) Index, 98, 243

Columbus Riflemen (vigilantes devoted to keeping blacks from voting), 248

Command of the Army Act, 64

Commissary system, 40

Commission on Louisiana, 278

Condition of Affairs in the Late Insurrectionary States, Joint Congressional Committee to Investigate the: hearings, commencement of, 105; dates, locations of, 105; testimony before, 105–217

Confederacy, postwar cabinet meeting of, 20

"Confederate aboveground": overt operations begun by, 91; terrorism, new format for, 239

"Confederate underground," 23; terrorist actions by, 87; white supremacy, ascendency of, 90

Confiscation Act: Lincoln's opposition to, 35–36; Thaddeus Stevens's impassioned plea for, 62. See also "Forty acres and a mule"

Congressional Reconstruction, 63

"Conservatives," 14

Conquest of a Continent, 12

Constitutional Amendments: Thirteenth, 48; 236; Fourteenth, 56, 63, 78–79, 100, 102, 252; Fifteenth, 91–92, 100, 102, 252, 258

Constitutional conventions: for whites only, 47; conventions of 1868, free election of delegates to, 75; ratification, Klan attempts to thwart, 76

Cooke, Henry: Reconstruction, opponent of, 220

Cooke, Jay, 232; Panic of '73, investment firm shut down by, 236; Deal of '76, influence upon, 255

Conduct of the War, Joint Congressional Committee on the, 44

Constitutional Union Guard, 201

Copperheads: Union war effort, opposition to, 5; Seymour described as "embodiment" of, 80; candidacy of Hayes, influence on, 269

Cornish, Reverend, 26

Cousahatta massacre, 263

Crazy Horse, Chief, exile of, 257

Crosby, D. M., 39

Custer, Gen. George A.: black murders in Texas, reports on, 56

Curtis, Justice Benjamin R., 29

Davis, President Jefferson: quoted, 19; Christmas 1868, amnesty of, 92; business dealings, resumption of, 255

Day, James L.: blacks rights, backing of, 233;

"Dead Books": compilation of, 243

Deal of '76: Civil War, marking actual ending of, 3; reality and legend, incorporated in, 6; Southern white supremacist version of Reconstruction "history," national acceptance of, 8; Johnson's soft peace, legacy of, 92; Enforcement Act, nonenforcement of, 220; white rule and segregation, acceptance of, 256; commission on disputed Hayes-Tilden election, appointment of, 268; payoff, rumors of, 270; Hayes, commission endorsement of, 271; the Deal as struck at Wormsley's Hotel, 272–74; implementation of, 273–76; black and other Republican office holders in South, purges and assassinations of, 276–80

"Death to all witnesses," 177

Declaration of Independence, 29

Demobilization and transfer of Union forces after Appomattox, 22

Democracy, "appointive": proposal for, 75

Democratic clubs, 239, 263. See also "Confederate aboveground"

"Democratic war department," 250

Dennison, William, 59

Department of Justice: founding of, 100; Klan terrorists, initial prosecution of, 102

Dissidents: determination of white supremacists not to tolerate, 106

Dixon, H. M., 245

Dixon, Thomas, Jr., 9

Donald, David: Dunning disciple, cited as, 223; quotation from, 232

Douglass Frederick: land distribution, demands for, 36; black delegation protesting to Johnson, led by, 52; Johnson's reaction to, 53; National Loyalist convention parade, integration of, 60

Draft dodging: northern "Copperhead" participation in, 5; Walter Brooks arrested for, 160

Dred Scott decision: excerpts from, 29; Johnson's pronouncement equated with, 45; hope for restoration of slavery based upon, 50; black status following troop withdrawal, augur of, 280

Du Bois, W. E. B.: "official" history of Reconstruction denounced as forgery by, 13; *Black Reconstruction,* authoritative account, cited as, 76

Dunn, Oscar: acting governor of Louisiana, takes office as, 224; integrity of, 259

Dunning, William A., 9

Dunning School, 9

Economic lynching: Fifteenth Amendment's proscription of, 100; Freedmen's Bureau as sole protection against, virtual abolition of, 220; econolynch of blacks voting against white rule, threat of, 242; nonvoting wives, inclusion of, 243

Emancipation Proclamation: ability to enforce, lack of, 25; as war measure, intent of, 28; revocation by USSC, Confederate hope for, 29

Emergency presidential powers: extension by Congress, 218

Enforcement Acts: First, 100; Second, 102; Third, 103, 218, 220; emasculated, 260

Ennis, Charles, 89

"E.S.," 23

Essay on the Inequality of the Human Races, 9

Evarts, William M., 275

Exploitation: changing forms of, 288

Fairfield (S.C.) Herald, 99

Ferry, T. W., 270

Fessenden, William P., 74

Field Order No. 15, 35

Fiery cross, 12

Fitzgerald, Brig. Gen. William F., 247

Florida Facts, 39

Floridian, The, 232

Forrest, Gen. Nathan Bedford: Fort Pillow massacre, role in, 69; Klan leadership, assumption of, 69; "Arm-in-Arm" convention, attendance at, 80; *Cincinnati Commercial,* interviewed by, 84–86; business, back in, 255; KKK Hearings, testimony at, 210–17

Fort Sumter: Union, Johnson remains loyal to, 44; "second secession" of 1872, analogous to firing upon, 229

"Forty acres and a mule": wartime promise of, 34; postwar Congressional denial of, 65; black voters, disappointment of, 68; last mention of, 75

Foster, Charles, 277

Foundations of the Nineteenth Century, 9

Four Freedoms, The, 29

Freedmen's Bureau: stay on plantations, freedmen urged to, 27; Black Codes, voided by, 32; Congressional renewal of, 35–36; 53, veto and overriding of, 55; extension, veto of, 61–62; KKK Hearings, testimony before, 182–89; abolition of, 220; last vestige, obliteration of, 281

Freedom, 27

Free elections in South: end of, 239

"Free persons of color": regulations governing, 32

Fremont, Gen. John C.: liberation of slaves by, 28

Frelinghuysen, Sen. F. T., 270

Fugitive Slave Act: adoption of, 30

Garfield, Rep. James A.: Deal of '76, initial and subsequent reactions to, 272; House Democrats, objections of, 284

Garrison, William Lloyd: Deal of '76, opinion of, 282; Hayes's policies, objections to, 283

"Gatherings": appelation given to, 28; resolutions adopted at, 63; opinions stated at, 67–68

"Generals' Agreement": stipulations set forth in, 43; violations of, 68

Genocide: Confederate threats of, 3; Nazi holocaust, as prototype of, 4; race war, prospect of, 51; black massacres, net result of, 58; terrorism, role of, 83; native Americans, fate of, 89; as final solution, pointed to, 98–99; black annihilation, prospect of, 254; Crazy Horse, example of, 257; "home rule," essential for, 282. *See also* Final solutions; Holocausts; Massacres; Negro hunts

"Gentlemen's Agreement of '66": private sector terrorism, proscription of, 100; state terrorism, attempts to delimit to, 104

George, J. Z., 248

Georgia legislature: purge of black members by, 78

Gettysburg Address, 19

Giant in Grey, 263

Gilbert, Willis, 118

Gillam, Gen. Alvic C., 71

Gillmore, Gen. Q. A.: Emancipation Proclamation implementation ordered by, 27

Global Sweatshop, 289

Gobineau, Count Arthur de, 9

"Gone to Texas," 184

"Good darkies," 14

"Good Ole Rebel," 24–25

Gordon, Gen. John B.: Grand Dragon Georgia Klan, appointment as, 69; regained affluence of, 255

"Grand Affairs," 244

Grand Army of the Republic, 85

Grant, Madison, 1–2

Grant, Ulysses S.: sobriety of, 18; black troops to West, transfer of, 22; state of the South, message by, 51; South, orders military rule of, 63; secretary of war, appointment as, 70; presidency, assumption of, 94; Confederate generals, still confronted by, 95; white rule, opposition to, 97; four states, readmission of, 99; atrocities list to Congress, submission of, 102; troops into Georgia, ordering of, 102; habeas corpus, suspension of, 104; second term, nomination for, 221; black voters, support by, 222; troops to Louisiana, sending of, 225; Texas intervention, refusal of, 241; troops for Mississippi, denial of, 247; S.C., ponders question of, 263; marshals of, 273; threatened coup, prevention of, 274

Gray, Richard, 246

Greeley, Horace: Seymour as "copperhead," branding of, 80; capital, go South," urging that, 220; "social equality forever out of reach," assertion that, 221; "Greeley Republicans," launching of, 225; revival by Southern Whigs, pondering of, 258; Hayes adopted by Democrats, charges that, 276

Griffith, D. W.: *Birth of a Nation*, White House debut of, 9

Halleck, Gen. Henry, W.: runaway slaves, return of, 28

Hampton, Gen. Wade: white rule, urges black support of, 67; S.C. Klan, Grand Dragon of, 69; Blair for vice presidency, nomination of, 80; affluence regained, 255; governorship, campaign for, 262; sworn in as, 266; Hayes, conferral with, 277–28; S.C. governor's office, occupation of, 282

"Hampton and Tilden Musical Club," 263

Hancock, Gen. Winfield Scott: Sheridan, his replacement of, 70; characteristics of, 279
Hardee, Gen. W. J., 69
Harlan, James, 59
Harper's Magazine, 44
Harris, Isham, G., 44
Hawley, Joseph R., 286
Hayes, Rutherford, B., 220, nomination of, 257; victory, declaration of, 273; inauguration of, 274; requests for troops, rejection of, 276; troops, withdrawal of, 278
Head tax, 38
Hemingway, W. L., 251
Hesseltine, William, 13
Hewitt, Abram, S.: Democratic party, chairman of, 270; quoted, 272; Tilden, attempted inauguration of, 274
Hill, Benjamin H., 69
Holmes plantation, 26
History of the United States since the Civil War, 89
Hitler, Adolf, 12
Hoard, George P., 286
Holocaust: European, comparison with, 3; threats of, 98; black rights, denial of, 99; unleashing of, 222; implementation of, 239–40. *See also* Final solution; Genocide; Massacres; Negro hunts
Home Guards, 37
"Home Rule": states' rights, restoration of, 78; instigation of, 231; account of, 249; return of, 274; opposition to delay of, 277; practice of, 282
Hostage-escort, 184
Houston Telegraph, 44
Howe, Timothy, O., 276
Humphreys, Benjamin, 32
Hunt, Justice Ward, 234
Hunter, Gen. David, 28
"H.V.N.B.," 23

Indians, American, 282
Ingersoll, Robert G., 276
"Innocents, The," 89

"Iron-clad oath": congressional adoption of, 43; veto and overriding of, 63; military enforcement of, 69
"Irrepressible conflict," 5, 50

Jackson (Miss.) Clarion, 247
Jenkins, Charles J., 66
Jim Crow segregation system: name, folksong origin of, 33
"Johnnie, Fill Up the Bowl!" 18
Johnston, Gen. Joseph E., 43, 255
Johnson, Patience, 26
Johnson Plan, 46
"Johnson Restoration": example of, 32; description of, 42–49
Jones, C. Winfield, 233
Josephson, Matthew, 13
"Jubilee," 26–27
Justice, Jim, 196–97
Just voters, 67

Kellogg, W. P., 225
Key, David M., 275, 285
King, Martin Luther, Jr., 3
Kirby-Smith, Gen. Edmund, 19
KKK, 233
Kloran, The, 10
Knights of the White Camelia, 215–16
Know-Nothing movement, 258
"Ku Klux Act," 191–92
Ku Klux Klan: founding of, 2; pitched battles with, 2; secret signs of, 163; disguises of, 176; membership, claims of, 197; *Prescript* of, 213
Ku Klux Klansmen: Altman, Peter, 127; Barnes, Tom, 121; Baxter, Henry, 134; Beacham, Dolph, 166; Brand, Charles, 138; Branham, Enock, 166; Briggs, Ben, 209; Burrows, Joseph, 168; Callahan, 141; Casey, James, 180; Casey, Thomas, 180; Cobb, James, 153; Coker, Billy, 127; Coker, Col. Jimmy, 128; Collins, Ed, 153; Cox, Jim Henry, 108, 180; Cummins, Captain, 143; Cummins, Doctor, 145; Deck, Mac, 193; DePriest, Jesse, 194; Dodson, Daniel, 163; Dogwood, George, 195;

Race war, 67, 254
"Radicals," 15
Railroads: Alabama & Chattanooga,
232; Louisville & Nashville, 231;
Pennsylvania, 269; Texas & Pacific,
234, 269, 281; "House owned by,"
273; in politics, 255; lobbying of,
271; Klansmen transported by, 215;
N. B. Forrest ownership of, 221
Raleigh Progress, 48
Randall, J. G.: Dunning School version
of Reconstruction, popularizer of,
12; Dunning, disciple of, 223; latter-
day views of, 232
Randall, Samuel J., 271
Randolph, A. Philip, 290
Ransier, Alonzo, 259
Rape, 172–73
"Readjusters," 283
Reconciliation: black-white, 233;
North-South, 233
Reconstruction Acts: First, 53; Second,
65; Third, 66
Reconstruction, Second, 284, 287
"Redeemers": frustrations of, 232;
white rule, restoration by, 254
Redfield, Horace, 286
Redheaded stepchildren, 256
Red Shirts: southern manhood, badge
of, 92; demonstrations by, 244; ter-
roristic acts of, 262; election eve
threats by, 266; leader, Wade Hamp-
ton as, 282
"Redskins, Pesky," 257
Reed, Isaac, 27
Reese, *U.S. v.*, 261
"Regulators," 37
Reign of terror: setting stage for, 6;
continuance of, 76
Reid Whitelaw, *Cincinnati Gazette*, re-
porter for, 21; *New York Times*, edi-
tor of, 265
Retreat of '73, 236
Rhodes, James Ford, 9
Rhodes, *U.S. v.*, 55
Richardson, Edwin, 71
Rising Tide of Color, The, 12

Rosecrans, William S., 83
Robeson, George M., 270
Rout of '72, 230
Runaway Capital Act, 289
Rutherford (N.C.) Star, 174
Rutherford Vindicator, 195–96

St. Louis Globe-Democrat, 280
St. Louis Republican, 277
Scalawags: defined, 14; misnomer for,
16; KKK Hearings, individuals
named in, 130; Franklin J. Moses, Jr.,
characterized as, 262
Schofield, Gen. John, appointment of,
64; interim secretary of war, as, 75
Schurz, Carl, 52, 220
Scott, Thomas, 269–70
Secession, Articles of, 47
"Second secession": white southern
rule, return of, 99; federal orders, de-
fiance of, 229; white rule, final
restoration of, 237
"Separate-but-equal," 288
Seward, William H.: Fourteenth
Amendment, involvement with, 78;
all-white militia, prevention of, 82
Seymour, Horatio, 80
Sharecropping system, 41
Sharkey, Gov. Robert P., 46, 58
Shellabarger, Samuel, 103
Sheridan, Gen. Phillip, 58, 64, 70, 264,
279
Sherman, John, 264, 274–75
Sherman, Gen. William T., 35, 43
Shotgun Plan, 238, 252, 262, 264
Sickles, Gen. Daniel E., 32, 64, 70, 266
Simmons, William Joseph, 9
Slaves, wage, 289; in situ, 290
Smith, Gerrit, 92
Smith, William, 20
Smythe, Augustine, 27
"Social equality," 57, 157–58, 182, 201,
234
Southern Cross, 58
Speed, James, 59
Souls of Black Folk, 13
Southern Argus, 215

164–69; Forson, Robert, 153–54; Justice, James M., 169–71; Martin, A. B., 178–81; Meason, John, 164–69
—"Carpetbaggers": Furman, Maj. W. J., 182–89; Harrill, John, 193–98; Shaffer, A. Webster, 189–93.
—"Kluxers": Durham, Plato, 198–202; Forrest, Gen. Nathan Bedford, 210–17; Hawkins, Isaac, 202–6; Tomlinson, John, 206–12

Woods, William B., 102

"Wormsley's Hotel, Treaty of": negotiation of, 272–73; ratification of; 274, 281; fulfillment of, 281